INTERPRETING
Everyday
Culture

INTERPRETING
Everyday
Culture

Edited by Fran Martin

Hodder Arnold

A MEMBER OF THE HODDER HEADLINE GROUP

First published in Great Britain in 2003 by
Hodder Arnold, an imprint of Hodder Education and
a member of the Hodder Headline Group, an Hachette Livre UK company,
338 Euston Road, London NW1 3BH

http://www.hoddereducation.com

Distributed in the United States of America by
Oxford University Press Inc.
198 Madison Avenue, New York, NY10016

The advice and information in this book are believed to be true and
accurate at the date of going to press, but neither the editor, the
contributors nor the publisher can accept any legal responsibility or liability
for any errors or omissions.

British Library Cataloguing in Publication Data
A catalogue record for this book is available from the British Library

Library of Congress Cataloguing-in-Publication Data
A catalog record for this book is available from the Library of Congress

ISBN 978 0 340 80852 8

3 4 5 6 7 8 9 10

Typeset in 9pt Baskerville by Tech-Set Limited, Gateshead
Printed and bound in Malta.

What do you think about this book? Or any other Hodder Arnold title?
Please send your comments to www.hoddereducation.com

CONTENTS

NOTES ON CONTRIBUTORS

Brett Farmer is Senior Lecturer in Cultural Studies at the University of Melbourne. He is author of *Spectacular Passions: Cinema, Fantasy, Gay Male Spectatorships* (Duke University Press, 2000).

Chris Healy is Senior Lecturer in Cultural Studies at the University of Melbourne. He is author of *From the Ruins of Colonialism: History as Social Memory* (Cambridge University Press, 1997), editor of *The Lifeblood of Footscray: Working Lives at the Angliss Meatworks* (1986), and co-editor of *Beasts of Suburbia. Reinterpreting Cultures in Australian Suburbs* (with Sarah Ferber and Chris McAuliffe, Melbourne University Press, 1994). He is co-editor of *Cultural Studies Review* <www.csreview.unimelb.edu.au>.

Annamarie Jagose is Associate Professor of English at the University of Melbourne. She is author of *Inconsequence: Lesbian Representation and the Logic of Sexual Sequence* (Cornell University Press, 2002), *Queer Theory* (Melbourne University Press and Otago University Press, 1996; simultaneously published as *Queer Theory: An Introduction*, New York University Press, 1996), and *Lesbian Utopics* (Routledge, 1994), as well as three novels, *Lulu: A Romance* (Allen & Unwin, 1998), *In Translation* (Allen & Unwin, 1994) and *Slow Water* (Vintage, 2003).

Fran Martin is Lecturer in Cultural Studies at the University of Melbourne. She is author of *Situating Sexualities: Queer Representation in Taiwanese Fiction, Film and Public Culture* (Hong Kong University Press, 2003), translator of *Angelwings: Contemporary Queer Fiction from Taiwan* (University of Hawai'i Press, 2003), and co-editor, with Chris Berry and Audrey Yue, of *Mobile Cultures: New Media and Queer Asia* (Duke University Press, 2003).

Greg Noble is Senior Lecturer in Cultural Studies in the School of Humanities and member of the Centre for Cultural Research at the University of Western Sydney. He is co-author of *Bin Laden in the Suburbs* (Institute of Criminology, 2003), *Kebabs, Kids, Cops and Crime: Youth, Ethnicity and Crime* (Pluto, 2000) and *Cultures of Schooling* (Falmer, 1990).

Audrey Yue is Lecturer in Cultural Studies at the University of Melbourne. She is co-editor with Chris Berry and Fran Martin of *Mobile Cultures: New Media and Queer Asia* (Duke University Press, 2003), and her essays on Hong Kong cinema, queer theory and diaspora cultures have been widely published.

ACKNOWLEDGEMENTS ☐

p. 15   Figure 2.1: Pioneer Plaque. Courtesy the NASA Ames Research Center.

p. 25   Figure 2.2: Public restroom sign. Photograph by Brett Farmer.

p. 27   Figures 2.3 and 2.4: Promotional images for late-Victorian programmes of physical culture. Public domain.

p. 28   Figure 2.5: Contemporary fitness magazine. Courtesy Muscle Media, Inc.

p. 29   Figure 2.6: Female bodybuilder. Polixeni Papapetrou, 'Miss Australia Competition', 100 × 100 cm gelatin silver print. Courtesy Polixeni Papapetrou.

p. 34   Figures 3.1 and 3.2: The idealization of the wealthy in advertising. Courtesy Hugo Boss, AG (3.1) and Doetsch Grether, AG (3.2).

p. 36   Figure 3.3: The Panopticon. Public domain.

p. 43   Figure 3.4: Urban graffiti. Photograph by Brett Farmer.

p. 44   Figure 3.5: Graffiti tags. Photograph by Brett Farmer.

p. 45   Figure 3.6: Tagging as resistant protest. Photograph by Brett Farmer.

p. 55   Figure 4.1: From *Roberto: The Insect Architect* by Nina Laden © published by Chronicle Books LLC, San Francisco. Courtesy Chronicle Books.

p. 56   Figure 4.2: From *Roberto: The Insect Architect* by Nina Laden © published by Chronicle Books LLC, San Francisco. Courtesy Chronicle Books.

p. 59   Figure 4.3: Film advertisement for *Mon Oncle*. Public domain.

pp. 76–83   Figures 5.1–5.16: Photographs of Anne Jagose's home by Annamarie Jagose.

p. 87   Figure 6.1: A workstation decorated with personal photographs, ornaments and non-standard screen-saver. Photograph by Fran Martin.

p. 89   Figures 6.2 and 6.3: The rise of the home office (6.2) blurs the distinction between home and workplace (6.3). Photographs by Fran Martin.

p. 94   Figures 6.4 and 6.5: 'Home things' on a bedside table; 'Work things' on a windowledge at the office. Photographs by Fran Martin.

p. 95	Figures 6.6 and 6.7: Home decoration and work decoration. Photographs by Fran Martin.
p. 112	Figures 7.1–7.4: Sanitarium breakfast cereals. Courtesy Sanitarium Health Food Company. Registered trademark of Australasian Conference Association Limited.
p. 115	Figure 7.5: The Nike ID sneaker. Copyright Nike, Inc., 2002. Nike and the swoosh design mark are registered trademarks of Nike, Inc. All rights reserved. Courtesy Nike, Inc.
pp. 119–20	Figures 7.6–7.8: Adbusters images. Couresy www.adbusters.org.
p. 127	Figure 8.1: Photograph taken in 1928 of the Grands Magasins du Bon Marché department store in Paris. Public domain photograph RIBA0333 accessed from Royal Institute of British Architects Library Homepage (20 January 2003) http://www.riba-library.com/imgranmagdub.html.
p. 136	Figures 8.2–8.3: Photographs taken in a produce and sundries market in Melbourne, Australia. Photographs by Audrey Yue, courtesy Centreway Management, Preston, Melbourne, Australia.
p. 137	Figure 8.4: Postcard advertisement for Preston Market, Melbourne, Australia. Courtesy Centreway Management, Preston, Melbourne, Australia.
p. 144	Figure 9.1: Page from *Marie Claire Australia*, March 2001, 141. Photographs by Jason Ell, courtesy *Marie Claire Australia*.
p. 146	Figure 9.2: Doc Martens classic boot. Courtesy Doc Martens.
p. 147	Figure 9.3: Doc Martens open-toed sandal. Courtesy Doc Martens.
p. 147	Figures 9.4 and 9.5: Doc Martens high boot and graffiti-style boot. Courtesy Doc Martens.
p. 167	Figure 10.1: Advertisement from Singapore Tourism Board. Courtesy Singapore Tourism Board.
p. 181	Figure 11.1: Bell telephone advertisement. Public domain.
p. 182	Figure 11.2: Bell telephone advertisement. Public domain.
p. 183	Figure 11.3: Bell telephone advertisement. Public domain.
p. 185	Figure 11.4: One.tel advertisement.
p. 191	Figures 12.1–12.3: Toyota Celica. Photographs by Audrey Yue.
pp. 192–8	Figures 12.4–12.23: Photographs of bumper stickers and decals. Photographs by Fran Martin.
p. 202	Figure 12.24: Women riding bicycles on Revere Beach driveway in the 1890s, Revere MA, USA. Courtesy Frances Loeb Library, Graduate School of Design, Harvard University. Photo sourced from public domain. The Library of Congress American Memory: Historical Collections from the National Digital Library http://lcweb2.loc.gov/house.html.

TEXT PERMISSIONS

pp. 38–40   From Michel Foucault, *The History of Sexuality, Volume 1: An Introduction*, 94–6.
Text reproduced with kind permission of Penguin, UK.

pp. 62–63   From Brian Morris, 2001: *Journeys in Extraordinary Everyday Culture: Walking in the Contemporary City*, unpublished PhD thesis, University of Melbourne. Text reproduced with kind permission of Brian Morris.

p. 67   From Barry Humphries, 'The Highett Waltz', from the sound recording Barry Humphries, *Wildlife in Suburbia Vol. 2* score © 1958. Text reproduced with kind permission of Barry Humphries.

Chapter One

INTRODUCTION

Fran Martin

Before you begin reading this book, take a moment to think about its title: *Interpreting Everyday Culture*. What kind of project does this title suggest? What's the definition of the 'everyday', and what sort of **culture** might characterize it? And, whatever definition we agree on, is 'everyday culture', in any case, amenable to interpretation? Or does the very ordinariness and taken-for-grantedness of the culture of our day-to-day lives make it inherently resistant to academic elucidation? Evidently, since you hold in your hands an entire book written by us on this subject, we're going to try to convince you that there is indeed much to be gained from subjecting everyday culture to intellectual scrutiny. But we want to start out by drawing your attention to what a strange, slippery, and paradoxical concept 'everyday culture' is, despite its deceptive obviousness. Consequently, the interpretation of everyday culture is often a counter-intuitive – even unsettling – endeavour. But in the pages that follow, we hope to show you how it's also a very rewarding project, one that can lead to unexpected and illuminating insight into the surprisingly complex significance of all the things we do, day after day, while barely noticing that we're doing them.

THE EVERYDAY IS OBVIOUS BUT ELUSIVE

What is the everyday? What kind of activities does this category encompass? You might think immediately of activities like brushing your teeth, travelling to work or college, chatting to a friend on the phone, eating lunch, buying groceries, getting dressed, tidying the house. All of these are certainly everyday activities, but what is it that *makes* them 'everyday'; what *defines* the everyday? The first thing that most studies of everyday life within **cultural studies**, sociology and philosophy do is acknowledge the difficulty of formulating a clear-cut or final definition of the everyday (Felski 1999/2000, Miller and McHoul 1998). The French philosopher Maurice Blanchot (1987) has written:

> [...] the everyday has this essential trait: it allows no hold. It escapes. It belongs to insignificance [...] It is the unperceived, first in the sense that one has always looked past it; [...] by another trait, the everyday is what we never see for a first time, but only see again [...]. (p. 14)

The difficulty Blanchot describes in defining, or in clearly 'seeing', the everyday arises partly because we are not trained to think of the repetitive activities and apparently banal objects that make up our everyday experience in an intellectual way. Instead, we tend to experience them as a kind of ubiquitous but unremarkable 'background' to the things in our life that we think *really* matter (usually these are more singular and momentous events, like graduating from school or college, giving birth, making a major trip, getting a job, winning a prize, dealing with the death of someone close to us). In contrast to all those 'important' moments in life, what is the everyday? Is it just everything else? Where are its boundaries? Even though it surrounds us completely and takes up the vast majority of our time, the everyday is extremely difficult to pin down. As well as the fact that we are not usually encouraged to take it seriously or give it much thought, this is because through sheer familiarity and repetition, everyday culture becomes so close to us, so taken-for-granted, that it becomes difficult for us to focus on it or even see it at all. The key task we hope to help you achieve with this book is to challenge common-sense assumptions about the essential insignificance of the everyday, in order to help you to see it afresh. In this way, we hope, those things that once appeared most banal and un-noteworthy might begin to reappear to you as productively strange and surprisingly new.

WHAT THE EVERYDAY ISN'T

In order to move a step closer to a provisional definition of everyday life, below is a list of occasions that various thinkers have argued should be distinguished from the everyday. Another, different list of what some scholars have argued the everyday isn't – a list of abstract qualities often constructed as antithetical to everyday experience – is discussed in the Introduction to Section 1. The list below simply distinguishes the everyday from rare or singular occurrences that demonstrably and by definition happen not 'every day', but only on particular days:

- the catastrophe (e.g. the occurrence and aftermath of an earthquake or a fire);
- the festival or sacred day (e.g. religious and popular festivals like Hanukkah, Easter, Ramadan and Chinese New Year);
- the carnival (in Mikhail Bakhtin's writing, carnival refers to special days like fairs or feast days, dating from but not limited to medieval times, when the structure of authority that usually rules a people's life is symbolically inverted);
- the holiday (e.g. public holidays when the usual routine of going to work or school is interrupted and we do other things, like drive to a beach, have a barbecue or sleep all day). *"everyday holidays"?*

SO WHAT IS EVERYDAY LIFE?

We can now outline some key elements of the general definition of the everyday that we will be assuming, and further elaborating, in the rest of this book. First, some more or less self-evident characteristics of everyday life that we have already touched upon briefly above.

1. THE TIME OF EVERYDAY LIFE IS REPETITIVE AND CYCLICAL, BUT PUNCTUATED BY THE UNPREDICTABLE

The activities we listed at the beginning of this Introduction (brushing your teeth, eating lunch, travelling to work or college, and so on) are activities that we repeat over and over again, at regular intervals. In their regular repetition these activities mark out a *cyclical time* – time marked out into days, nights, weeks and months that form the repetitive cycles which, in turn, are a central feature of everyday life (Lefebvre 1987). However, although repetition and a predictable cyclical structure characterize the everyday, this structure is nonetheless punctuated by moments of surprise and broken routine (you receive a phone call from a long-lost friend; you lock your keys in your car and have to enlist the help of a stranger; an unexpected insight strikes you while you're riding your bike to school). While it is predictable in some ways, day-to-day life is also full of unexpected events – events of an intellectual and psychic nature as well as material events – and as a consequence, is probably less boring and banal than some writers have assumed.

2. THE SPACES OF EVERYDAY LIFE ARE SPACES OF FAMILIARITY

Since we inhabit them as the normative 'default-spaces' of our daily lives in the urban, **postindustrial** cultures in which most of us live, the everyday life spaces discussed in this book (the city, the suburb, the home and the workplace) are characterized by their familiarity: the almost 'home-like' feel they acquire for us (Felski 1999/2000: 22). These everyday spaces stand in contrast to other kinds of space that exude a sense of novelty or strangeness: for example, a foreign city or other distant location visited on a holiday; or spaces visited only irregularly or on special occasions, such as a funeral centre or the central offices of your national government.

3. THE FEEL OF EVERYDAY LIFE IS THE FEEL OF 'NORMALITY'

Taken together, the activities, objects, and experiences of everyday life are usually felt by us to be utterly 'normal', quite unremarkable, 'the most natural thing in the world'. *The apparent 'naturalness' of the particular forms of everyday life that we are used to is what this book seeks most urgently to complicate and challenge.*

I want to continue my list by adding two propositions that are not quite so self-evident as the three statements above.

4. EVERYDAY LIFE HAS A HISTORY

This is another one of those paradoxical statements that, as we'll see, seem to proliferate around the concept of the everyday. How can everyday life have a history, you might ask, when it's simply an aggregate of the various, mundane, unremarkable things we all do in the course of our daily lives? One of the most influential interpreters of everyday life, the French scholar Henri Lefebvre (1971, 1987), argued that the kind of 'everydayness' that we know and inhabit today is a distinctly **modern** phenomenon. He argued that the rise of the middle **class** in modern Europe, together with mass migration to its urban centres, led to the *standardization* of once-diverse life **practices**, and to the unprecedented *perceptibility* of something called 'everyday life' (Kaplan and Ross 1987: 2). Lefebvre's work will be discussed in more detail in the Introduction to Section 3 of this book, Everyday life and commodity culture. For now, the salient points to note are:

3

- the *lived forms* of everyday life familiar to us at the beginning of the twenty-first century have been enabled by and produced out of the history of **industrial capitalism** and the rise of **commodity culture**;
- the *popular concept* of an 'everyday life' that is notionally more or less shared across class and other social divisions within a given society is a distinctively *modern* concept;
- the *academic concept* of 'everyday life' as an object of sociological and philosophical inquiry also has a considerable history, dating back to the mid-twentieth century. This intellectual history is centrally informed by the work of European scholars including Lefebvre with his books *Critique of Everyday Life* (published in French as *Critique de la vie quotidienne* in 1947) and *Everyday Life in the Modern World* (published as *Vie quotidienne dans la monde moderne* in 1968), and Michel de Certeau, with his book *The Practice of Everyday Life* (published as *Arts de faire* in 1974). You will learn more about the history of the study of everyday life in the chapters that follow.

5. EVEN THOUGH IT FEELS 'NATURAL' AND INNOCENT, EVERYDAY LIFE IS ACTUALLY INHABITED AND SHAPED BY POLITICS AND POWER

This proposition is elaborated fully in Section 1 of this book, Theorizing the everyday. Our argument in that section, following thinkers including Louis Althusser, Antonio Gramsci and Michel de Certeau, is that if we subject the terrain of the everyday to critical scrutiny we find that far from being 'just natural', our everyday life worlds are actually organized by the material and **ideological** dominance of particular groups, and riven by the competing desires and demands of the subordinated. Instead of being 'natural', 'normal', or 'just the way things are', we'll argue that the minutiae of the everyday are structured by fully historical, fully **political** organizations of domination and subordination, and of **power** and **resistance**.

INCONCLUSIVE CONCLUSION: EVERYDAY LIFE IS RIDDLED WITH PARADOXES

We have already observed three of the paradoxical aspects of the everyday:

- that the everyday is obvious yet elusive;
- that everyday life appears to be outside history but in fact is a product of history; and
- that everyday life appears to be 'just natural' but is in fact the result of the machinations of power.

In fact, everyday life is just as notorious for its paradoxical and contradictory character as it is for resisting definition. Highlighting this, Lefebvre (1987) muses: 'the everyday is [...] the most universal and the most unique condition, the most social and the most individuated, the most obvious and the best hidden' (p. 9).

What is perhaps the most significant paradox of everyday life today, though, relates to points 4 and 5 above, about everyday life in the era of commodity culture, and everyday power and resistance, respectively. This paradox results from an irresolvable tension between what we will call *structural and institutional constraint*, on the one hand, and *individual **agency** and **res̩tance***, on the other. Many theorists of everyday life have commented on this tension (Blanchot 1987; de Certeau 1984; Fiske 1991; Silverstone 1994). Alice Kaplan and Kristin Ross (1987), paraphrasing one of Lefebvre's key arguments which is informed by a **Marxist** critique of commodity culture, put it well:

> The quotidian is on the one hand the realm of routine, repetition, reiteration: the space/time where constraints and boredom are produced [...]. Even at its most degraded, however, the everyday harbors the possibility of its own transformation; it gives rise, in other words, to desires which cannot be satisfied within a weekly cycle of production/consumption. (p. 3)

Rewording and generalizing this point slightly, we might say that whilst our everyday lives are centrally organized by structural and institutional constraints (for example those of schools, legal systems, and advanced **capitalism** as an economic and cultural system), these constraints are nevertheless always productive of resistant behaviours by us: the embodied social subjects of these systems (for example students who tune out and carve graffiti into their desks during school, passengers who evade ticketing procedures and ride on public transport for free, people who reject the ideology of **consumer** culture and produce their own food). Similar examples will be discussed in detail in the chapters that follow. The important point to bear in mind for now is that the everyday lives of all of us are shaped by this crucial, irresolvable tension, whereby *institutional constraint is always answered by individual acts of resistance; and individual agency is everywhere conditioned by structural constraints*. In fact, as you'll see in Section 1, several influential theorists have argued that *institutional constraint is itself productive of resistance*: hence constraint and resistance are always locked in an inseparable, paradoxical embrace. If you follow up the suggested Further Reading listed at the end of each of the main chapters in this book, you will find that some scholars of everyday life emphasize institutional constraint over individual agency (Adorno and Horkheimer 1993; Lefebvre 1971, 1987, 1991), while others concentrate on individual agency and downplay structural constraints (Fiske 1991). Like Roger Silverstone (1994), though, we're committed to recognizing the importance of *both* constraint *and* agency and resistance, and of attempting to unravel the effects of the productive tension between them at the level of everyday life.

WHAT IS THE 'CULTURE' IN 'CULTURAL STUDIES'?

Up to this point, we have been using the terms 'the everyday', 'everyday life' and 'everyday culture' reasonably loosely. It's now time to consider the term '**culture**' in more detail, since what we're working towards is a definition of the 'everyday culture' that this book proposes to interpret. The methodology (more precisely, methodolog*ies*) that we employ and aim to teach in this textbook are multiple and varied but, overall, the book speaks to that broad agglomeration of interpretative approaches known as 'cultural studies'. Institutionally speaking, cultural studies is a set of scholarly practices that first appeared as a field of study in Great Britain in the late 1950s. Since then, it has spread as a discipline from Britain and the Centre for Contemporary Cultural Studies (CCCS) at Birmingham in the 1960s, to the United States, Europe, Australia, New Zealand and, more recently, also to Japan, South Korea, Singapore, Hong Kong and Taiwan. In the process of this dispersion, 'cultural studies' has come to mean different things to different people in different places. For example, for some, cultural studies is a discipline in its own right; for others, cultural studies is inherently anti-disciplinary, or else simply designates an amalgam of approaches drawn from a broad sweep of disciplines across the humanities and social sciences. Methodologically, some cultural studies practitioners concentrate on close textual analysis of films, books or television shows; others on ethnographic research; others on cultural policy studies. Leaving aside these debates for the moment (I'll say more about our own methodologies in this book at the end of this Introduction), the important task for us right now is to define what 'culture' means for us: since this is a *cultural studies* textbook about *everyday culture*, clearly 'culture' is a key term.

As it is used in everyday speech, the word 'culture' has many different meanings and associations – making it, like 'the everyday', difficult but important to define. To take a few random examples, 'culture' can refer to:

- **popular culture** (like pop music, television game shows, karaoke singing, bingo nights, or folk art);
- national culture (in the USA, markers of national culture include the rhetoric of 'freedom', 'democracy' and global military dominance; in Taiwan, national culture bears a complex and controversial relation to the 'Chinese culture' of mainland Chinese languages, cuisines, festivals and so forth);
- 'other cultures' (as in the sentence, 'in other cultures, women's rights are understood differently': this is a proto-anthropological view of cultures as discrete wholes, demarcated neatly by political, religious or geographic boundaries).

All of these different meanings of 'culture' and various objects of cultural analysis are relevant to the project of cultural studies. But to define more precisely what we understand the 'culture' of 'cultural studies' to refer to, it's worth taking a step back to consider two more influential – and competing – definitions of 'culture'. The first comes from the English poet and humanist scholar, Matthew Arnold (1966). In a series of lectures published as a book, *Culture and Anarchy*, in 1869, Arnold praised 'men of culture' who sought to spread:

> the best knowledge, the best ideas of their time; who have laboured to divest knowledge of all that was harsh, uncouth, difficult, abstract, professional, exclusive; to humanize it, to make it efficient outside the clique of the cultivated and learned, yet still remaining the best knowledge and thought of the time, and a true source, therefore, of sweetness and light. (p. 70)

This definition of culture – still an influential one today – defines 'culture' in terms of *excellence*: only that which can be described as 'the best' knowledge and thought qualifies, for Arnold, as true culture that is worth preserving and popularizing. This definition has a lot in common with the idea of culture as **high culture** as opposed to '**mass culture**' or '**popular culture**': this is the kind of 'culture' embodied in arts like, say, classical ballet, BBC drama series and 'quality' literature. Despite Arnold's expressed hopes that such culture might be made popular and rid of its taint of exclusiveness, the fact remains that such high cultural forms still tend to be enjoyed by a limited audience only. These forms of high culture are thus exclusive in so far as particular levels of training, or **cultural capital**, are a prerequisite to their appreciation.

A second and quite different definition of 'culture' comes from another British intellectual: Raymond Williams (1965), a very influential figure in the early history of British cultural studies. In Williams' definition from his 1965 book, *The Long Revolution*, 'culture' refers to:

> a particular way of life which expresses certain meanings and values, not only in art and learning, but also in institutions and ordinary behavior. The analysis of culture, from such a definition, is the clarification of the meanings and values implicit and explicit in a particular way of life, a particular culture. (p. 57)

For Williams, then, 'culture' means not only the ballet and sonnets of high culture, nor only the television and folk art of popular culture, not only the rhetoric, cookery and festivals of a 'national culture', nor the strange and exotic rituals and customs often attributed to 'other cultures' but left unexamined in our own. Instead, *culture is a whole way of life – including, and most importantly, our own.* In our approach to everyday culture in this book, it is this definition of culture that will prove most useful.

Ellen Rooney (1996) gives another definition of culture that helps explain our approach to everyday culture in this book. She writes:

> to speak very generally, those scholars and critics pursuing Cultural Studies are united by the desire that their students [...] see culture, not as a 'canon' or a 'tradition', but as the embodiment and site of antagonistic relations of domination and subordination, that is, as a productive network of power relations. (p. 212)

Perhaps you can see how Rooney's definition of culture as *a productive network of power relations* links up with what we proposed earlier: that *everyday life is inhabited and shaped by politics and power*. Don't be too anxious if this argument is a bit difficult to grasp fully at this stage: the whole of Section 1 is dedicated to illustrating what we mean in asserting that everyday culture is saturated by relations of power. For now, it's enough that you read and digest the following summary that arises out of the discussion of *everyday life* and *culture* so far.

Summary

In this Introduction, we have argued that everyday culture is:

- not an artistic canon or tradition, but a whole way of life;
- not the same thing as 'popular culture', because it includes the regulatory effects of institutions;
- repetitive, cyclical, familiar and 'natural-feeling' – though also punctuated by breaks in routine;
- the product of particular social and intellectual histories;
- shaped by relations of power that at once constrain the possible forms that culture can take, and produce particular forms of culture – including resistant ones.

HOW TO USE THIS BOOK

This book is divided into four sections, and each section comprises two to three chapters, as well as a brief section introduction. There are two ways in which you can use this book. The first is to work through the chapters sequentially, starting with Section 1, 'Theorizing the everyday', moving through 'The spaces of everyday life' and 'Everyday life and commodity culture' and on to 'Everyday practices'. It would make sense to approach the book this way, because that is the way we've written it: the sections work cumulatively, each one building on concepts introduced previously. 'Theorizing the everyday' functions as a broad conceptual grounding for the book as a whole. 'Everyday spaces' begins the nitty-gritty work of analysing specific everyday sites with attention to one of the most basic conceptual and lived realities of the everyday (yet one that we probably seldom think about in detail): geographical, architectural and imagined forms of space. 'Everyday life in commodity culture' outlines some of the basic historical and cultural specificities of the forms of everyday life most of us are familiar with in early twenty-first-century, post-industrial societies. 'Everyday practices' moves on from there to consider the everyday practices that take place in and define these particular kinds of society: practices including eating, using **technologies**, and everyday travel. Thus, each section sets up the context for the one that follows, and if you read the book in this way you'll find that you accumulate a rich 'tool kit' of concepts and analytic frameworks as you go along. Working through the book in this way, you might read one chapter per week from this book, as well as one or more of the additional readings listed at the end of each of the main chapters. If you're using this book as part of a college course in cultural studies, you might then use your class time to discuss the further questions listed at the end of each chapter, and maybe undertake some of the suggested activities for homework or in class. As part of this process, we also suggest that you organize ahead of time to watch the films that are referred to in some of the chapters – all of these films are easy to find on DVD or video (films discussed are listed at the start of each chapter). Using the book in this methodical way should leave you with a very solid understanding of the basic approaches to contemporary everyday life within cultural studies.

The book can also be used in a less rigidly organized way. Because it contains a comprehensive Glossary of specialized terms (at the back), it is quite possible for you to 'dip into' the book at a particular point – say, the chapter on 'Everyday work', or the one on 'Fashion' – and read and discuss the chapter quite effectively by referring to the Glossary in cases where you're not quite sure of the meaning of terms you haven't yet met. Words and phrases contained in the Glossary appear in **bold text** the first time they appear in a chapter. In this way, the book can be used piecemeal to complement your other readings in a particular area, or as a resource kit for researching an essay, for example. (Of course, we hope the Glossary will also be useful for those readers who work through the book sequentially – it should be seen as a resource kit of commonly used terms and concepts that can easily be referred to in the process of your reading.)

Whichever way you use the book, we hope it will leave you with fresh understandings of quotidian cultures that resonate meaningfully with your own personal experience as a **subject** in those cultures. Ideally, this book will serve as your starting point for unravelling the complex webs of cultural meaning that comprise that excessively obvious, yet all too elusive object known as everyday life.

REFERENCES

ADORNO, T. and HORKHEIMER, M. 1993: The culture industry: enlightenment as mass deception. In During, S. (ed.), *The Cultural Studies Reader*. London and New York: Routledge.

ARNOLD, M. 1966: *Culture and Anarchy*. In Wilson, J.D. (ed.), Cambridge: Cambridge University Press.

BAKHTIN, M. 1984: *Rabelais and His World*. Iswoldsky, H. (trans.), Bloomington: Indiana University Press.

BLANCHOT, M. 1987: Everyday speech. *Yale French Studies* 73, 12–20.

DE CERTEAU, M. 1984: *The Practice of Everyday Life*. Randall, S. (trans.), Berkeley: University of California Press.

FELSKI, R. 1999/2000: The invention of everyday life. *New Formations* 39, 15–31.

FISKE, J. 1991: *Reading the Popular*. London and New York: Routledge.

KAPLAN, A. and ROSS, K. 1987: Introduction. *Yale French Studies* 73, 1–4.

LEFEBVRE, H. 1971: *Everyday Life in the Modern World*. Rabinovitch, S. (trans.), London: Penguin Press.

LEFEBVRE, H. 1987: The everyday and everydayness. Levich, C., Kaplan, A. and Ross, K. (trans.). *Yale French Studies* 73, 7–11.

LEFEBVRE, H. 1991: *Critique of Everyday Life*. Moore, J. (trans.), London and New York: Verso.

MILLER, T. and McHOUL, A. 1998: Introduction to popular culture and everyday life. *Popular Culture and Everyday Life*. London: Sage.

ROONEY, E. 1996: Discipline and vanish: feminism, the resistance to theory, and the politics of Cultural Studies. In Storey, J. (ed.), *What is Cultural Studies? A Reader.* London and New York: Arnold.

SILVERSTONE, R. 1994: Television, technology and everyday life. *Television and Everyday Life.* London and New York: Routledge.

WILLIAMS, R. 1965: *The Long Revolution.* Harmondsworth: Penguin.

Introduction to section 1

Theorizing the everyday

Fran Martin

WHAT THIS SECTION AIMS TO DO

This first section, on theorizing the everyday, is slightly different from the other three sections of this book. While each of those sections is organized around analysis of a series of *sites* and ***practices*** within everyday **culture**, this section is organized around an introduction to some of the most influential *theories* of everyday culture. Chapters 1 and 2 also include real-life examples, of course, to ground and illustrate the general, conceptual arguments being advanced. But the real point of this section is to equip you with a kind of theoretical 'tool kit' which, we hope, will prove equally useful in analysing everyday spaces, everyday life and commodity culture, and everyday practices: the subjects of the rest of this book. To that end, the two chapters that follow introduce the work of thinkers who have been highly influential in accounts of everyday life within **cultural studies**, including Karl Marx, Louis Althusser, Roland Barthes, Antonio Gramsci, Judith Butler, Michel Foucault and Michel de Certeau. The key concepts covered in these chapters include:

- **ideology**;
- **myth**;
- **hegemony**;
- **gender performativity**;
- **disciplinary power** and **resistance**;
- **strategies** and **tactics**.

HOW CAN ONE THEORIZE THE EVERYDAY?

It's possible that as you read this introduction you're reflecting, maybe with some puzzlement, on the apparently peculiar logic of beginning a book on everyday culture with a section on theory. How does 'theory' relate to the everyday? Isn't 'theory' pretty much the *opposite* of 'everydayness'? Isn't theory academic, abstract and intellectualized, while the everyday is down-to-earth, concrete and practised? Certainly that's the way the relationship between theory and everyday life is often constructed. Below is a list, similar to the one in this book's Introduction, of things that many people assume the everyday *isn't*. This list is more speculative and open to query than the earlier, more straightforward, list of special occasions that simply don't fit into the category of that which happens every day. This list distinguishes the everyday from modes of thought and behaviour that are often presumed to be elevated above the supposed banality and ordinariness of everyday experience. These include (according to Featherstone 1992):

- the spiritual;
- the artistic;
- the philosophical;
- the heroic.

Maybe you can see how this set of assumptions about the supposedly unreflective, non-intellectual character of everyday experience contributes to the difficulty we noted in this book's Introduction of taking the everyday seriously as an object of intellectual inquiry. There exists an influential tradition of thinking that constructs the everyday, in what is assumed to be its unconsidered mundaneness, as inherently antithetical to rational interpretation. There may be a small grain of truth in this: certainly the modes of thought we engage in when wandering through the mall or preparing a meal tend to be quite different from those we exercise in writing an academic essay. However, as we'll try to demonstrate both in this section and throughout this book, we don't believe that this means those everyday activities are therefore by nature impermeable to academic analysis. On the contrary, we're convinced that intellectual critique and everyday experience have the capacity to illuminate each other in very productive ways. Along with Lefebvre (1987:9), we would pose the rhetorical questions: 'Why should the study of the banal itself be banal? [...] Why wouldn't the concept of everydayness reveal the extraordinary in the ordinary?'

To help you see one way in which the extraordinary might be revealed in the ordinary unfolding of your own everyday life, try asking yourself is your own day-to-day existence (as you do the grocery shopping, sit on a bus, get dressed in the morning) really characterized by a complete absence of spiritual, artistic or philosophical experience and reflection. Many scholars of everyday life within cultural studies contest the influential dichotomization of experience into 'spiritual/artistic/philosophical' et cetera *versus* 'everyday', arguing instead that people's everyday lives, even in all their mundane repetitiveness, can also be saturated with these modes of experience. A case in point is provided in Chapter 2, which introduces Paul Willis's direct challenge to the orthodox conceptual distinction between 'art' and 'the everyday' in his work on the role of 'symbolic creativity' in daily life. Brett Farmer illustrates the implications of Willis's idea through a discussion of the practice of graffiti writing in cities. In general, then, we reject that way of thinking that opposes intellectual, artistic and spiritual pursuits to everyday life. Not only are we, like Willis, convinced that in their everyday lives people engage in modes of thought and experience that can indeed be described as intellectual, artistic and even spiritual; but we also believe that everyday life, complex and unpredictable phenomenon that it is, abundantly deserves intellectual attention just as rigorous as that which is routinely accorded to other cultural objects (for example, those of '**high culture**').

Hence, we commence the book with this section on theory. However, as we hope you'll find as you read on, the theories introduced in Chapters 1 and 2 are not the dry, abstract tracts of decontextualized verbiage you may fear, but instead remain always intimately tied to the familiar, lived, concrete experience of everyday life itself. We hope that the examples we have selected – including public toilet signage, gym culture, advertising, schools and school uniforms, **subcultural** style and urban graffiti – serve to highlight, throughout, the links between cultural theory and everyday practice.

EVERYDAY POWER

The key term that draws together the conceptual concerns of this section of the book is **power**. In this book's Introduction, we proposed that *even though it feels 'natural' and innocent, everyday life is actually inhabited and shaped by politics and power.* This section is concerned with elaborating some of the nitty-gritty specifics of just how such inhabitation and shaping takes place. It offers some preliminary answers to questions that include:

- What is everyday power?
- Through what mechanisms is such power exercised?
- Who and what does everyday power privilege, and who and what does it disadvantage?
- What drives power's privileging and disadvantaging of these particular groups?
- What fields of difference (**gender**, **ethnicity**, age …) does everyday power polarize most sharply?
- How do people respond to power in their everyday lives?

THE SHADOW OF MARX

While everyday culture is a field of power relations, there is not only one kind of power, but many; equally, there are many different theories of power and resistance. However, many of the theories discussed in what follows share a common intellectual ancestry that can be traced back to the work of the German economist and philosopher, Karl Marx (1818–83). In popular understandings, '**Marxism**' denotes a tradition of leftist thought that is primarily economic and/or narrowly political in focus. While many cultural studies practitioners want to retain the impulse towards social critique that is so central to Marxist philosophy, and hence also to retain the link with '**politics**' in its broadest sense, the type of Marxist thought that has been most influential for cultural studies is that which concentrates on the question: *How is the inequitable logic of* **cap$_i$tal$_i$sm** *as an* *economic system expressed and shored up at the level of society and culture?* Thus, the theorists introduced in this section take a **materialist**, historicist view of culture, and assume late capitalism and its inequities as the omnipresent, structuring background to contemporary cultures. For many of them, 'power' is first of all the power of capitalism: for example, its power to enforce a system in which some people are paid more than others for their labour; and its power to divide people, without their consent, into economic classes arranged hierarchically according to who gets how much money and which related privileges. These concerns are reflected most clearly in the work discussed in Chapters 2 and 3 by Karl Marx and Frederick Engels, Louis Althusser and Antonio Gramsci.

POWER IS NOT THE EFFECT OF CAPITALISM ALONE

However, we must recognize that if economics and class distinction are one, extremely important, axis along which power works within the everyday cultures we inhabit, this is not power's only axis. Accordingly, in the chapters that follow we also consider cultural power exercised through formations of **gender**, ethnicity and generation (of course, this list could be extended). While the theories introduced in the chapters that follow in general take Marxist thought as a starting point, referencing Marxism either explicitly or implicitly, we would discourage the assumption that all forms of cultural power are reducible to effects of capitalism alone. For example, in the case of the **patriarchal** power that underlies the ideology of gender dimorphism (Chapter 1), the system of patriarchy of course interacts in many, mutually advantageous ways with the system of capitalism, but notwithstanding this, we assume that patriarchy and **sexism** also operate with a logic that is *specific* to the field of gender relations. Similar arguments could be made for **racism** and the relations of ethnicity, or ageism and generational relations, discussed elsewhere in the chapters that follow.

REFERENCE:

FEATHERSTONE, M. 1992: The heroic life and everyday life. *Theory, Culture and Society* 9, 159–82.

Chapter Two

THE IDEOLOGIES OF ▢
EVERYDAY LIFE

Brett Farmer

INTRODUCTION

In the early 1970s, the US space agency, NASA, embarked on what was the most ambitious project of space exploration to that date. In a bid to discover and chart the farthest reaches of the universe, it committed to sending a series of crewless space-crafts on a one-way fact-finding mission into outer space. In March 1972 the first of these crafts, Pioneer 10, was officially launched. Travelling at speeds in excess of 50,000 km per hour, the craft rocketed through space, passing the Moon in just 11 hours and Mars in a little under 12 weeks. As of March 1997 when the mission officially concluded and NASA ceased monitoring the ship's radio transmissions, Pioneer 10 had travelled an astonishing 10 billion km from Earth (Lasher 2001). Because it was the first terrestrial object created to go beyond the limits of our solar system, NASA affixed to the side of the craft a pictorial plaque that was intended to signal the ship's function and provenance to any extraterrestrial life forms that might intercept it.

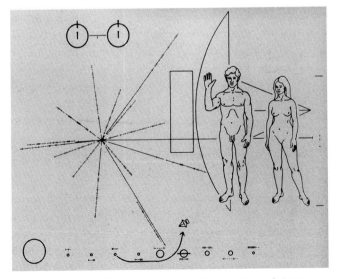

Figure 2.1: Pioneer Plaque. Courtesy the NASA Ames Research Center.

Designed by the eminent astronomers Dr Carl Sagan and Dr Frank Drake, and executed by Linda Salzman Sagan, the plaque was unveiled amid much fanfare as a scientifically calculated document that, in the words of the official NASA description, was 'determined from results of a computerized analysis of the average person in our civilization' and would therefore offer to 'scientifically-educated inhabitants of some other star system' a perfectly objective and universally legible mapping of the Earth, its position in the solar system, and its human inhabitants (Lasher 2001).

Despite this lofty rhetoric of scientific objectivity, the plaque is actually loaded with all sorts of assumptions and biases that give the lie to any claims of absolute **universalism**. Not only is the whole exercise premised on the rather shaky assumption that, if there is intelligent life in the universe, it must necessarily have evolved in the same way as humans with a similar physiological capacity for vision and correlative systems of pictorial representation, that would allow the plaque to be seen and understood in the first place, but the actual images that make up the plaque are patently skewed in both cultural and historical terms. This is especially evident if we focus on the representation of the two human figures that dominate the plaque. Computerized creations or not, the figures are shaped extensively by basic cultural ideals and prejudices of the time and place in which they were produced. They are for example represented in accordance with **modern** Western ideals of physical health and attractiveness, being young, mesomorphic and able-bodied. They are depicted without any form of body hair, a Western convention of nude portraiture, and both sport facial features and hairstyles heavily weighted toward white European physiognomy and fashion. In addition, the two figures are represented through culturally specific notions of **gender** and sexuality, implicitly constituting a monogamous heterosexual couple in which the man is dominant and the woman subordinate. It will be noted, for instance, that the man is bigger than the woman and, through his stance and gesture, assumes an active position of strength and leadership, while she conversely stands demurely to one side, arms supine and legs splayed. If any extraterrestrials were to encounter this plaque, therefore, they'd more than likely assume that on Earth, men are the natural dominant leaders and women their passive auxiliaries. Admittedly, there may even be 'earthlings' who would subscribe to this reading, but most of us would recognize this as a very conservative conception of sexual relations that was outmoded even by 1970s standards. Thus, far from offering a purely neutral statement of objective fact as NASA scientists would have us believe, this plaque is ridden with biases and beliefs that reflect the specific cultural contexts within which it was produced.

I start with this brief reading of the Pioneer 10 plaque because it serves as a neat example of one of the guiding postulations of **cultural studies**: *that meaning, knowledge and truth are always cultural* **constructs**. Contrary to the claims of **rationalism** and **positivism** that 'the truth is out there' as a natural given that can be known and communicated in absolute terms, cultural studies argues that all knowledge is discursively produced: that it is constructed by and relayed through **discourses**, or culturally regulated ways of speaking and thinking about the world. Forming part of the broader **relativist** critique of objectivity that has been revolutionizing Western traditions of critical thought, cultural studies holds meaning to be culturally and historically contingent and thus partial to the values and belief systems of the society from whence it comes. *There can be no mode of meaning or knowledge that is universally true; no single understanding or representation of reality.* What we have instead are plural and competing productions of knowledge, different cultural conceptions of reality and different truth claims. It is an argument that has been explored most fully in cultural studies through the category of **ideology**.

DEFINING IDEOLOGY

No doubt, ideology is a term that is already familiar to you. It is often used in popular speech to refer to the ideas or philosophies of a particular group, generally of a political nature. Thus, for example, one often hears people talk of a 'communist ideology', or 'the ideology of the British Conservatives', or 'the ideology of the Canadian Liberal Party'. In this understanding, ideology is generally associated with a singular agency or group and it is nearly always externalized, seen as something that belongs to others and rarely to oneself. In cultural studies, by contrast, ideology is used to refer to *our* ideas and beliefs, the collective and common ideas and beliefs of the whole **culture**. To put it more forcefully, cultural studies understands ideology as *the network of ideas and beliefs through which culture and its members order, represent and make sense of reality.*

As members of a given culture, we share certain ideas about the nature of the world and our relations to it. For example, most of us would hold in common broadly comparable ideas about the nature of selfhood; the value of family and friendship; the significance of romance and sexuality; the responsibilities of citizenship; the meanings of work, home and leisure, and so on. Many of these ideas are so integral to our ways of being and thinking that they don't even appear to us as ideas, but instead seem to be natural givens. They're not beliefs; they're just 'the way things are'. It is precisely this core complex of shared structures of thought and feeling that cultural studies nominates through the notion of ideology. As Stuart Hall (1986), a key figure in British cultural studies, defines it, ideology is 'the frameworks of thinking and calculation about the world – the "ideas" which people use to figure out how the social world works, what their place is in it, and what they ought to do' (p. 97).

MARXIST THEORIES OF IDEOLOGY

This understanding of ideology as common cultural frameworks of thought and meaning comes to us largely through **Marxist** theory. Karl Marx himself used the term in this general sense in his own writings. In *The German Ideology*, a critique he co-wrote in 1846 with Frederick Engels, Marx (1977) defines ideology broadly as the 'production of ideas, of conceptions, of consciousness as [...] directly interwoven with [...] the language of real-life' (p. 47). Following the central concern in all of his work with the determining role of social conditions, especially economic conditions, Marx promoted a reading of ideology as shaped and governed by socioeconomic forces. As he saw it, the primary role of ideology is the direct translation of social and economic structures, or what he termed 'the material conditions of existence', into ideational form. Ideology, he writes in a classic formulation, is 'the ideal expression of the dominant material relationships, the dominant material relationships grasped as ideas' (p. 64). Thus in **capitalist** societies, for instance, which were generally the primary focus of Marx's analysis, ideology operates to transpose the *economic relationships and imperatives of free market capitalism* – competition, private ownership, **class** distinction, and so forth – into *ideas and beliefs*. The ideological discourse of **individualism** is a good case in point and one that is actually cited by Marx. In capitalist societies, we hold all sorts of beliefs based on the idea of the individual as an active agent of free will; it is an idea that forms the cornerstone of not only our political and legal systems but our very concept of human **identity**. For Marx, the ideology of individualism works ultimately to reflect and uphold the capitalist system. As it declares universal rights and freedom of choice of all human beings, individualism presupposes and naturalizes a society of atomized subjects – the very social structure that makes possible the capitalist principle of private property in the means of **production** – and it represents individuals as free agents interacting in a market, thus ensuring the ready availability of both workers and consumers to fuel the circuits of capitalist exchange. At the same time, it submerges from view the bases of class **power** that under-gird the social relations of capitalism.

As this example suggests, a key aspect of ideology for Marx is the reproduction and naturalization of the status quo, most specifically social hierarchies of **power**. As he writes in a much-cited passage:

> The ideas of the ruling class are in every epoch the ruling ideas, i.e. the class which is the ruling material force of society, is at the same time its ruling intellectual force. The class which has the means of material production at its disposal, has control over the means of mental production, so that thereby, generally speaking, the ideas of those who lack the means of mental production are subject to it (p. 64).

We will be returning to the question of ideology, power and domination in the next chapter; for the present we want to focus on the constitutive link that Marx forges here between ideology and social reproduction. As Marx suggests, ideas are never independent of the real, material conditions of culture and history but are always products of those conditions. Thus, ideas are active agents in the perpetuation of society, its modes of production and its core belief systems.

This argument is taken up and developed further by the French structuralist critic, Louis Althusser (1971), in his widely influential revisions of Marxist theory. Like Marx, Althusser understands ideology as the ideational translation of social realities. As he puts it in his classic reworking of Marx's original formulation, ideology is 'the imaginary relation of individuals to the real relations in which they live' (p. 155). But he develops a rather more complex and flexible understanding than Marx of this process and its effects. Indeed, much of Althusser's theoretical work on ideology aims explicitly to circumvent the more simplistic and reductive elements of Marx's original thought on the subject. It does this in three interrelated ways.

1. First, Althusser stresses the *relative autonomy of ideology*. Unlike Marx, who saw ideology as a direct reflection of the economic structures of society, Althusser argues that ideology has its own 'logic and rigour' and thus can't simply be reduced to or read off from socioeconomic factors.

2. Second, he moves the focus away from thinking of ideology as a static set of ideas to thinking of it in terms of *processes and* ***practices***. Ideology for Althusser is not so much a system of ideas fully formed in people's heads as a complex 'material practice' through which people live and negotiate their relations to society as a whole.

3. Third, he foregrounds the role of ideology in the production of *cultural identity or* ***subjectivity***. In Althusser's reading, ideology functions as both the agency and site of acculturation or socialization: it works to constitute human beings as cultural subjects and is, as such, the necessary condition of being and action in the social sphere. Through ideology we acquire and articulate our sense of social selfhood; who we are, what we represent, and how we think and act.

The term Althusser uses for this process of **subject** construction through ideology is **interpellation**, a word that means 'calling' or 'hailing'. According to Althusser, the practices, discourses and representations that make up the field of ideology call or interpellate us into particular formations of subjectivity which we assume and internalize as fundamental components of our identity. Take for example ideologies of national identity. The concept of the nation has been a vital category of social organization for much of the modern era and most of us would identify with some category or other of national identity. In fact, the hold of national identity can be so strong that some people are prepared to go to war and even die for it. Obviously we are not born with a sense of nationality; it is something that we must acquire and assume as our own. In other words, nationality is something into which we must be interpellated. This process of national interpellation occurs in multiple ways: through language (learning a national tongue, speaking with a national accent); rituals (observing national celebrations, voting in national elections); customs (wearing national dress, eating national dishes); images and artifacts (national media, currency, stamps), and so forth. Partaking of these various cultural forms and practices, we are consistently and subtly interpellated into a specific formation of national identity and, if the process is successful, we come to internalize that identity as a core part of our social self.

Take some time now to read the following excerpt from Althusser, where he outlines his notion of ideological interpellation. It isn't an easy passage: the writing style is rather stiff and the argument can appear opaque and circuitous, but it is worth your perseverance. To clarify some terminology, Althusser makes a theoretical distinction between the category of 'the individual' and the category of 'the **subject**', where the former refers to the pre-social human monad and the latter the fully formed social self. As Althusser acknowledges, in real terms these two are indissociable – indeed, the crux of the reading here is that ideology produces us as subjects even before birth – but the distinction enables him to theorize the operations of ideology.

Ideology interpellates individuals as subjects

This thesis is simply a matter of making my last proposition explicit: there is no ideology except by the subject and for subjects. Meaning, there is no ideology except for concrete subjects, and this destination for ideology is only made possible by the subject: meaning by the category of the subject and its functioning.

By this I mean that [...] the category of the subject [...] is the constitutive category of all ideology, whatever its determination (regional or class) and whatever its historical date [...] I say: the category of the subject is constitutive of all ideology, but at the same time and immediately I add that the category of the subject is only constitutive of all ideology insofar as all ideology has the function (which defines it) of 'constituting' concrete individuals as subjects. In the interaction of this double constitution exists the functioning of all ideology, ideology being nothing but its functioning in the material forms of existence of that functioning [...].

[I]n order to represent why the category of the subject is constitutive of ideology, which only exists by constituting concrete subjects as subjects, I shall employ a special mode of exposition: 'concrete' enough to be recognized, but abstract enough to be thinkable and thought, giving rise to knowledge.

As a first formulation I shall say: all ideology hails or interpellates concrete individuals as concrete subjects, by the functioning of the category of the subject [...].

This is a proposition which entails that we distinguish for the moment between concrete individuals on the one hand and concrete subjects on the other, although at this level concrete subjects only exist insofar as they are supported by a concrete individual.

I shall then suggest that ideology 'acts' or 'functions' in such a way that it 'recruits' subjects among individuals (it recruits them all), or 'transforms' the individuals into subjects (it transforms them all) by that very precise operation which I have called interpellation or hailing, and which can be imagined along the lines of the most commonplace everyday police (or other) hailing: 'Hey, you there!'

Assuming that the theoretical scene I have imagined takes place in the street, the hailed individual will turn round. By this mere one-hundred-and-eighty-degree physical conversion, he becomes a subject? Why? Because he has recognized that the hail was 'really' addressed to him, and that 'it was really him who was hailed' [...].

Naturally for the convenience and clarity of my little theoretical theatre I have had to present things in the form of a sequence, with a before and an after, and thus in the form of a temporal succession...But in reality these things happen without any succession. The existence of ideology and the hailing or interpellation of individuals as subjects are one and the same thing.

I might add: what thus seems to take place outside ideology [...], in reality takes place in ideology. What really takes place in ideology seems therefore to take place outside it. That is why those who are in ideology believe themselves by definition outside ideology: one of the effects of ideology is the practical denegation of the ideological character of ideology by ideology: ideology never says, 'I am ideological' [...] As is well known, the accusation of being in ideology only applies to others, never to oneself [...] Which amounts to saying that ideology has no outside[...].

Thus ideology hails or interpellates individuals as subjects. As ideology is eternal, I must now suppress the temporal form in which I have presented the functioning of ideology, and say: ideology has always-already interpellated individuals as subjects, which amounts to making it clear that individuals are always-already interpellated by ideology as subjects, which necessarily leads us to one last proposition: individuals are always-already subjects [...].

That an individual is always-already a subject, even before he is born, is [...] the plain reality, accessible to everyone [...] simply by noting the ideological ritual that surrounds the expectation of a 'birth', that 'happy event'. Everyone knows how much and in what way an unborn child is expected. Which amounts to saying, very prosaically, [...] the forms of family ideology (paternal/maternal/conjugal/fraternal) in which the unborn child is expected: it is certain in advance that it will bear its Father's Name, and will therefore have an identity and be irreplaceable. Before its birth, the child is therefore always-already a

> subject, appointed as a subject in and by the specific ideological
> configuration in which it is 'expected' once it has been conceived. I
> hardly need add that this familial ideological configuration is...highly
> structured, and that it is in this implacable...structure that the former
> subject-to-be will have to find its place, i.e. 'become' the sexual subject
> (boy or girl) which it already is in advance [...] [through] the rituals of
> rearing and then education in the family.
>
> Louis Althusser, Ideology and Ideological State Apparatuses, pp. 160–5.

On the basis of this passage and the preceding overview of Althusser's theory, we may draw a number of broad conclusions about the nature and functions of ideology.

- *Ideology is productive*; it produces us as subjects and enables us to make cultural sense both to ourselves and others.
- *Ideology is everywhere*; it informs and saturates every aspect of cultural life.
- *Ideology is inescapable*; because we can never move outside our social sense of self and knowledge, we can never move outside of ideology, to do so would be literally 'unthinkable'.
- *Ideology is heterogeneous*; it is a process that involves multiple discourses and produces multiple and often unpredictable effects.

THE MYTHS OF EVERYDAY LIFE

One of the major significances of Althusser's theory of ideology for cultural studies is its highlighting of everyday life as a vital arena for the reproduction and negotiation of social meanings. As the condition and site of subjectivity, the very field through which we are produced and function as social beings, ideology grounds everything we think, do and say. It therefore exists not simply in large-scale institutions and systems such as government, mass media and religion but also, and perhaps more importantly, in the myriad forms and practices that constitute everyday cultural existence. *Indeed, it is precisely through the mundane and seemingly trivial practices of everyday life that ideology works most freely and effectively.*

In a book titled *Mythologies*, originally published in 1957, the French critic Roland Barthes (1973) offers an early and particularly influential analysis of some of the reproductions of ideology in everyday life. Surveying a broad and seemingly disparate range of ephemera – advertisements, celebrities, toys, foodstuffs, sports, holidays, cleaning products, and so on – Barthes attempts to reveal how the mundane artifacts and practices of daily life assume supplementary social meanings and values – or **connotations** to use his preferred term – beyond those of their immediate functional significance. Thus, for example, in a reading of the latest Citroën model, he argues that, more than just a vehicle for transportation, the car signifies an expansive array of supplementary meanings pertaining to social obsessions of the time with modernity, progress and consumerist affluence. These supplementary meanings are so vital to the car's cultural significance that they overtake the original use-value of the **commodity** as an automobile and turn it into a social fetish, 'a transformation of life into matter' that communicates something quite distinct about the concerns and desires of postwar French culture (p. 88). In this sense, the Citroën car operates as the site of an ideological practice; it works to reproduce social systems of meaning and belief, and to interpellate its **consumer** – whether owner, driver or simply onlooker – into those systems.

The name given by Barthes to the various sites of everyday ideological practice that he analyses is **myths**, hence the title of his book. This might seem an odd choice of terminology, but Barthes uses it to suggest that the forms and practices of everyday life in contemporary culture function analogously to the myths of classical or pre-modern cultures by narrativizing and communicating collective social belief systems. We may no longer sit around the tribal meeting place and relay our common social beliefs and ideals through the literal telling of fables, but, according to Barthes, we continue to reproduce our core ideologies through the displaced mechanisms of everyday life. In particular, we continue to use the objects and rituals of daily existence as symbolic agents through which to naturalize our ideological worldviews and value systems. If, as Barthes asserts, the primary principle of myth has always been to naturalize discursively produced formations of social reality, 'to transform history into nature', then for contemporary culture, everyday life is arguably our collective mythology (p. 129).

IDEOLOGIES OF GENDER AND EVERYDAY LIFE

To illustrate the points covered so far, let's look at ideologies of **gender** and some of the ways in which they might be seen to function at the level of everyday life. Gender is a particularly rich category to explore in terms of ideology both because it is such an integral component of cultural identity, and because it is one that is routinely thought of as a pre-social, 'natural' given. Most of us have a sense of ourselves as gendered beings, of belonging to or having a particular sex, most typically male or female. For many of us, this sense of gendered identity seems an unproblematic given; we think of it as something existing in nature, written at the level of the body and biologically fixed. In other words, we think of gender in **essentialist** terms, as an immutable property of our selfhood that is universal and unchanging. But in fact, our categories and understandings of gender are discursive constructs that are culturally and historically specific. Different cultures and different historical eras have often produced vastly different forms of gender. In contemporary Western cultures, we generally work with an understanding of gender as *dimorphous*: as consisting of two distinct categories, male/female, that are defined in opposition and mutually exclusive. Other cultures, however, can work with very different systems of sexual difference that do not always correspond to our categories of male and female or the meanings that we ascribe to them (Laqueur 1990; Herdt 1994; Brettle and Sargent 1997).

To help focus the constructed character of systems of sexual difference, some critics suggest that we should make a distinction between **sex** and **gender**, where the former refers to nature and the latter to culture. In this distinction, sex is generally thought of as the biological or anatomical 'ground' on which cultural constructions of gender are produced. We may all have a biological sex, but what that means and how it is interpreted is culturally specific (Oakley 1993). Other critics question the utility of this distinction because, as they argue, it implies that biology and anatomy are somehow free from cultural constraints, free from the taint of ideology. By contrast, these critics contend that even something as seemingly natural and immutable as anatomical sex is in fact discursively produced, and thus ideological. Not only is it the case that, as behavioural scientists point out, cultural conditions can directly impact on biological elements of sexual difference – such as hormonal fluctuations, say – but *the very categories through which biological sex is routinely determined are themselves constituted culturally*. Bodies, for example, which have long been taken as the primary sign and guarantor of anatomical sex, are irrevocably enmeshed with cultural discourses of gender to the point where it becomes nonsensical to think of them separately. *What bodies mean and how they are experienced are always determined culturally and historically* (Gatens 1996). These debates are challenging and complex, and a full discussion of them is not possible here, but they point to the extent to which our understandings of sex and gender are always contingent and ideologically informed.

Judith Butler (1990) develops a suggestive account of these constructionist theories in terms of what she dubs **gender performativity**. She argues that we should stop trying to locate a definitional ground for either sex or gender because it perpetuates an essentialist account of identity and thus prevents a full recognition of the diverse possibilities of sexual expression. Instead, she suggests we develop a relational account of how gender is variably produced in material contexts. For Butler, gender is not a property or attribute of subjects or their bodies but a shifting effect of ideological practices; not so much something we have as something we do. This is what she means by performativity. *Gender is something that is produced performatively; it is constructed through multiple 'acts' of gendered practice.* In an argument that echoes Althusser's notion of ideological interpellation, Butler suggests that from the moment of birth when the doctor or midwife issues the categorical statement: 'It's a girl/boy', we are ensnared in ideological discourses of gender that encourage – if not demand – certain forms of social practice and behaviour. We are encouraged to dress, to speak, to act, even to think, in a fashion that is deemed 'appropriate' to our assigned gender. The constant repetition of these gendered practices over an extended period of time coheres to the point where we think of and experience them as the natural expression of a unified sexual essence.

As Butler (1990) writes: 'Gender is the repeated stylization of the body, a set of repeated acts within a highly regulatory frame that congeal over time to produce the appearance of a substance, of a natural sort of being' (p. 33).

EVERYDAY INTERPELLATIONS OF GENDER

Given the ingrained character of gendered behaviour and the constant reiteration of ideological discourses that encourage us to think of gender as an immutable essence, it is not easy to look at everyday practices of gender with a dispassionate eye. There is a persistent tendency to think of these practices as natural and inevitable, which is of course the principal effect of ideology. As we have seen, the function of ideology is precisely to naturalize and universalize a particular cultural understanding and arrangement of social reality, to transform a discursive **construct** into a natural given. In the case of sexual difference, ideology serves to mask the cultural contingency of our understandings and practices of gender, encouraging us to think of them as simply 'the way things are'. Take for example the following:

Figure 2.2: Public restroom sign. Photograph by Brett Farmer.

This is an image that we would all encounter on a regular basis. It is a ubiquitous and routinized feature of the contemporary urban landscape. Based on what the psychoanalyst Jacques Lacan (1977) terms 'the laws of urinary segregation' (p. 151), this sign works to effect a gendered division of social practices and spaces whereby men and women are separated for the public discharge of bodily waste. Such a division is a central custom of modern, Western cultures that is widely practised and rigorously enforced. Indeed, in many places, it is a criminal offence punishable by law for a person of one gender to use public restrooms designated for the opposite gender. For all its routinized pervasiveness, however, this practice of gender-specific restrooms is both culturally and historically specific. Not all cultures recognize such a practice and even in the West it wasn't implemented with any degree of consistency much before the modern era. Yet we assume

25

and engage this practice as if it were a natural inevitability, and by so doing we enforce the particular ideological systems of dimorphous sexual difference on which it is based. Every time we encounter the sign above, we are required to make an identification with a cultural discourse of gender: we are required to nominate ourselves as either male or female and to fashion our social practice accordingly. Thus even a humble trip to the bathroom becomes an instance of everyday gender performativity, and a form of ideological practice.

A slightly more complex example of the performative reiteration of gender ideologies in everyday life may be offered by contemporary cultures of physical fitness. A cursory glance at any modern Euro-American city with its daily tides of people jogging, cycling and hitting the local gym would reveal that ours is a culture obsessed with physical fitness. Indeed, the fitness industry today is a massive transnational business worth billions of dollars. This contemporary obsession with fitness derives in large part from late nineteenth-century practices of 'physical culture'. Throughout the late Victorian era, there was a widespread interest in the cultivation of good health and physique through exercise, which led to the establishment of many of the institutional foundations of modern fitness such as gymnasiums, physical education programmes and sporting associations.

Some cultural historians suggest that the explosion of physical culture in the *fin de siècle* period was a direct response to seismic shifts in the social organization of gender. Nineteenth-century society was staunchly **patriarchal** and was organized by an explicitly gendered division of social life. Men and women were understood to be polar opposites and were assigned mutually exclusive roles and capacities. Men were seen as 'naturally' dominant and superior, and were accorded control of the public realm, while women were regarded as the 'naturally' gentle, loving caretakers of home and hearth. Towards the end of the century, however, this system of gender-divided social spheres underwent serious revisions. With the rapid expansion of industrialization, urbanization and consumer cultures, women increasingly moved from the confines of domesticity to take a more active role in public life. In concert with these material changes went correlative shifts in social and political discourse as women started to contest traditional, patriarchal ideologies of gender. It was in this period, for example, that modern **feminism** emerged with the movement for female emancipation and enfranchisement. Not surprisingly, these changes provoked profound anxieties, especially for many men, who felt that the very foundations of the social system were under assault. The development of physical culture, it is argued, was a response to these anxieties, designed to restore traditional, patriarchal ideologies of gender through the production and idealization of sexually differentiated bodies.

In the case of men, physical culture served to re-emphasize traditional notions of **masculinity** as strong and authoritative through the development of body musculature and bulk. The neo-classical cult of male bodybuilding, for example, was routinely endorsed in this period as an antidote to the enervations of modern life, promoting what Tamar Garb (1998) describes as 'the myth that modern masculinity could be

Figures 2.3 and 2.4: Promotional images for late-Victorian programmes of physical culture.

redeemed through the emulation of a classical body type … that was strong [and] heroic' (p. 72). For women, by contrast, the emphasis in physical culture was on the cultivation of traditional **femininity** through gender-specific exercise regimes such as dance and callisthenics that, as Sheila Fletcher (1984) observes, 'aim[ed] to develop the beauty of the figure and to promote a graceful carriage' (p. 13). As such, the birth of modern physical culture was intimately connected to ideological discourses of gender. It was, at least in part, a symptomatic reaction to profound social anxieties about the changing nature of gender roles that attempted to assuage those anxieties through the production of distinctively gendered bodies.

It is revealing, therefore, that the resurgence of interest in physical culture in the contemporary era should coincide precisely with another period of profound transformation in Euro-American economies of sexual difference. The late twentieth century again saw sweeping changes to social conceptions of gender and sexual discourses with the emergence of second-wave feminism and sexual liberation movements. There were equally profound changes to gendered labour and social relations, as the increase in female higher education and the emergence of **postindustrial** societies meant that for the first time in modern history men and women were effectively working in the same jobs interchangeably. It was during this period of radical transformation that the modern fitness revolution emerged, with gymnasiums and health clubs springing up all over the world, and popular exercise regimes like aerobics, jogging and rollerblading winning millions of adherents. While it would be grossly reductive to claim that the complex cultures of modern fitness are nothing more than a latter-day reaction to changes in ideologies of gender and sexuality, they certainly serve in part to represent and negotiate these changes.

27

Anyone who has frequented a modern gym will attest that they are nothing if not sites of rigorously gendered practice. The spaces, clothing, exercises, equipment and even foodstuffs of contemporary gym culture are all frequently organized in explicitly gendered ways. Furthermore, much like their Victorian antecedents, contemporary fitness regimes more often than not have as a principal aim the production of visibly gendered bodies. Thus, men pump iron and down protein supplements in the pursuit of muscular mass, while women sweat in the aerobics room and tone up on exercise machines to achieve a desired svelte litheness. As caricatural as this account may seem, one need only look at the plethora of popular fitness magazines that have emerged in recent years to see the extent to which contemporary gym cultures are invested in the production of bodies coded in traditionally gender-distinctive ways. Their auratic images of hulking muscle-bound he-men and curvaceous svelte women bathed in a mock-religious glow are striking testament to the fact that, as Joanne Finkelstein (1994) writes:

> Struggling at the gym, sweating at aerobics, spending vast quantities of money on equipment, racing bicycles, handweights, lycra leggings, sports bras, inflatable shoes, is the way we have chosen today to make differences in sex visible and important (p. 103).

Figure 2.5: Contemporary fitness magazine. Courtesy Muscle Media, Inc.

IDEOLOGICAL SUBVERSION ...?

The manifold forms of contemporary gym culture cannot of course be reduced to or exhausted by this ideological operation of traditional gender embodiment. Like any social practice, gym cultures assume multiple ideological functions and effects. The issue of ideological variability and negotiation is the focus of the next chapter, but it would be remiss to leave this brief exploration of physical fitness practices without at least signalling their potential for ideological diversity. The modern gym may be a vital site for processes of ideological reproduction and gender performativity, but how those processes are realized at the level of everyday life is open to all sorts of permutation. As a striking example one need only consider the following image of a female bodybuilder. It is an image that is certainly confronting and, in its flagrant transgression of conventional modes of female embodiment, possibly even disturbing, but it highlights the fact that gym cultures need not always function in the service of orthodox ideology. Indeed, they may even subvert it.

Figure 2.6: Female bodybuilder. Polixeni Papapetrou, 'Miss Australia Competition'. Courtesy Polixeni Papapetrou.

Summary

In this chapter, we have argued that:

- ideology refers to the collective ideas and beliefs through which a given culture constructs its forms of reality;
- ideology is vital to the reproduction of society and the naturalization of its relations;
- ideology constitutes the very grounds of our sense of self by interpellating us into predefined categories of cultural identity;
- ideology pervades all aspects of social life, and works through the diverse practices and rituals of everyday life;
- ideology is a complex field of competing discourses that generates diverse and often conflicting meanings.

EXERCISES

1. Select an image from a newspaper or magazine and see if you can identify how it might be informed by ideology. Look for evidence of ideological conventions and assumptions in its choice of subject matter, its representation and framing, its reference to broader social issues, and so forth. List your findings and discuss what it reveals about the image and its meanings. Would you have noticed these things ordinarily? What does this tell us about ideology?

2. Using as a guide the brief analysis in this chapter of how national identity is constituted through interpellation, discuss how other categories of identity such as class, **race/ethnicity**, religion, generation, etc. may also be produced through interpellation. Think not only of the obvious sites or rituals associated with these identity categories but the seemingly trivial practices of everyday life that help constitute them.

3. On a blank piece of paper, mark two columns with the headings 'masculinity' and 'femininity' and then list the sorts of things you associate with these two terms. Get a friend to do the same thing and then compare your lists. Do you see any patterns in what you have written? What does this reveal about our common social understandings of gender? Do you think these understandings have changed and/or are still changing?

4. Think about your own sense of gender. What does it mean to you? How do you perceive and experience it? Has it shifted at various stages of your life? Do you think that ideological discourses of gender impact on how you act and behave? Is your gender behaviour different in certain contexts: for example, at home alone; with your family; among friends; on a date; at college; at work? Do you find it difficult to think about your gender in these terms? If so, why? What do you think your answers to these questions reveal about gender?

REFERENCES

ALTHUSSER, L. 1971: Ideology and ideological state apparatuses (Notes towards an investigation). *Lenin and Philosophy and Other Essays*. Brewster, B. (trans.), London: NLB.

BARTHES, R. 1973: *Mythologies*. Lavers, A. (trans.), London: Granada.

BRETTLE, C.B. and SARGENT, C.F. (eds) 1997: *Gender in Cross-Cultural Perspective*. 2nd edn. Upper Saddle River, NJ: Prentice Hall.

BUTLER, J. 1990: *Gender Trouble: Feminism and the Subversion of Identity*. London and New York: Routledge.

FINKELSTEIN, J. 1994: *Slaves of Chic: An A–Z of Consumer Pleasures*. Melbourne: Minerva.

FLETCHER, S. 1984: *Women First: The Female Tradition in English Physical Education 1880–1930*. London: Athlone Press.

GARB, T. 1998: *Bodies of Modernity: Figure and Flesh in Fin-de-Siècle France*. London: Thames & Hudson.

GATENS, M. 1996: *Imaginary Bodies: Ethics, Power, Corporeality*. London and New York: Routledge.

HALL, S. 1986: Signification, representation, ideology: Althusser and the post-structuralist debates. *Critical Studies in Mass Communication* 2(2), 91–113.

HERDT, G. (ed.) 1994: *Third Sex, Third Gender: Beyond Sexual Dimorphism in Culture and History*. New York: Zone Books.

LACAN, J. 1977: The Agency of the letter in the unconscious or reason since Freud. *Écrits: A Selection*. Sheridan, A. (trans.), New York: Norton, 146–78.

LAQUEUR, T. 1990: *Making Sex: Body and Gender from the Greeks to Freud*. Cambridge, MA: Harvard University Press.

LASHER, L. 2001: Mission descriptions. *Pioneer Project Homepage*, <http://spaceprojects.arc.nasa.gov/Space_Projects/pioneer/PNhome.html>. Accessed 15 January 2002.

MARX, K. and ENGELS, F. 1977: *The German Ideology*. London: Lawrence & Wishart.

OAKLEY, A. 1993: *Sex, Gender and Society*. Revised edn. Aldershot: Arena.

FURTHER READING

BARKER, C. 2000: *Cultural Studies: Theory and Practice*. London: Sage.

BUDD, M.A. 1997: *The Sculpture Machine: Physical Culture and Body Politics in the Age of Empire*. London: Macmillan.

EAGLETON, T. 1991: *Ideology: An Introduction*. London: Verso.

EDGAR, A. and SEDGWICK, P. 1999: *Key Concepts in Cultural Theory*. London and New York: Routledge.

GREEN, H. 1986: *Fit for America: Health, Fitness, Sport and American Culture*. New York: Pantheon Books.

HAWKES, D. 1996: *Ideology*. New York and London: Routledge.

HEBDIGE, D. 1993: From culture to hegemony. In During, S. (ed.), *The Cultural Studies Reader*. London and New York: Routledge.

LEWIS, J. 2002: *Cultural Studies: The Basics*. London: Sage.

PAYNE, M. 1997: *Reading Knowledge: An Introduction to Foucault, Barthes, and Althusser*. Cambridge, MA: Blackwell.

STEWART, M.L. 2001: *For Health and Beauty: Physical Culture for Frenchwomen, 1880s–1930s*. Baltimore, MD: Johns Hopkins University Press.

THOMPSON, K. 1986: *Beliefs and Ideology*. London: Tavistock.

Chapter Three

THE POLITICS OF
EVERYDAY LIFE

Brett Farmer

One of the more significant developments of recent history has been the expansion of our understanding of what constitutes **politics**. The emergence across the postwar period of new political groups and struggles around such diverse issues as **gender**, sexuality, **race** and the environment has forced a reconceptualization of politics as not simply a matter of public governance and policy making, but an expansive field of action that encompasses and informs all facets of social life. Variously dubbed the turn to 'identity politics', '**postmodern** politics' or simply 'cultural politics', this transformation has highlighted everyday life as a central site of political articulation and contest, demonstrating that, as the popular catch cry of 1970s **feminism** put it, the personal is indeed political.

Cultural studies has been an integral component of this sea change in social and political thought. With its emphasis on locating and reading **culture** at the level of everyday **power** networks, cultural studies advances a reading of everyday life as a profoundly political arena. Indeed, cultural studies itself may even be thought of as an avowedly political project, for its primary aim is not just theoretical or academic but, as Graeme Turner (1990: 5–6) notes, 'it is also political, to examine the power relations that constitute [...] everyday life and thus to reveal the configuration of interests its construction serves'.

In the last chapter, we saw how this attention to the political dynamics of everyday life is articulated in cultural studies through questions of **ideology**. We argued that by referencing common cultural ideas and beliefs, the forms of everyday life serve to reproduce and naturalize ideological constructions of reality and the social systems they support. In this chapter we extend our understanding of this process by thinking more carefully about everyday life and its political relations to networks of social power.

GRAMSCI AND HEGEMONY

One of the major critical influences on how cultural studies thinks about the politics of everyday life is Antonio Gramsci's theory of **hegemony**. Gramsci was an Italian **Marxist** whose work was centrally concerned with how social systems of power operate under **capitalism** and why those who are disadvantaged or oppressed by these systems acquiesce to their ongoing subordination. Writing in the late 1920s and early 1930s,

Gramsci was deeply disheartened by the apparent failure of socialism and the popular embrace of anti-democratic systems such as fascism in Italy and elsewhere. *Why was it, he pondered, that so many people seem prepared willingly to accept a system – whether capitalist or fascist – that depends on their subjugation and clearly compromises their political interests?* The concept of hegemony is Gramsci's theoretical response to this dilemma.

As Gramsci (1971) argues, power in **modern** societies is not generally exercised through coercion or force but through consensus. There may be coercive agencies such as the police and the military that will physically enforce social conformity if required, but for the most part, social equilibrium is achieved and maintained through voluntary consent. We actively and willingly consent to abide by the rules and conventions that govern social life, and to accept our relative position within existing structures of social power and hierarchies of dominance. Hegemony is the term Gramsci uses for this process, a process he describes as the 'spontaneous consent given by the great masses of the population to the general direction imposed on social life by the dominant fundamental group' (p. 12). To state it more baldly, hegemony is: *the process of consensus whereby members of a society agree to existing networks of social power by accepting the cultural authority and dominance of the ruling group or groups.*

Taking his cue from Marx's argument, introduced in the last chapter, that 'the ideas of the ruling **class** are in every epoch the ruling ideas', Gramsci contends that the process of hegemony occurs largely through ideology. Dominant ideology works to ensure popular consent to existing power structures by naturalizing and legitimating the claims of the ruling classes to social and moral leadership. In particular, cultural institutions such as schools, political groups, religious bodies and the mass media espouse and promulgate the ideas and beliefs of the ruling elite, and by so doing create a cultural economy that favours the interests of the dominant classes and fosters general acquiescence to their rule.

In contemporary culture, advertising is an obvious instance of this process of hegemony at work. Not only is advertising openly engaged in the promotion of capitalism as an economic system, it equally promotes and naturalizes the inequitable hierarchies of class-based power upon which capitalism rests. For example, advertisements constantly bombard us with images and signs associated with upper-class **lifestyles** and **taste** formations, and they encourage us to view these as eminently desirable symbols of social and personal prestige. Everything from cars to bathroom products is sold in advertisements through a persistent ideological association of the upper classes with cultural power and achievement.

The underlying logic at work in these advertisements is that *wealth = success = power* and that the rich therefore have a natural claim on positions of cultural leadership. Far from questioning a social system that concentrates power in the hands of the wealthy few, these advertisements imply that such a system is somehow natural and inevitable, and that we should all happily play by its rules and aspire to climb its hierarchical ladder. In

Figures 3.1 and 3.2: The idealization of the wealthy in advertising. Courtesy of Hugo Boss, AG (3.1) and Doetsch Grether, AG (3.2).

this way, advertising may be seen to work in the service of hegemony by idealizing the upper classes as 'naturally' privileged, and legitimating their hold on social power and authority.

Class is not, of course, the only form of social power that advertising serves to idealize. It equally endorses interrelated systems of social power and privilege defined in terms of gender, race, nationality, generation, and so forth. The advertisements above, for example, might be seen to work equally in the service of hegemonies of class, gender, sexuality and race. The first advertisement's representation of a smiling man and woman coupled together in a romantic waltz references and supports traditional ideologies of heteronormativity; while the second advertisement's image of a slender, young woman gazing dreamily off-frame as she prepares to disrobe for her bath reproduces standard **patriarchal discourses** of femininity as eroticized and narcissistic, while equally promoting prescriptive ideals of female beauty as young, thin and white. Indeed, it should not go unnoticed that both advertisements feature exclusively Caucasian models and thus may be seen to buy into ideological discourses of white hegemony. How different would these advertisements be, for example, if they featured black models, or a lesbian couple waltzing in the street, or a muscular man about to slip into his bubble bath? That these imagined alternatives might seem less 'natural' or 'spontaneous' is not because they have any less plausibility than the existing images but because they less clearly relay dominant ideologies and expectations. The varied forms of social distinction and privilege reproduced through advertising should alert us to the fact that hegemony is a process invested not just in class-based power, but power in all its multiple and heterogeneous articulations. Put simply, hegemony is *a process for the maintenance of the social status quo and its diverse regimes of power*.

In fact, much of the usefulness of Gramsci's theory of hegemony stems from its complication of traditional Marxist readings of power in simple terms of economics. Unlike Marx, who equated the ruling class almost exclusively with the owners of economic capital or the bourgeoisie, Gramsci argues that the ruling elite is a shifting alliance made up of many 'class factions': rural landowners, priests and clergy, intellectuals, civil servants, aristocrats, and so on. Other critics have extended this reading to attend to the hegemonic operations of such competing systems of social power as **sexism** or **phallocentrism**, the cultural privileging of men over women, and **racism** or **Eurocentrism**, the cultural privileging of white Europeans over other races and ethnicities. In all of these instances, hegemony works to naturalize the dominance and leadership of one social group over others.

In addition to highlighting the plural forms assumed by social power, Gramsci's theory of hegemony also underscores the heterogeneous and conflicted character of the operations of power in everyday life. Because it works through consensus to engage diverse factions and interests, hegemony is a complex and often unpredictable phenomenon. Far from a monolithic structure in dominance with predetermined outcomes, hegemony is what Gramsci describes as 'a continuous process of formation and superseding of unstable equilibria [...] between the interests of the fundamental group and those of the subordinate groups – equilibria in which the interests of the dominant group prevail, but only up to a certain point' (p. 182). As the final clause here suggests, the exercise of power through hegemony is never assured, but is a *process of constant struggle* that, by definition, is *perpetually open to contestation and change*. Hegemonic regimes of power must strive actively to win the support of all social groups and prove their cultural currency. This is how and why societies and their power structures alter over time. Hegemonic alliances shift, incorporating new factions in the social corpus and responding to new ideas. Furthermore, there is always the possibility that hegemony will fail: that subordinate groups will refuse its naturalizing operations and seek to effect a renegotiation of social power. One need only consider, for example, the way in which **feminism** has challenged patriarchy, or indigenous rights movements have combated (post)colonialism, to see that hegemony is almost always open to **resistance** and dissent.

FOUCAULT AND DISCIPLINARY POWER

Another theorist who has had an enormous influence on critical understandings of social power in cultural studies is the French historian Michel Foucault. A fiercely innovative thinker whose work traverses a wide range of fields and topics, Foucault develops an original understanding of power as a dispersed network of disciplinary production. Like Gramsci, Foucault (1977) argues that power in modern societies is *consensual rather than coercive*. Indeed, he traces a historical shift from an earlier system of **sovereign power** where social authority was located in a central agency such as the crown or the state and was physically enforced by deputized representatives, to a more diffuse and consensual system of **disciplinary power**. This latter system, which Foucault argues emerged in the seventeenth and eighteenth centuries with the rise of modern capitalism, is largely predicated on forms of *individual surve$_i$llance and discipline*. Where earlier societies used brute force or terror to control populations, modern society has cultivated a much more indirect and effective system of social control, where each **subject** internalizes ideological conventions and imperatives, and then unconsciously uses these as regulatory yardsticks with which to measure and modify social **identity** and comportment.

As a metaphoric exemplar of disciplinary power, Foucault cites the Panopticon, a model prison conceived by Jeremy Bentham in the nineteenth century as a modern replacement for older punitive systems of dungeons and torture chambers. Consisting of a circular structure in which individual prison cells are arranged around a central watchtower with one-way windows, the Panopticon was designed according to a uniquely modern rationale of psychological surveillance. The theory was that, because they were constantly subject to the potential scrutiny of guards in the tower, individual prisoners would eventually internalize the watchful gaze of the Panopticon and monitor their own behaviour accordingly. It is a system of incorporated surveillance that, according to Foucault, provides the *modus operandi* for modern regimes of disciplinary power where *subjects are trained to police their own identities through internalized mechanisms of social control.*

Figure 3.3: The Panopticon.

The ways that these processes of internalized disciplining occur are, according to Foucault, complex and manifold. There exists a whole battery of interacting ideological discourses and **practices** – what Foucault terms *technologies of discipline* – that work to inculcate dominant norms of social **subjectivity** and ensure the reproduction of power networks. Foucault does, however, accord special significance to various institutional agencies such as prisons, hospitals, asylums and schools, which he argues function as privileged sites for the disciplining of modern subjects.

It is fairly apparent how schools, for example, play a vital role in disciplinary power. As primary agents of socialization, schools are essential training grounds for the inculcation of ideological norms and values. They work to educate or 'school' young people in appropriate modes of social being. In particular, schools place a premium on moulding young minds and bodies to meet the dual purposes of social obedience and productivity, or what Foucault (1977) calls 'docility-utility'. The whole culture of schooling is implicitly geared towards the production of 'docile bodies that may be subjected, used, transformed and improved', and that will, precisely in their compliancy, emerge as useful members of and resources for society (p. 137).

Consider, for example, the accent on surveillance and normalization in school cultures. With its uniform rows of desks under the elevated and ever watchful gaze of the teacher and its regulatory practices of monitors, supervisors, inspections and examinations, the school classroom is strikingly similar to Bentham's Panopticon and, like its penal correlative, is explicitly designed for the production of well-behaved, docile subjects who have learned to monitor and regulate their behaviour in accordance with hegemonic norms. Given the highly regimented practices of corporeal and mental regulation that dominate school cultures in everything from clothing and physical training to timetabling and academic curricula, the modern school is a particularly forceful site of disciplinary power.

The school uniform is a good case in point. With a history dating back to the early modern period, the school uniform has long functioned as a sartorial symbol and tool of social discipline. Designed to identify the wearer as a member of a particular educational establishment, the uniform effectively subsumes the student and his or her individual sovereignty within the collective school body and seeks to brand him or her – quite literally in the case of uniforms that feature crests and mottoes – with the core ideological values promoted by the school.

That the principal function of school uniforms is the exercise of social discipline was neatly evidenced in 1996 when President Clinton instructed the US Federal Education Department to distribute manuals on how to enforce a school uniform policy legally in 16,000 school districts. In the context of a highly public debate on youth violence and facing an up-coming election, Clinton (1996) vigorously promoted a renewed commitment in public educational institutions to the wearing of uniforms, 'to create an atmosphere in our schools that promotes discipline and order' and that assists students in learning 'basic American values and the essentials of good citizenship'.

Yet, the case of uniforms and other practices of contemporary schooling might also serve to demonstrate that the exercise of disciplinary power is not always straightforward or successful. Far from being sausage factories of social control that churn out perfectly docile subjects, schools are more often than not terrains of intense power struggles and dissent. School cultures may be organized to foster student submission, but this doesn't automatically translate into practice. Whether modifying uniforms to reassert individual style, skipping classes, passing notes behind the teacher's back, or enjoying an illicit cigarette in the school restroom, students the world over are enormously resourceful when it comes to evading the power and control of school authorities. Indeed, from Tom Sawyer to Bart Simpson, there is a long tradition in modern Western cultures of celebrating as folk hero the 'naughty' school child that bucks the system and, by so doing, resists social power.

The question of resistance is actually vital to Foucault's theory of disciplinary power. In a way that nicely complements Gramsci's theory of hegemony, Foucault (1978) stresses that *the exercise of power in everyday life is a site of endless struggle that is always open to resistance and negotiation.* As he famously asserts, 'where there is power, there is resistance'. However, in concert with his understanding of power as diffuse and multiple, Foucault argues that resistance needs to be thought of in equally multiform ways. In fact, Foucault is generally pessimistic about the possibility of huge revolutionary changes in social power. Because modern power is disseminated across the whole social corpus and is thus by definition unlocalizable, it is naïve, he suggests, to think that power could be simply overthrown or eradicated. To change systems of disciplinary power, we must fight it from within, and cultivate multiple points of resistance at the level of daily praxis. It is an argument that has been singularly important to cultural studies and its readings of everyday life as a site of political struggle. Before proceeding to explore how the question of resistance has been taken up in cultural studies, take some time to read the following excerpt from Foucault, in which he summarizes his primary arguments about power and resistance.

MICHEL FOUCAULT ON POWER AND RESISTANCE

Continuing this line of discussion, we can advance a certain number of propositions:

- Power is not something that is acquired, seized, or shared, something that one holds on to or allows to slip away; power is exercised from innumerable points, in the interplay of nonegalitarian and mobile relations.
- Relations of power are not in a position of exteriority with respect of other types of relationships (economic processes, knowledge relationships, sexual relations), but are immanent in the latter; they are the immediate effects of the divisions, inequalities, and

disequilibriums which occur in the latter, and conversely they are the internal conditions of these differentiations; relations of power are not in superstructural positions, with merely a role of prohibition or accompaniment; they have a directly productive role, wherever they come into play.

- Power comes from below; that is, there is no binary and all-encompassing opposition between rulers and ruled at the root of power relations, and serving as a general matrix – no such duality extending from the top down and reacting on more and more limited groups to the very depths of the social body. One must suppose rather that the manifold relationships of force that take shape and come into play in the machinery of production, in families, limited groups, and institutions, are the basis for wide-ranging effects of cleavage that run through the social body as a whole. These then form a general line of force that traverses the local oppositions and links them together; to be sure, they also bring about redistributions, realignments, homogenizations, serial arrangements, and convergences of the force relations. Major dominations are the hegemonic effects that are sustained by all these confrontations. [...]

- Where there is power, there is resistance, and yet, or rather consequently, this resistance is never in a position of exteriority in relation to power. Should it be said that one is always 'inside' power, there is no 'escaping' it, there is no absolute outside where it is concerned, because one is subject to the law in any case? Or that, history being the ruse of reason, power is the ruse of history, always emerging the winner? This would be to misunderstand the strictly relational character of power relationships. Their existence depends on a multiplicity of points of resistance: these play the role of adversary, target, support, or handle in power relations. These points of resistance are present everywhere in the power network. Hence there is no single locus of great Refusal, no soul of revolt, source of all rebellions, or pure law of the revolutionary. Instead there is a plurality of resistances, each of them a special case: resistances that are possible, necessary, improbable; others that are spontaneous, savage, solitary, concerted, rampant, or violent; still others that are quick to compromise, interested, or sacrificial; by definition, they can only exist in the strategic field of power relations. But this does not mean that they are only a reaction or rebound, forming with respect to the basic domination an underside that is in the end always passive, doomed to perpetual defeat. Resistances do not derive from a few heterogeneous principles; but neither are they a lure or a promise that is of necessity betrayed. They are the odd term in relations of power; they are inscribed in the latter as an irreducible opposite. Hence they too are distributed in irregular fashion: the points, knots, or focuses of resistance are spread over time and space at varying densities, at times mobilizing groups or individuals in a definitive way, inflaming certain points of the body, certain moments in life, certain types of behaviour. Are there no great radical ruptures, massive binary divisions, then? Occasionally, yes. But more often one is dealing with mobile and transitory points of resistance, producing cleavages in a society that shift about, fracturing unities and effecting regroupings, furrowing across individuals themselves, cutting them up and remoulding them, marking off irreducible regions in them, in their bodies and minds. Just as the network of power relations ends by forming a dense web that passes through apparatuses and institutions, without being exactly localized in them, so too the swarm of points of resistance traverses social stratifications and individual unities. And it is doubtless the strategic codification of these points of resistance that makes a revolution possible, somewhat similar to the way in which the state relies on the institutional integration of power relationships.

Michel Foucault, *The History of Sexuality, Volume 1: An Introduction*, pp. 94–6.

(Text reproduced with kind permission of Penguin, UK.)

TACTICAL RESISTANCE IN EVERYDAY LIFE

The combined theoretical traditions of Gramsci and Foucault offer a productive framework through which to analyse the politics of everyday life. Their dual emphasis on everyday cultures as a locus of both domination and dissent has inspired a wealth of work in cultural studies on how subjects negotiate the operations of power in the contexts of their daily lives. In particular, this work has, as Simon During (1993) notes, been 'most interested in how groups with least power practically develop their own readings of, and uses for, cultural products – in fun, in resistance, or to articulate their own identity' (p. 7).

Cultural studies' interest in forms of popular resistance is arguably nowhere more apparent than in its long tradition of **subcultural** studies. Starting in the 1970s, many critics seized on subcultures as particularly striking examples of cultural resistance at work. In a seminal contribution, Dick Hebdige (1977) argues that youth subcultures are engaged in an indirect 'challenge to hegemony' that is 'expressed obliquely, in style' (p. 17). The distinctive and often aberrant fashions and associated **consumption** practices of subcultures operate, he suggests, as forms of resistant **bricolage**: the **appropriation** and reconfiguration of mainstream forms and objects in ways that 'disrupt and reorganize' hegemonic systems of social order. In the case of a spectacular subculture like punk, for example, its anarchic music, chaotic dances, and confrontational clothing and hair-dos are read literally by Hebdige as a 'revolting style': a challenge to hegemonic power through subversive practices of consumption that does 'more than upset the wardrobe', it 'undermine[s] every relevant discourse' (p. 108). As he writes:

> Style in subculture ... is pregnant with significance. Its transformations go 'against nature', interrupting the process of 'normalization'. As such they are gestures, movements towards a speech which offends the 'silent majority', which challenges the principle of unity and cohesion, which contradicts the myth of consensus. (p. 18)

Subcultures certainly offer spectacular displays of counter-hegemonic dissent, but it is important to recognize that popular resistance can and does occur in far more prosaic ways as well. Indeed, if as we have argued through Foucault, power is an unlocalizable network dispersed across the social landscape, then it is precisely at the small-scale level of the everyday and the mundane that 'the micro-circuitry of power' is most fully encountered, and therefore 'the micro-politics of resistance' most decisively waged.

The French sociologist Michel de Certeau (1984) uses the term **tactics** to refer to the multitude of minor moments and points of resistance that are practised by everyday people in the contexts of their everyday lives. In opposition to the large-scale **strategies** of domination that are the preserve of the powerful, tactics are the *little ways of 'making do'* used by the powerless to combat their subjection; an 'art of the weak' that jams the operations of power and helps restore some measure of value in the lives of the disenfranchised. As de Certeau sees it, because of the massified and impersonal nature of **postindustrial** society, the modern subject is essentially a latter-day 'poacher' who, barred from positions of real cultural power and **production**, must make raids across the fields of **consumer** culture, purloining what she or he can from the commodities and spaces on offer, and redirecting them in the service of personal empowerment. Thus he cites by way of example the modern office worker who uses company resources – telephone, stationery, photocopier – for personal ends, or the renter who redecorates the rented apartment in order to personalize the 'borrowed space' in which she or he lives. These are undeniably small and trivial occurrences, but they are precisely the sorts of ephemeral tactics that people employ to resist the full oppressive force of hegemonic subordination. They are, as de Certeau puts it, minor, everyday 'victories of the "weak" over the "strong" (whether the strength be that of powerful people or the violence of things or of an imposed order, etc.), clever tricks, knowing how to get away with things, "hunter's cunning", manoeuvres, polymorphic simulations, joyful discoveries, poetic as well as warlike' (p. xix).

The productive and imaginative force of these daily tactics of resistance is nicely encapsulated by Paul Willis's (1990) evocative description of them as forms of symbolic creativity. In a trenchant critique of orthodox distinctions between 'art' and 'the everyday', Willis asserts that creativity and 'imagination [are] not extra to daily life' but 'part of the necessariness of everyday symbolic and communicative work' (p. 10). He contends that we should recognize and celebrate the 'artistry' of daily living, 'the extraordinary symbolic creativity of the multitude of ways in which ... people use, humanize, decorate and invest with meanings their common and immediate life spaces and social practices' (p. 2).

While the 'everyday arts' of symbolic creativity are potentially practised by all, they may be seen to assume increased urgency and significance in the case of marginal or minority social groups for whom creative resistance is often nothing less than 'a question of cultural survival' (p. 12). To develop this argument, Willis attends in his study to how young people from lower socioeconomic backgrounds cultivate symbolic creativity in their daily lives as a way of combating the dehumanizing effects of their cultural and economic marginalization. Faced with a social system that barely recognizes and seldom values them, working-class youths have developed a range of creative tactics in everyday practices, from speech and fashion to media consumption, that enable them not only to valorize their identities 'but also to forge new resistant, resilient and independent ones to survive in and find alternatives to the impoverished roles proffered by modern state bureaucracies and rationalized industry' (p. 14).

'TAGGING' AS SOCIAL RESISTANCE

While neither theorist explicitly mentions it, graffiti may be read as a striking example of the sort of ephemeral counter-hegemony dubbed tactical resistance by de Certeau and symbolic creativity by Willis. Understood in its literal sense as the scratching or daubing of marks on a wall, graffiti is a practice that has been around for millennia. There is, for example, evidence of graffiti in the ancient ruins of Rome and Pompeii. However, the rise of mass urbanization in the modern period and the widespread availability of inexpensive, transportable tools of inscription have made graffiti an increasingly ubiquitous and characteristic feature of the contemporary urban landscape. From Sydney to São Paulo, the (post)industrial city is marked indelibly with the distinctive signs of modern urban graffiti.

While there has been a limited acceptance of some forms of urban graffiti as 'art', most mainstream commentators are categorical in their representation of graffiti as a social problem in need of urgent redress. These negative responses are particularly intense in relation to practices of graffiti writing or so-called 'tagging': the multiple inscription in a public space of a person's name, marker or 'tag'. Where other forms of graffiti generally have some pictorial component and are thus recuperable – even if only partially – to traditional notions of aesthetic value, tagging strikes most observers as entirely value-less. The apparent aim of tagging seems to be less the production of a recognizably artistic creation than the rapid and multiple scrawling of a graffiti signature on as many surfaces as possible. Like a manual stamp, the graffitist's tag is

Figure 3.4: Urban graffiti. Photograph by Brett Farmer.

imprinted again and again to the point where it resembles more a multi-xeroxed mess than a traditionally conceived work of art. In the absence of a readily perceptible aesthetic function, tagging is almost universally denounced as utterly worthless and inane. Indeed, it is not uncommon for tagging to be described in the most damning of terms such as 'a social blight', 'an eyesore' and 'an urban scourge'. Civic and corporate authorities frequently talk about 'waging war' on graffiti writing, and spend billions of dollars in aggressive campaigns to erase its presence from buildings and streets. Many cities, for example, have set up dedicated anti-graffiti police units that employ a veritable arsenal of sophisticated surveillance and control techniques, from helicopter patrols and infrared cameras to undercover 'sting' operations and telephone hotlines, in an effort to curb graffiti writing.

Regardless of one's personal opinion of graffiti, the extraordinary vehemence of anti-tagging responses and measures can only be described as entirely disproportionate to the seriousness of the actual practices against which they are targeted. Using even the most conservative criteria, tagging would have to rate pretty low on the overall scale of human wickedness. If it is a crime, it is a relatively petty and harmless one. So why does it provoke such extreme ire and condemnation?

Tim Cresswell (1996) offers a possible answer to this question in his reading of graffiti as a form of counter-hegemonic spatiality, or what he terms 'heretical geography'. Cresswell argues that the reason graffiti is so offensive to many people is because it contravenes hegemonic systems of social order and propriety. 'Graffiti,' he writes, 'flagrantly disturbs notions of order. It represents a disregard for order and, it seems to those who see it, a love of disorder – of anarchy, of things out of place' (p. 42). In particular, graffiti upsets

43

Figure 3.5: Graffiti tags. Photograph by Brett Farmer.

dominant systems of social space. Like any cultural environment, the city is constructed in and through a complex set of hegemonic discourses that imbue its spaces with 'appropriate' meanings and uses. There are spaces deemed correct for work, for play and leisure, for production and consumption; some that are public, others that are private, and so on. Graffiti flagrantly disrupts this dominant mapping of civic space by turning public places into private notebooks, scrawling playful markers across surfaces of commercial business, and generally contravening the governing boundaries and norms of social **geography**. As such, it can seem an affront to the meanings and stability of civic hegemony, 'a massive and continuing defacement … of the carefully controlled facades of the urban environment' (1996: 46).

It is within this context that we might also begin to apprehend the function and value of graffiti writing for its practitioners. *By transgressing the norms and 'proper' uses of social space, graffiti offers its proponents a way of disrupting systems of cultural authority.* It is a symbolic breaking of society's rules and a thumbing of the nose at the powers-that-be. As such, graffiti potentially acts as a significant tactic of popular resistance: a way of combating hegemony and domination. It is, for example, instructive that tagging is a form of graffiti most frequently practised by members of disadvantaged social groups, notably urban working-class youths and/or youths of colour. Indeed, historically, tagging first developed in the 1970s among the poor black, Latino and immigrant communities of

New York City. Using broad-tipped felt pens, poor youths of colour started to scrawl their names on the stations and train carriages of New York's underground in small but defiant gestures of personal anger. It was a metaphoric form of expression through which the city's most brutally oppressed minorities could tell the civic authorities, which seemed largely indifferent to their plight, that 'we are here and we will not go away'. These first few acts initiated a wave of graffiti writing that, as Jeff Ferrell (1997) notes, quickly spread to 'a remarkable variety of world settings' where tagging is used by disadvantaged 'kids (and others) … as symbols or representations of resistance' (p. 71).

In this sense, tagging is arguably a vital practice of political protest. It is a way for those with minimal access to the means of cultural and political representation to signal their presence in the social body. Working-class youths and youths of colour are seldom made visible in public culture and, in the rare exceptions when they are made visible, they are invariably demonized. Tagging is their way of asserting a public visibility and legitimacy in defiance of a social system that would render them unseen and unheard. It is, as Cresswell argues, 'a "tactic" of the dispossessed – a mobile and temporary set of meanings that insert themselves into the interstices of the formal spatial structures (roads, doors, walls, subways, and so on) of the city' (p. 47). This is why tagging is so controversial: it breaches the fundamental rules about who should be visible and who should not in the realms of public life. After all, the urban environment is saturated with all sorts of 'tags' – government and municipal markers, corporate brands, company logos – but these are the signatures of the powerful, and as such they are officially sanctioned and accepted. Graffiti tags by contrast are the signatures of the weak, those without social power and authority, and thus their presence in the cultural landscape is an aberration that poses, if not a serious threat, then a palpable challenge to the norms and operations of hegemony.

Figure 3.6: Tagging as resistant protest. Photograph by Brett Farmer.

It would be wrong to over-romanticize tagging as some sort of pure poetic voice of the disenfranchised or exaggerate its resistant dynamics. Graffiti is undoubtedly performed for all sorts of different reasons and produces all sorts of different effects, many of which would be far removed from the political reading advanced here, and the subversive effects that may be claimed for tagging are at best minimal and fleeting. At the end of the day, the cleaners move in and erase the offending marks, and the hegemonic systems of social power continue more or less intact. Nevertheless, it would be equally wrong to dismiss tagging – or for that matter any tactic of resistance – as merely trivial and inconsequential. It isn't easy navigating a life course through the frenetic and ever-changing waters of contemporary culture, especially for those who are most disadvantaged by its inequitable distributions of power. Under such conditions, the little ephemeral ploys that people develop in order to resist domination and attain some measure of personal **agency** can be crucial to a functional sense of self-identity and worth. It is precisely the small moments of resistance that enable all of us to negotiate and survive the very real – and often very fraught – politics of everyday life.

Summary

In this chapter, we have argued that:

- everyday life is a vital arena of social politics – a site for the reproduction and negotiation of power networks as these are organized around diverse axes of social difference such as class, gender, race, age and sexuality;
- power is exercised in contemporary culture through processes of consensual accord or hegemony whereby cultural subjects actively consent to uphold social hierarchies and accept their relative position in them;
- hegemonic consent is often won through practices of social discipline – as part of their cultural training, subjects are disciplined into internalizing the rules of society and the power systems they support;
- because of its dispersed and refracted nature, power is never singular or absolute but always open to negotiation and change;
- subjects routinely develop and use tactics of resistance in their everyday lives through which to combat the oppressive operations of power.

EXERCISES

1. Select a series of advertisements from magazines or newspapers and analyse how they might function in the service of hegemony. What sort of social power relations do they presuppose and naturalize? Are their images and representations grounded in social divisions such as class, gender, race, nationality and/or generation? Do they idealize dominant social groups and thus help legitimate their claims to power? How do you feel about these ads: indifferent, envious, angry, included, excluded?

2. Drawing from your own experience, discuss how educational institutions work as tools of social discipline. How are they organized in order to promote surveillance and submission? It might help to think about specific spaces such as classrooms, lecture theatres, locker rooms, libraries; or specific practices such as school assemblies, games and sports, examinations, report cards, and awards ceremonies. Now consider how other social institutions such as the family, the legal system, medical and health systems might also function as sites of social discipline.

3. Using your responses to the preceding exercise as a framework, discuss how people may resist or evade the operations of social discipline in particular contexts. Again you may want to draw on your own experiences whether current or past as, for example, a student at school or university, a child in a family, a medical patient, and so on.

4. What are your thoughts on graffiti? Do you agree that graffiti can serve as a form of political resistance? Have you ever engaged in graffiti writing? If so, what prompted you to do it and how did you feel about it afterwards; if you haven't, why haven't you? What about other so-called social youth problems such as drugs, vandalism, street gangs, and so on; do you think these also have a dynamic of social resistance? Does this put a different complexion on how we should think about and deal with these issues?

REFERENCES

CLINTON, W. 1996: Manual on school uniforms. *Office of the Press Secretary*, <http://www.inet.ed.gov/ updates/uniforms.html>. Accessed 26 January 2002.

CRESSWELL, T. 1996: *In Place/Out of Place: Geography, Ideology and Transgression*. Minneapolis: University of Minnesota Press.

DE CERTEAU, M. 1984: *The Practice of Everyday Life*. Rendall, S. (trans.), Berkeley: University of California Press.

DURING, S. (ed.) 1993: *The Cultural Studies Reader*. London and New York: Routledge.

FERRELL, J. 1997: Urban graffiti: control, resistance, and alternative arrangements. In Lang, K. S. and Nadelhaft, M. (eds), *America Under Construction: Boundaries and Identities in Popular Culture*. New York: Garland.

FOUCAULT, M. 1977: *Discipline and Punish: The Birth of the Prison*. Sheridan, A. (trans.), New York: Pantheon Books.

FOUCAULT, M. 1978: *The History of Sexuality, Volume 1: An Introduction*. Hurley, R. (trans.), New York: Pantheon Books.

GRAMSCI, A. 1971: *Selections from the Prison Notebooks*. Hoare, Q. and Nowell Smith, G. (ed. and trans.), New York: International Publishers.

HEBDIGE, D. 1977: *Subculture: The Meaning of Style*. London: Methuen.

TURNER, G. 1990: *British Cultural Studies: An Introduction*. Boston: Unwin Hyman.

WILLIS, P. 1990: *Common Culture: Symbolic Work at Play in the Everyday Cultures of the Young*. Milton Keynes: Open University Press.

FURTHER READING

AHEARNE, J. 1995: *Michel de Certeau: Interpretation and its Other*. Cambridge: Polity.

BOCOCK, R. 1986: *Hegemony*. London: Tavistock.

EDGELL, S. 1993: *Class*. London and New York: Routledge.

GELDER, K. and THORNTON, S. (eds) 1997: *The Subcultures Reader*. London and New York: Routledge.

HALL. S. and JEFFERSON. T. 1976: *Resistance through Rituals: Youth Subcultures in Post-War Britain*. London: Hutchinson.

HEARN, J. and ROSENEIL, S. (eds) 1999: *Consuming Cultures: Power and Resistance*. New York: St Martin's Press.

JERMIER, J., KNIGHTS, D. and NORD, W.R. (eds) 1994: *Resistance and Power in Organizations*. London and New York: Routledge.

McNAY, L. 1994: *Foucault: A Critical Introduction*. Cambridge: Polity.

O'BRIEN, J. and HOWARD, J.A. 1998: *Everyday Inequalities: Critical Inquiries*. Malden, MA: Blackwell.

Introduction to section 2

The spaces of everyday life

Fran Martin

To suggest out of the blue that there is a need for a 'critique of space' is liable to seem paradoxical or even intellectually outrageous. In the first place, it may well be asked what such an expression might mean; one normally criticizes a person or thing – and space is neither.
[... Nevertheless] there would certainly seem to be a need for such criticism: its 'object' is at least as important and interesting as the aesthetic objects of everyday consumption. We are talking, after all, of the setting in which we live.

Henri Lefebvre, *The Production of Space*

WHAT THIS SECTION AIMS TO DO

In Section 1 of this book we introduced you to some of the key conceptual tools and analytic frameworks for interpreting everyday **cultures**. Now it's time to get down to the business of examining in detail the everyday worlds that we all inhabit, and the first aspect on which we want to focus is that of *space*. But as the epigraph above from Henri Lefebvre (1991) suggests, the study of everyday spaces, like the study of everyday cultures more generally, can be a difficult and counter-intuitive project. This is because it's hard to adjust our customary ways of thinking in order to see that:

- *the spaces of everyday life are produced by everyday culture and **power** relations*; and also
- *the spaces of everyday life are active in producing our everyday cultural experience.*

It's difficult at first to see just how this is so because most of us are accustomed to thinking of the everyday spaces that we live in and move through as 'just being there': we take space for granted and tend to treat is as a kind of empty container or neutral backdrop for the activities of our lives. Analysing spatial forms seems more difficult than analysing other, more obviously textual and discrete, cultural forms like literary texts, films or television because spatial forms seem to give us less to 'hold onto'; it can be hard to see space as a separate, meaningful object of analysis and critique. This section's primary aim is to show you how the spaces of everyday life are in fact absolutely saturated with cultural meanings and the effects of everyday power relations. Relatedly, we also aim to help you see how the spaces of your own everyday life can provide richly productive objects of cultural analysis and critique.

The three chapters that comprise this section examine:

- how the *city* is a paradigmatically **modern** cultural space that functions not only as physical, built environment saturated with relations of regulatory power and popular **resistance**; but also, powerfully, as an *imagined* space replete with cultural fantasies, **utopian** dreams, and unpredictable desires as well as enduring fears and anxieties;
- how the *suburban homes* and domestic spaces that many of us inhabit enable us to express and construct our own **identities** through displays of **taste**, a cultural phenomenon that is itself constructed through the complex workings of **cultural capital**;
- how the *workplace* works as an everyday space riven by the contradictory movements of *regulation* and *resistance*; *enforced conformity* and *personal expression*; and how contemporary work **practices** reinforce yet also complicate the historically entrenched distinctions between *public* and *private*, work and home.

The key concepts covered in these chapters include:

- **cultural imaginaries** – especially those of the city and the suburb;
- modernity;
- **identity** formation;
- taste;
- cultural capital;
- spatial power relations.

SPACE AND IDEOLOGY

In his widely influential study of spatiality and social power, *The Production of Space*, originally published in French in 1974, Henri Lefebvre wrote the following about the apparent neutrality of everyday space:

> Vis-à-vis lived experience, space is neither a mere 'frame', [...] nor a form or container of a virtually neutral kind, designed simply to receive whatever is poured into it. [...] To picture space as a 'frame' or container into which nothing can be put unless it is smaller than the recipient, and to imagine that this container has no other purpose than to preserve what has been put in it – this is probably the initial error. But is it error, or is it ideology? The latter, more than likely. If so, who promotes it? Who exploits it? And why and how do they do so? (1991: 93–4)

In this passage, Lefebvre points to that mistaken tendency many of us have to assume that space is no more than a neutral 'container' divorced from the effects of power and ideology. Further than that, though, his argument is actually that *the very tendency to see space as ideology-free is in itself an ideological effect*. (This shouldn't surprise you: recall from Chapter 2 the fact that ideology generally works by effacing the fact that it is ideological and appearing as 'natural' instead.) So, let's consider Lefebvre's questions: what benefit is to be had, and by whom, from the promotion of the commonly held conception of space as value-free? A concrete example may help us consider this.

EXAMPLE: INTERPRETING THE LECTURE THEATRE

Consider the everyday spaces of the educational institution you currently attend or have attended in the past (perhaps you have already begun to consider the arrangement of space in educational institutions as part of one of the exercises at the end of Chapter 3). In particular, think about those lecture theatres commonly used as teaching spaces for undergraduate subjects with large enrolments – you may attend such a room for the subject in which you are using this textbook, or perhaps you have seen or used such a space at another time. Commonly, large lecture theatres are designed with rows of raked student seating radiating outwards and upwards from a central point at the front of the theatre where the lecturer stands, sometimes highlighted by a spotlight; usually with a microphone; and generally equipped with the means to control any audiovisual equipment, such as slides or videos, used during lecturing. Students are seated in tightly packed rows of identical seats, often equipped with functional, fold-down desks; while the lecturer stands in a highly differentiated space marked out by a large table, lectern, and/or computer and audiovisual console, and proximity to a screen and/or whiteboard. Students may sit under dimmed lights while the lecturer is highlighted with a spotlight. Students' voices are not amplified, while the lecturer's voice rings out to fill the space with the aid of electronic amplification and speakers positioned around the theatre. Students' eyes are encouraged by the alignment of their seats to face forwards and not to look at other students; in contrast, the lecturer's central position enables her or him to take in all of the students with a single sweep of the eyes. Obviously, such a spatial arrangement tends to *privilege* the lecturer, lending her or him a distinct aura of importance and authority; while at the same time *depersonalizing* and *de-privileging* the individual student, making her or him only one of a mass of bodies that are rendered uniform by the architectural layout of the theatre.

Now compare this lecture theatre situation with a smaller class group in which you are asked to sit in a circular formation, and where the teacher sits in the circle along with all the students. For many lecturers, the logic behind asking students to sit this way in small classes is in order to effect a kind of 'democratization' of the teaching space, so that the physical layout of the room does not privilege teacher over students, and in this way, to facilitate an easier and more relaxed flow of discussion. Consider, too, other spaces of your everyday life – your living room at home; a polling booth at a government election; outdoor areas at the college you attend; a local park or civic square. How does the spatial arrangement of each of these areas encode particular power relations? Which people are privileged, which people de-privileged? What kinds of activities does each space encourage, and what activities does it tend to discourage? Has an attempt been made to create a 'democratic' space where all people are positioned equally? Do you think this works effectively?

SPACE, PLACE, PRACTICE

You have already been introduced to the work of Michel de Certeau in Chapter 3, in which Brett Farmer discussed de Certeau's theorization of **strategies** and **tactics** in everyday life. In the same book that Farmer drew on in Chapter 3, *The Practice of Everyday Life* (1984), de Certeau also advances what has become a very influential theory about spatial practice. In particular, de Certeau suggests a definitional distinction between *space* and *place*. A place, he writes, is 'an instantaneous configuration of positions. It implies an indication of stability' (p. 117). In other words, for de Certeau, *a place is the physical arrangement of geographic or architectural elements*; for example, a street geographically defined by the practice of urban planning is a *place*. Space, on the other hand, 'exists when one takes into consideration vectors of direction, velocities, and time variables. [...] *Space is practiced place*' (p. 117). *Space*, in other words, *is physical, geographic place, as it is lived by the people that inhabit it*. For example, the street of the urban planners becomes a *space* when it is traversed by walkers. This definition of space is crucial to the kinds of work we'll be doing in this section of the book. In the chapters that follow, we encourage you at all times to keep in mind (at least) two aspects of the everyday spaces we are considering. These are:

1. the *physical* layout; the geographical and architectural elements (the elements of place, in de Certeau's terms);
2. the way the space is *used* – space as *practised* (the elements of space, in de Certeau's terms).

In the questions I suggested above about the layout of educational and other spaces, I've already suggested how we might begin to consider the relations between these two elements, by asking: to what extent does the physical layout of a space determine the ways in which it's used; and how do certain spaces enable certain practices, and discourage others? As you will discover in the chapters that follow, there is also another, very important, related question: *are there perhaps ways of inhabiting spaces that resist the 'intentions' of the spaces themselves?* Through consideration of these and related questions, we hope in this section to show you some of the many ways in which the apparently banal spaces of our everyday lives in fact function as rich sources of cultural meaning, encoded power relations, and opportunities for resistance and the fashioning and expression of personal identities.

REFERENCES

DE CERTEAU, M. 1984: *The Practice of Everyday Life*. Rendall, S. (trans.), Berkeley: University of California Press.

LEFEBVRE, H 1991 (originally published in French, 1974): *The Production of Space*. Nicholson-Smith, D. (trans.), Oxford: Blackwell.

Chapter Four

THE CITY

Chris Healy

Films discussed in this chapter:
- *Mon Oncle* (*My Uncle*, Jacques Tati, 1958);
- *Blade Runner* (Ridley Scott, 1982).

Cities, like dreams, are made of desires and fears

(Italo Calvino)

DREAMING THE CITY

Nina Laden's fabulous children's book, *Roberto: The Insect Architect* (2000) tells the story of Roberto, a termite, who, even when he was little, dreamed of being an architect. His fellow termites regard these aspirations as fanciful but, undeterred, Roberto decides that he has to start a new life somewhere else:

> So Roberto packed his bags and took the train to Bug Central Station, in the busy, buzzing hive of the big city. The city was a place where you could build your dreams. It was a place where you would be accepted. It was a place where the other termites wouldn't bug you. Roberto beamed hope like a lit-up skyscraper.
>
> But hope didn't come cheap in the big city. Neither did a place to live. Roberto had no choice but to rent a room in a flea-bag hotel run by a nervous tick. He shared the room with a family of bed bugs. Roberto introduced himself. Then he built the bed bugs their very own beds. (n.p.)

In the big city, Roberto tries to find a job as an architect, trawling, unsuccessfully, through the offices of Hank Floyd Mite, Fleas Van Der Rohe and others. Jobless, miserable and alone on the sidewalk, he is confronted by homeless insects. He realizes that he is not the only insect in the city with problems and so decides to use the waste of the city to build a neighbourhood for those without homes. Anonymously, Roberto transforms a block filled with junk into extraordinary homes that he gives to the homeless. This creates a storm of media interest in the big city with Steven Shieldbug desperate for the movie rights and the *Insect Inquirer* posting a reward for the first bug to bring the builder to light. Roberto is outed by a click beetle who gets the shot that appears as front-page news the next morning under the by-line, 'Termite Chips New Homes out of Old Blocks'. Roberto becomes an instant celebrity, feted by the mayor and honoured with a likeness in stone. He becomes 'the most famous architect in the insect world' and some of his houses even become museums. The story closes with these lines:

> But best of all, when little termites play with their food, now their parents say: 'Be creative. Maybe someday you'll grow up to be just like Roberto'.
> (n.p.)

This illustrated story skilfully brings together a number of ideas about city cultures. In the first place, the city is a magnet for Roberto, who, born into a small-town world that is clearly constraining, needs to find a place in which to realize his dreams. Thus for Roberto, as for many people across the globe since the mass urbanization of the nineteenth century, the city already existed as an imaginary place that had been talked about in conversation, consumed in a guidebook or gazed upon as an image. While this is certainly the case for many famous or iconic cities – think of the ubiquity of the Manhattan skyline or Hong Kong harbour in film and television – it is also the case, in a more abstract sense, for the city in general. *Cities exist for us as a set of ideas, images and ways of thinking about scale and density, about social relationships and community, about mobility and **power**, and about ways of being in the world.*

Figure 4.1: From Roberto: The Insect Architect *by Nina Laden © published by Chronicle Books LLC, San Francisco. Courtesy Chronicle Books.*

Figure 4.2: From Roberto: The Insect Architect *by Nina Laden © published by Chronicle Books LLC, San Francisco. Courtesy Chronicle Books.*

In this sense, then, we can regard city cultures as consisting of *both* **cultural imaginaries** and lived cultural experiences. By cultural imaginaries we mean the ensemble of images and fantasies, thoughts and expectations, feelings and values that we mentally attach to the idea of a city. In this chapter, we will look at both of these aspects, and will suggest that our urban cultural imaginaries actually affect our lived experience of cities. That is, our cultural imaginaries both about cities in general and about particular cities underpin the ways in which we organize our lives in cities, and may determine, for example, the kinds of transport we use, the kinds of interactions we initiate on a street, or the buildings we enter. In Roberto's case, he imagines that it's in the 'big city' that he will find what Georg Simmel (1997) called the freedom of the urban world. The 'big city' is where Roberto believes he will be able to become the kind of person he wants to be: an architect. And, of course, an architect is precisely a bridge between 'ideas' (ideas that take the form of plans, programmes, models, drawings, specifications and job costings) and actual spaces (homes, roads, public places, shops, offices, car parks, and so on). Similarly, cultural processes are in train when planners create differentiated precincts for factories or entertainment, for rubbish dumps or pedestrian traffic; when landscape architects design and workers run a path this way rather than that through a park, or choose between different materials in a playground; when local government authorities facilitate or prohibit certain kinds of activities, or install street lighting, or when engineers site roads, bridges, harbours and airports. More broadly, we can say that *cultural* **pract*i*ces** *and cultural understandings of cities actually take material form in the built environment of the city, and in how different people use the city.* Thus, from the outset, the story of Roberto the insect architect understands the city as a place where dreams come together with the sensual activity of making city culture.

But it's not long before Roberto is forced to confront some of the absences or tensions in his imaginary city. It turns out that the city is a place where the mere desire to work and to 'be something' (an architect) does not guarantee success. On the contrary, the city itself is an alienating place of anonymity where Roberto is nothing but one of the crowd. It is a place of scarcity, where jobs, housing, food and even a bed in which to sleep are hard to come by. It's a place where the scale of buildings, the speed of movement, the ways in which things work (and don't work) make life a misery for many. Roberto confronts these contradictions in a manner that, within Western **culture** at least, has been one of the key **ideologies** associated with **modernity** and the city (MacPherson 1962). Using what seems to be only his talent, hard work, plus determination and junk, he actually makes architecture and hence makes himself into an architect. Roberto becomes a modern individual by using what he possesses (his labour) in an environment that enables a new kind of productive transformation. Thus far, Roberto's story shares many of the key features of any number of narratives about self-made people: businessmen, migrants or artists who come to the 'big city' and make themselves anew. These familiar narratives are drawn on directly in the book: 'Like a magician, he transformed the block of junk into a street of extraordinary houses. Each one was a work of art' (Laden 2000: n.p.). There are, however, a number of twists, in that Roberto's self-making is both anonymous and philanthropic, and that he uses junk to make the houses that he gifts to the homeless, so that Roberto transforms not only himself but the city itself by using the materials that the city regards as waste. In this sense, *Roberto: The Insect Architect* literally enacts what Marshall Berman (1983) calls 'the intimate unity of the modern self and the modern environment' (p. 132), an environment that is, by definition, urban.

The final twist of Roberto's big adventure, however, relates to events of a more recent origin. Roberto's new houses made from junk are instantly noticed in the city – and not only by those he made them for. In this story, his creations inspire a mini media frenzy. As I've said, the mystery of who built the houses is solved when Roberto's identity is divulged and he goes on to be feted and acclaimed (although for what, exactly – his architecture, his philanthropy or both? – the book does not tell us). This part of the story suggests two aspects of contemporary city life that are worth recognizing immediately. The first is that Roberto's city (and, allegorically, those in which many of us live today) is a *mediatized city*. This is not a new phenomenon. Indeed, it could be argued that Henry Mayhew, the London journalist whose collected articles – part reportage, part ethnography and part oral history – on the poor of Victorian London were eventually published as *London Labour And The London Poor* (1861–2), began a tradition in which modern forms of **surveillance** and city life went hand in hand. Indeed surveillance by instruments of the state, from the police forces to census collection, has been central to the governance and control of the masses of humanity huddled together in urban centres since the nineteenth century. However, in the case of Roberto's 'big city', the circulation of information about the city is instantaneous, much more like the hourly traffic reports broadcast on the radio, or the constantly updating webcam placed at central locations in some major cities today. Not only this, but once Roberto is outed as the mystery house-building termite, he is fed into the loop of urban media culture: the Mayor unveils a statue of Roberto and he becomes 'the most famous architect in the insect world [...] Some of his houses even became museums' (Laden 2000: n.p.). In this respect, Roberto is a thoroughly contemporary urban hero. His impact on the world of the city begins with the everyday life of the insects whom he re-houses. But his impact extends much further than this, as well. Through the mediatization of his work, his celebrity status, and the museumification of his houses, Roberto's image – like the image of the Sydney Opera House or the Golden Gate Bridge – becomes one of the mechanisms by which the city represents, differentiates and markets itself to the world of urban consumers.

'EVERYTHING COMMUNICATES': THE CITY AS SECOND NATURE

A long history of the city would emphasize the ways in which cities have, for hundreds (and in some cases thousands) of years, been important as material concentrations of economic, political and cultural energies and forces. As fixed places of settlement, cities have tended to impose their own rationality, their own time and space, not only on the land on which they are sited, but also on the hinterland on which they depend for resources. Cities have produced and depended on **technologies** and social arrangements necessary to enable people to live together in high concentrations: capital, food and water, shelter, sanitation, transport, division of labour, economic, political and cultural institutions, and so on. However, from the mid-nineteenth century, cities became important not only in and of themselves but because they began to define the dominant form of life. As Richard Sennett (1994) argues:

> The modern geographic transformation swept over all the Western nations during the latter half of the nineteenth century. In 1850, France, Germany, and the United States, like Britain, were dominantly rural societies; a century later they were dominantly urban, highly concentrated at their cores. Berlin and New York grew at the same headlong rate, roughly, as did London, and both cities grew as the national countryside submitted to the flux of international trade. For good reason the hundred years spanning 1848 to 1945 are called the age of 'urban revolution'. (p. 320)

This urban revolution, allied to the industrialization of **production**, transformed the everyday life of many people. Marshall Berman (1983) describes it as a:

> dynamic new landscape in which modern experience takes place. This new landscape of steam engines, automatic factories, railroads, vast new industrial zones; of teeming cities that have grown overnight, often with dreadful human consequences; of daily newspapers, telegraphs, telephones and other mass media, communicating on an ever wider scale; of increasingly strong national states and multinational aggregrations of capital; of mass social movements fighting these modernizations from above with their own modes of modernization from below; of an ever expanding world market embracing all, capable of the most spectacular growth, capable of appalling waste and devastation, capable of everything except solidity and stability. (pp. 18–19)

As Berman suggests, the modern city is the centrepiece of this 'dynamic new landscape'. In this section we will outline some of the parameters of the modern city by discussing *Mon Oncle* (Tati, 1958) and *Blade Runner* (Scott, 1982), two films that offer rich and distinctive visions of everyday life in the city. We begin by arguing that *this new world of urban experience is what history and culture have made 'second nature' for most urban dwellers.*

Figure 4.3: Film advertisement for Mon Oncle.

Jacques Tati's film *Mon Oncle* (also released with the English title *My Uncle*) brings together two seemingly antithetical worlds in postwar Paris: the world of the Mme and Gérard Arpel, and the world of the uncle, Hulot. Both are urban worlds, but Hulot's is 'a traditional, cramped and twisted "old quarter" of Paris' and the Arpels' a 'modern, suburban villa' (Bellos 1999: 206). The film follows Hulot, who passes between these two urban worlds; a transition that he (and a pack of dogs that accompanies him almost everywhere) makes by crossing a wasteland on the fringe of a huge tower-block development of the kind that was very common in postwar France and elsewhere. The old quarter of Paris, where Hulot lives, is lovingly presented in the film. It is an integrated and seemingly organic place where work and home co-exist, where human relationships are profound, where time and labour have not been subordinated to the logic of money and mere **exchange value**, and where the use of things is more important than their **spectacular** status as commodities. By contrast, the modern suburban villa is self-consciously designed to be modern: it is a feminized space of domestic work separated from the public world of masculine labour; it is occupied by a dysfunctional nuclear family isolated from its neighbours, it is a place of bourgeois values in which time is money and commodities are worshipped. Thus, from the outset, *Mon Oncle* presents different kinds of cities as forming, shaping and determining different practices and experiences of everyday life in the city.

Like many of Tati's films, *Mon Oncle* can be regarded as a historical record of a particular moment in twentieth-century Europe. By this I do not mean that Tati's films are documentary films or period pieces, but that they are films that are fundamentally concerned with particular problems that were central to the historical world that Tati occupied. Chief among these concerns are those to do with *the rise of modern, (sub)urban, consumer lifestyle*. In general, we can identify this with the post-Second World War period in which the **mass culture** critique became widespread. Elaborated most influentially during the interwar period by the Frankfurt School, this model of critique identified **capitalism** in the twentieth century as having extended its domain and influence from production to **consumption** so that all aspects of life have been subordinated to **commodity** relations. The result, for Adorno and others, was that Western capitalist culture had become one in which people's most intimate relationships were with commodities rather than each other; in which passive consumption, standardization, false desires and alienation dominated cultural life. While Tati was neither a **Marxist** nor influenced directly by such work, his films responded to and engaged with the 'lifestyle' of mass suburban consumption. Kristin Ross (1996) argues that *Mon Oncle* provides a 'critique of the kind of life it is possible to live inside hypermodern suburban architecture'. She identifies Mme Arpel's home as a kind of temple to a consumer lifestyle: it is 'an assemblage of standardized, interconnected components [which] create the "total ambiance" of the modernized home [...] the stove-sink-refrigerator flowing together in a seamless, white-and-chrome unit, the design of the objects and their context mutually reinforcing each other in a seamless ambiance' (p. 192).

> 'Everything communicates.' In Jacques Tati's treatise on the anxieties of
> modernization, *Mon Oncle*, the obsessively clean housewife character,
> Mme. Arpel, repeats this line over and over whenever she shows off her
> home to guests. 'Everything communicates': the line proudly sums up a
> space designed to promote efficiency of movement, the flow of bodies from
> one room to another, a kind of interior circulation or traffic like the one we
> see automobiles involved in outdoors. The joke, of course, is that
> communication is exactly what is lacking in this sterile, precise, fenced-in
> suburban home where parents relate to their sullen, silent child in a series of
> compulsive directives about hygiene: don't mess up your room, put your
> books away, wash your hands, hang up your clothes, and so forth. (p. 105)

While *Mon Oncle* looks nostalgically to the 'old quarter' world of Hulot for a sense of
how we live a meaningful life in **modernity**, for our purposes it also offers a second
thread that enables us to further our discussion of everyday life and the modern city.
Although Tati allows the viewer of *Mon Oncle* many pleasures in mocking the
commodities that dominate the Arpels' lives, in the end it is not the commodities
themselves but the uses to which they are put that seem most important. So when Hulot
is baby-sitting Gérard, rather than acquiescing to the design of a ludicrously
uncomfortable couch, Hulot simply inverts it to make for himself a comfortable bed. In
other words, while the commodities of modern consumer culture seek to impose a
particular 'lifestyle', cultural practices – in this case the ways in which people use, make-
do, transform and live with a piece of furniture – remain not only a source of humour,
but a **tactic** of survival.

If a humanist, nostalgic, anti-modern and playful critique of post-Second World War
France can be recognized in Tati's films, then Ridley Scott's 1982 film *Blade Runner*
provides a very different vision of the urban life – post-humanist, **dystopian**,
postmodern and bleak. *Blade Runner* tells the story of Deckard, a Blade Runner who, in
Los Angeles in 2019, hunts and destroys a group of four replicants: androids who are
on the run and in search of their maker. However, for our purposes it is more the *mise-
en-scène* than the narrative of *Blade Runner* that offers us a powerful vision of a
postmodern city. The filmic urban world of *Blade Runner* seems the antithesis of both
the clean, bright suburbia and the quaint, quiet 'old quarter' of *Mon Oncle*:

> This is a dark city of mean streets, moral ambiguities and an air of
> irresolution. *Blade Runner's* Los Angeles exemplifies the failure of the
> rational city envisioned by urban planners and science fiction creators ... If
> the metropolis in noir was a dystopian purgatory, then in *Blade Runner*,
> with its flame-belching towers, it has become almost literal Inferno.
> (Bukatman 1997: 50)

Here consumerist gadgets and highly ordered 'nature' have given way to a world in
which hi-tech gadgets control and dominate human subjects, and nature seems to have

been overwhelmed by not just buildings, bitumen and pavement but the suffocating waste of hyper-capitalism. Here the city itself seems to be out of control: the street is dark, wretched, teeming and incomprehensibly hybrid; the built environment is a pastiche of decaying modernist icons and impossibly large skyscrapers housing the bio-industrial elite who, God-like, look down from on high. Here second nature is an extreme version of the managed order of *Mon Oncle*; both the city and the way of life it enables seem in-human.

This city is a place of *terminal identity*: 'the modernist, human subject is hollow, while replicants, with their implanted memories and false photographs, are permitted a luxurious illusion of wholeness' (Bukatman 1997: 57). Scott Bukatman uses the notion of terminal identity to describe two parallel tendencies exemplified in *Blade Runner*: the first is what he calls 'the end of the traditional subject'; the second, the augmentation of urban space by cyberspace. The ideal **subject** of the modern city, as we saw in Roberto, was a subject who would make itself in a struggle with the contradiction of urban freedom. Free of the tyranny of its past (the un-freedom of rural life, the constraints of family background, kinship ties, and so on), the individual emerges from the anonymity of the crowd. This particular ideological understanding of modern urban life as the space in which 'fully developed personalities' can be created has strong links to both romantic and revolutionary traditions (Hunter 1993). These traditions are undone in *Blade Runner* through confusion as to the human-ness of the androids and Deckard; androids are seeking to answer the question, 'Where do I come from?'; they cherish their memories, support and care for each other; and they worry, grieve, laugh and cry: they are passionate. Deckard, on the other hand, is an isolated individual, seemingly without a past, whose work consists of killing. In the imaginary of *Blade Runner*, the city is a place of nightmares. Yet for Bukatman, borrowing from Georg Simmel, this is the key to understanding cities – the metropolis produces a place for conflicting versions of what it is to be human:

> Cities, at least images and stories of cities, continue to represent the human position within a still-increasingly technologized, commodified world. City films and urban science fictions like Blade Runner 'make a place' in which to test the tensions, and play out the contradictions, of concentrated cities, spectacular societies and the continuing struggle to exist in the bright dark spaces of the metropolis. (p. 86)

DANCING IN THE STREET AND LIVING ON VOLCANOES

> As the shuttle bus brings me in from the airport to my Kings Cross hotel we happen to drive along Oxford Street, Sydney's 'gay mile' and part of tonight's parade route. This street, like a select number of others around the globe, is marked by its history of queer practices. The pavements of such streets are 'wandered by a multitude of pilgrims and adventurers: Old Compton Street in London, [C]anal [S]treet in

Manchester, Christopher Street in New York, Santa Monica Boulevard in Los Angeles' (Bell and Binnie 1998: 132). Today, the 'pilgrims' are out in force and the palpable sense of excitement in Oxford Street invades the bus [...] Bodies spill out of hip cafés and over sidewalk barriers onto the streets; old friends embrace and catch up with each other while checking out this year's visitors. There simply isn't enough sidewalk to accommodate everyone and a collective desire to take over the street seems to be only just kept in check [...]

The size of the gathering crowd is daunting and remains insistently out of reach of my experiential grasp [...] I'm no longer simply a spectator in the crowd – instead, I am strangely aware of being one tiny node in an immense collective mass spreading from the inner city outwards [...]

I settle on a vantage point for watching the parade and supervise some milk crates for a Vietnamese-Australian teenager and some of his friends in exchange for a temporarily better view and a plastic cup of wine. Then, finally, like medieval trumpets, the deafening roar and ride-by of at least two-hundred motorcycle-riding-lesbians (or 'dykes on bikes' as they are popularly known) officially 'herald' the beginning of the parade [...] The next few hours leaves me, like Eric Michaels in 1988, struggling to describe: 'it was so vast, so diverse, so, so ultra, even compared to previous years [...] No longer just a gay parade, it has become a theatrical event gay people perform as an offering to the city at large' (Michaels 1988: 4). When Michaels wrote of the parade [...] it was estimated to have been seen by more than one hundred thousand spectators. Tonight, by eight o'clock, approximately seven hundred thousand people will either be pressing in on the barriers that mark out the parade route or watching from available roofs, balconies and other overhangs along the parade route as a staggering assortment of 274 floats and walking groups move past us all.

(Morris 2001: 106-9) (Text reproduced with kind permission of Brian Morris.)

This excerpt describes the beginnings of the 1998 Sydney Gay and Lesbian Mardi Gras, an annual parade of gay pride and celebration. This parade provides us with one of two closing examples of contemporary city cultures. Up to this point, we have been concerned with stories about and images of the city: we have focused on how cities have communicated and encapsulated various cultural imaginaries. In observing some of these re-presentations we have stressed the ways in which cities are formed by, and in turn produce, powerful material forces – massive economic and demographic transformations – and potent ideological forces – the destruction of some identities and the creation of entirely new **subjectivities**. But, in the end, these are not merely abstractions but in fact ways of describing (abstractly) the actual, ordinary, everyday practices of living in the city. Morris argues that the Mardi Gras parade 'transforms the everyday practice of "walking down the street" into something extraordinary' (p. 110). By using the carnivalesque **strategies** of exaggeration, Mardi Gras is able to 'highlight the socially constructed nature of the everyday with particular reference to normative forms of sexuality and gender ... and the rights of marginalized social groups to use "public space" ' (p. 110). What emerges from Morris's analysis is a rich understanding of how urban queer communities provide a model for re-claiming and re-imagining everyday activity in the city.

Mike Davis's book *City of Quartz* (1990) is a marvellous exploration of what the history and present of the city of Los Angeles might offer its future. Davis introduces some of the key ideas of the book by describing how, in 1990, he visited the few physical traces that remained of Llano del Rio outside of Los Angeles. Built as a socialist **utopia** in the early part of the twentieth century, Llano del Rio is, for Davis, 'the ruins of Los Angeles' alternative future' (p. 3). In 1990, Davis found two 20-year-old building workers camping out there. He describes the encounter:

> We talked about the weather for a while, then I asked them what they thought about Los Angeles, a city without boundaries, which ate the desert, cut down the Joshua and the May Pole, and dreamt of becoming infinite. One of my new Llano compañeros said that L.A. already was everywhere. They had watched it every night in San Salvador, in endless reruns of *I Love Lucy* and *Starsky and Hutch*, a city where everyone was young and rich and drove new cars and saw themselves on television. After tens of thousands of daydreams like this, he had deserted the Salvadorean Army and hitchhiked two thousand five hundred miles to Tijuana. A year later he was standing at the corner of Alvarado and Seventh Street in the MacArthur Park district near Downtown Los Angeles, along with the rest of yearning, hardworking Central America. No one like him was rich or drove a new car – except for the coke dealers – and the police were as mean as back home. More importantly no-one like him was on television; they were all invisible.
>
> His friend laughed, 'If you were on TV you would just get deported anyway and have to pay some coyote in Tijuana $500 to sneak you back to L.A.'. He argued that it was better to stay out in the open whenever possible, preferably here in the desert, away from the center. He compared L.A. and Mexico City (which he knew well) to volcanoes, spilling wreckage and desire in ever-widening circles over a denuded countryside. It was never wise, he averred, to live too near a volcano. 'The old gringo socialistas had the right idea.' (pp. 12–14)

Cities as volcanoes is a metaphor that also appears in the opening scene of *Blade Runner*, as exploding fireballs fill the screen and the soundscape: cities are threatening and awesome, dangerous and spectacular. But, as we have seen, that is only half (or perhaps less than half) of the story of cities that are also Emerald Cities over the rainbow; places of promise and plenty, of belonging and comfort. How we make sense of everyday life in cities is not a question of choosing one set of metaphors over another, but of negotiating the productive tensions between the alluring promise and the arduous experience of urban life.

Summary

In this chapter, we have argued that:

- over the last 150 years, modern cities have been created by massive environmental, economic, demographic and cultural transformations that have produced the dynamic landscape that forms the terrain for a dominant form of life;
- the cities we live in today are paradigmatically modern environments, enabled by the rise of industrial capitalism;
- cities are imagined as well as material, lived places;
- cities spatialize cultural tensions between dystopia and utopia, hope and fear, possibility and constraint, abundance and scarcity.

EXERCISES

1. Many people still have some connection to non-urban environments and life experiences. Drawing on these experiences, try to produce a list of the key distinctions between urban and rural life. Once this had been done, consider whether it's possible to think of the urban and the rural as connected rather than antithetical.

2. Find some examples, concerned with a city you live in or know, which rely on a **cultural imaginary** of the city as utopia or dystopia: such examples might be found in stories or photographs, film or advertising, civic or tourist materials. Is it also possible to identify cultural texts that work between or beyond these characterizations?

3. Try to map and describe some of the ways in which cultural practices within 2 km of where you live or work are determined by, negotiate or subvert particular urban spatial constraints or configurations.

REFERENCES

BELL, D. and BINNIE, J. 1998: Theatres of cruelty, rivers of desire: The erotics of the street. In Fyfe, N.R. (ed.), *Images of the Street: Planning, Identity and Control in Public Space*. London: Routledge.

BELLOS, D. 1999: *Jacques Tati: His Life and Art*. London: Harvill Press.

BERMAN, M. 1983: *All That Is Solid Melts Into Air: The Experience of Modernity*. London: Verso.

BUKATMAN, S. 1997: *Blade Runner*. London: BFI.

DAVIS, M. 1990: *City Of Quartz: Excavating the Future in Los Angeles*. London: Verso.

HUNTER, I. 1993: Setting limits to culture. *New Formations* 4, Spring, 1988. Reprinted in Turner, G. (ed.), *Nation, Culture, Text. Australian Cultural and Media Studies*. London: Routledge.

LADEN, N. 2000: *Roberto: The Insect Architect*. San Francisco: Chronicle Books LLC.

MACPHERSON, C.B. 1962: *The Political Theory of Possessive Individualism: Hobbes to Locke*. London: Oxford University Press.

MAYHEW, H.H. 1967 (first published 1861–2): *London Labour And The London Poor: A Cyclopaedia Of The Condition And Earnings Of Those That Will Work, Those That Cannot Work, And Those That Will Not Work*. New York: A.M. Kelley.

MICHAELS, E. 1988: Carnival in Oxford St. *New Theatre: Australia*, 5, 4–8.

MORRIS, B. 2001: *Journeys in Extraordinary Everyday Culture: Walking in the Contemporary City*. Unpublished PhD thesis, University of Melbourne.

ROSS, K. 1996: *Fast Cars, Clear Bodies: Decolonization and the Reordering of French Culture*. Cambridge, MA: MIT Press.

SENNET, R. 1994: *Flesh and Stone: The Body and the City in Western Civilization*. New York: W.W. Norton.

SIMMEL, G. 1997 (first published 1903): The metropolis and mental life. In Frisby, D. and Featherstone, M. (eds), *Simmel on Culture: Selected Writings*. London: Sage.

FURTHER READING

ABBAS, A. 1997: *Hong Kong: Culture and the Politics of Disappearance*. Minneapolis: University of Minnesota Press.

DONALD, J. 1999: *Imagining the Modern City*. Minneapolis: University of Minnesota Press.

DUTTON, M. 1998: *Street Life China*. Cambridge: Cambridge University Press.

HARVEY, D. 1989: *The Urban Experience*. Oxford: Blackwell.

LOW, S.M. 1999: *Theorizing the City: The New Urban Anthropology Reader*. New Brunswick, NJ: Rutgers University Press.

MASSEY, D., ALLEN, J. and PILE, S. (eds) 1999: *City Worlds*. New York: Routledge.

MILES, M., HALL, T. and BORDEN, I. (eds) 2000: *The City Cultures Reader*. London: Routledge.

ROSS, A. 1999: *The Celebration Chronicles: Life, Liberty and the Pursuit of Property Values in Disney's New Town*. New York: Ballantine.

SORKIN, M. (ed.) 1992: *Variations on a Theme Park: The New American City and the End of Public Space*. New York: Hill and Wang.

ZUKIN, S. 1996: *The Culture of Cities*. Oxford: Blackwell.

Chapter Five

AT HOME IN THE SUBURB ☐

Annamarie Jagose, Fran Martin and Chris Healy

I have lived all my life, schoolgirl mother and wife
In decent suburban seclusion;
But the call of the sea has created in me
A curious restless confusion.

For it's so beautifully quiet in Highett
Where my daughter and son-in-law dwell,
They've severed the bonds with beloved Moonee Ponds
And I don't see why I can't as well.

Ooh it's so beautifully quiet in Highett,
So beautifully cosy and clean,
The folks who live there never gossip or stare,
They're too busy watching the screen.

Barry Humphries, 'The Highett Waltz'

INTRODUCTION

The words of Edna Everage – internationally renowned suburban housewife and alter ego of the Australian performer Barry Humphries – refer to specific suburbs in the Australian city of Melbourne, at a particular moment in the city's postwar cultural history. Yet the affective and **ideological** significance conveyed by the lyrics of 'The Highett Waltz' nevertheless relates recognizably to the ways in which the idea of 'suburbia' continues to be understood across many contemporary societies. Evoking the sense of uncanny, creeping horror for which her satirical representations of 'suburban-ness' are famous, Dame Edna rhapsodizes over the pleasures of suburban life – the quiet, the cleanliness and the sense of living 'decently' – while at the same time intimating an ominous dark side to this imagined ideal: the numbness, apathy and tedium that are equally strongly associated with the idea of suburbia.

The suburb, home to many of us at one time or another, and familiar to all, is a key location to consider for this book's project of helping you make sense of everyday life in contemporary, **postindustrialized** societies. This chapter aims to help you think through the centrality of the suburb as both a *lived* and an *imagined* location of everyday life today. As Dame Edna's example suggests, the suburb, like the city discussed in the previous chapter, does not consist solely in the materiality of its characteristic built forms (roads, shopping centres, schools, domestic homes, convenience stores, petrol stations, local council facilities, and so forth) and the ways we live in and with these architectural forms. It also consists of a powerful and complex **cultural imaginary**: all of the various and sometimes conflicting ways in which we understand, think about and represent the suburb to ourselves. It may be helpful, then, to distinguish two separate terms to refer to these different aspects. We'll use:

1. 'suburb' to refer to the material, built, and lived environment of a *particular* suburb (the physical and experiential materiality of the suburb in which many of you will actually live); and
2. 'suburbia' to refer to the imagined and representational **construction** of 'the suburbs' *in general* (what has colloquially been called a 'state of mind', and which we might refer to more precisely as a cultural imaginary or a set of **ideological** understandings and representations of 'the suburbs').

As we argued in relation to the city in the previous chapter, with the suburb, too, these aspects exist in a symbiotic relationship of inter-penetration and mutual cross-influence: the ways in which we *imagine* suburbia have a significant impact on our real everyday life experience of *living in* (or even making the decision *not* to live in) a suburb. As Chris Healy has written elsewhere:

> [S]uburbia has been a way of talking about other things; about change, family, community, childhood, and the tenuous habits we sometimes imagine as tradition. Suburbia names an imagined place which can hold together and enunciate a sometimes attenuated sense of self in the world.
> (1994: xvii)

This chapter starts out with a discussion of the historical, ideological and lived specificities both of the suburb as a type of built environment with a particular history, and of suburbia as a cultural imaginary. It then moves on to offer a detailed case study of one of the most iconic suburban sites: the domestic suburban home. In particular, the latter part of the chapter explores the ways in which everyday **practices** of interior decoration and the display of **taste** in the suburban home index the cultural processes of **identity** formation.

HISTORIES: SUBURB AND CITY

In the last chapter we discussed the historical processes of industrialization and urbanization that have seen the **modern** city become the dominant environment for human life worldwide since the mid-nineteenth century. Although the first suburban developments occurred in the USA as early as the 1850s, these were elite enclaves well out of the reach of the mass of the population (Jackson 1985: 73–86). The historical context for the large-scale rise of the suburb as we know it today emerged about a century later – post-Second World War. The spread of low-density housing development around the commercial centres of larger cities in the USA, Western

Europe and Australasia can be linked to a number of social changes taking effect post-1940s. These include:

- increased demand for housing postwar due both to returning servicemen and women and to population expansion through a sharp increase in birth rates – the so-called 'baby boom';
- relative postwar affluence leading to an expanding middle **class** with income available to spend on home ownership;
- a rising rate of car ownership and the development of freeway systems, enabling convenient transport from city workplaces out to 'dormitory suburbs' distant from the city centres;
- along with postwar economic growth, booming real-estate markets and building industries fuelling a surge in residential development (Jackson 1985: 231–45).

Kenneth T. Jackson lists five key characteristics of the subdivisions typical of suburban development in postwar America, characteristics that are also echoed to varying degrees in the suburbanization of European and Australasian cities at around the same time. These include:

- peripheral location – outside or on the edges of the major urban centres;
- low density – detached dwellings surrounded by garden plots; though this is in contrast to the predominance of apartment developments in Europe;
- architectural similarity – to lower the cost and simplify the process of design and construction;
- easy availability – the new, relatively inexpensive suburban developments put home ownership within the reach of a significantly larger section of the population than had previously been the case;
- economic and racial homogeneity – some of the new developments in the USA, for example, actually had policies of refusing to sell houses to black people (Jackson 1985: 238–43).

Although the precise historical background and characteristics of postwar suburbanization cannot easily be generalized across nations – or even across particular suburbs within a given nation – nevertheless, the factors outlined above delineate the basic historical and cultural context that produced the suburban environments that, for many of us today, are so familiar as almost to seem like a kind of 'second nature'.

SUBURBIA: BANALITY AND UTOPIA

Having sketched out this basic historical context for the rise of the suburb in the postwar West, what more can we say about suburbia, the cultural imaginary decisively linked to this set of lived and material places? What does suburbia mean to us as a field of representational practices and ideological significances? First and most straightforwardly, many argue that suburbia is defined by a paradigmatic 'in-between-ness'. If the city has frequently been seen as the central symbolic location of modernity, then the contemporary suburb – historically and culturally the location, more precisely, of **postmodernity** – is frequently presumed to be the very antithesis of the modern metropolis. Equally surely, however, suburbia is understood to be distinct from rural areas, 'nature' and the countryside. Neither urban nor rural; neither city nor country; both a 'product of urban expansion and [...] a protest against it' (Silverstone 1997: 5) the suburb and its cultural imaginary are characterized not only by a sense of geographic and cultural in-between-ness, but by a pervasive *ambivalence*.

The dominant tone of the representations of suburbia in both the quote from Dame Edna above, and the Jacques Tati film *Mon Oncle* (1958) discussed in the previous chapter, is a pessimistic one: suburbia is represented in a markedly **dystopian** light. Dame Edna conjures images of an eerily anaesthetized population in the bayside suburb of Highett, quietly and uniformly transfixed by their television screens. The suburban home of the Arpel family in *Mon Oncle*, as we have seen, is characterized by the similarly anaesthetic effects of the **commodification** of everyday domestic life and the insipidness of a **culture** built around the bourgeois values of consumption, display, organized leisure and 'nice' taste. In fact, even without needing to hear Dame Edna's song or watch Tati's film, we're probably all already familiar with the sometimes caricatural disparagement of suburbia as an imagined place characterized, among other attributes, by:

- cultural homogeneity;
- whiteness;
- straightness and heterosexual coupledom;
- political conservatism;
- a narrow, parochial view of the world;
- materialism;
- self-satisfaction;
- social isolation;
- subjective alienation;
- spiritual impoverishment.

We're not suggesting that such a strongly dystopian characterization is straightforwardly 'true' (or untrue) of *actual* suburbs, but it's undeniable that in our contemporary cultures, suburbia the *imagined* place is often heavily freighted with such associations.

Equally, though, suburbia may be *optimistically* associated with a range of positive ideas: in some representations, it is seen as a **utopia** where human social life may flourish both materially and spiritually. In fact, the earliest proponents of the idea of the suburb in mid-nineteenth-century America belonged to a religious cult called the Perfectionists, which maintained a romantic view of the suburb as the ideal human environment enabling a 'perfect existence' (Jackson 1985: 77). Llewellyn S. Haskell, developer of America's first suburb at Llywellyn Park, New Jersey, in the 1850s, described the suburb idealistically as 'a retreat for a man to exercise his own rights and privileges' (Haskell quoted in Jackson 1985: 77) This optimistic view of the suburb as enabling the happiness and well-being of individuals is echoed in slightly different ways in some forms of contemporary media culture. We might think, for example, of the 1960s American television series *The Brady Bunch* or, in a more contemporary example, the popular Australian soap opera *Neighbours*. Both of these programmes represent the suburb as a place of community, family, friendship, and general healthiness of body and spirit: a veritable model of the 'suburban dream' (though it might be interesting to consider how both programmes also imply – and arguably glorify – the overwhelming whiteness of this 'dream' by the near-total exclusion of non-white characters). In representations like these, far from signifying the nightmare vision of spiritual anaesthesia, political apathy and cultural conservatism of the dystopian accounts, suburbia is associated on the contrary with:

- family;
- community;
- neighbourliness;
- connection with others;
- a clean environment;
- peacefulness and safety
- health and 'good living';
- communal activities – car pools; dog-walking circles; local sports teams;
- public facilities – recycling programmes; child-minding centres; parks;
- local clubs and community associations – Girl Scouts; veterans' associations; rotary clubs.

Whatever you may personally think about the meanings and values of suburbia, it's clear that popular understandings of this idea in our contemporary cultures is markedly split – in ways comparable, if not identical, with understandings of the city discussed in the previous chapter – between the poles of utopianism and dystopianism. Suburbia is an idea about which our contemporary cultures feel profoundly *ambivalent*.

In the remainder of this chapter, we will move on from this general discussion of the history and meanings of the suburb to a more tightly focused consideration of a key site of suburban experience and expression: the domestic home. In doing so, we hope to help you think through in more detail exactly what it means, and how it feels, to experience everyday life in that particular and idiosyncratic yet almost by definition familiar contemporary environment known as the suburb.

DOMESTIC SPACE

Perhaps the most distinct and recognizable suburban site is the domestic space of the house. The cultural iconography of the suburban house is such that versions of the same dwelling – a squarish fully detached house with chimney – are recognizable across a range of cultural references including the small plastic moulded figures that represent property in the Monopoly board game or the icon you click on in some web browser interfaces to return to your computer's home page. The architectural space of the suburban house is heavily freighted with cultural meanings. This can easily be seen in the semantic conflation of house and home where 'house' refers to a building designed and used for private residence while 'home' inflects the material residential space with **connotations** of belonging, refuge and privacy.

> The concept of 'home' embraces both a physical and a social space; the house itself is home, as are the social relations contained within it. The concept of 'home' also carries a heavy ideological burden; it can be seen as part of an ideological trinity: 'family', 'home', and 'community'. Ideas of what constitutes a 'proper' family have shaped the ways in which individuals relate to one another in the intimacy of their domestic life, and the same ideas have influenced the physical design of the housing within which these social relations are lived. The home thus provides an important locale within which individuals negotiate their daily lives. (Munro and Madigan 1999: 107)

Commonly the home is understood as a privatized refuge from the world, an autonomous space for the individual or family defined in contradistinction to the spaces of work or more generally the world at large. This is the sentiment of the cross-stitched sampler 'Home Sweet Home' or the gruffer admission, usually made in a bid to limit public behaviours deemed indecent or unpalatable, that people may do what they like *in the privacy of their own homes*. In these everyday usages, the space of the home is synonymous with a seclusion from the public sphere, connoting a sanctuary for the maintenance of individual identity and domestic relationships.

This idea of the home as a private space is a historical one, secured in large part by the separation of work from the domestic sphere:

> The result of this separation was that – as far as the outside world was concerned – the house was becoming a more private place. Together with this privatization of the house arose a growing sense of intimacy, of identifying the house exclusively with family life. (Rybczynski 1986: 39)

The historical transformation Rybczynski is describing is a long one, beginning after the Middle Ages, and care must be taken to ensure that our ideas of home are attuned to the specific conditions of the early twenty-first century. For example, notions of the home as inviolably private, a retreat from the outside world, are rendered problematic by such everyday phenomena as the mass-media penetration of the home by television broadcasts and the telephone and, more recently, Internet access or communication **technologies** such as e-mail (Silverstone 1994). Moreover, the privacy and sanctuary allegedly guaranteed by the home is not extended equally to all, but is **overdetermined** in terms of one's normative positioning in relation to such categories as class, **race** and sexuality. For instance, as Rybczynski's naturalized specification of 'family life' indicates, the concept of heterosexuality frequently underwrites the ideal of domestic privacy.

TASTE AND THE HOME

The important conceptual point in this distinction between architectural and ideological representations of domestic space is that our ideas of public and private are mutually informing, not just at the semantic level, as each other's opposites, but in terms of everyday understandings of what the terms delineate. In order to think of the home as a space whose meanings are derived from both individual 'private' forces and cultural 'public' ones, we want now to think about **taste**, the exercise of intensely held and seemingly personal aesthetic judgements which, despite appearing purely personal, in fact simultaneously map **hegemonies** of the social order. In large part because of its ambiguous status in terms of the subjective and the hegemonic, the individual and the sociocultural, taste has long been an object of critical fascination, an intellectual tradition continued in the study of everyday life where the practices of aesthetic discernment are negotiated daily.

By the practices of aesthetic discernment we refer to those everyday discriminations between different orders of object which are naturalized as expressions of individuality, but which equally classify the discerning **subject** in terms of pre-existing social orders such as **gender**, sexuality and class. The practices of aesthetic discernment are equivalent to:

> the making of cultural choices, in every dimension of daily life, which differ in relatively systematic ways according to the kind of person you are – or rather the kinds of person, because all these differences occur along a number of different axes of social being. We all have a sense that these choices – preferring yum cha to McDonald's, or living in the city rather than living in the suburbs, or wearing silver instead of gold, or listening to Bach rather than Wagner or Pearl Jam rather than Elton John – are significant; they go to the core of who we are, and we are likely to feel that anyone who is blind enough to make the opposite choices is in some sense deficient or even downright strange. Bennett *et al.* 1999: 8)

Taste, then, is an important signifier of social identity. More than just an idiosyncratic marker of individual aesthetic preference, taste relates also to the way we, as social subjects, signify our position in relation to existing networks of social **power** and privilege. The home is an important staging of the aesthetic claims of individual taste. Before considering some specific everyday examples of domestic taste – the arrangement of domestic objects, for example, or styles of interior decoration – we need to think about how taste negotiates relations between the subjective and the hegemonic.

BOURDIEU'S DISTINCTION

Pierre Bourdieu, the French sociologist whose work *Distinction: A Social Critique of the Judgement of Taste* is central to these discussions of domestic taste and cultural hegemony, describes most succinctly the doubled capacity of taste when he describes its cultural function as the *classification of the classifier*: 'The social agents whom the sociologist classifies are producers not only of classifiable acts but also acts of classification which are themselves classified' (Bourdieu 1984: 467). Bourdieu's study is based primarily on two large-scale ethnographic studies undertaken in France in the 1960s in which more than 12,000 respondents were surveyed about their taste formations and cultural knowledge. Here we offer a brief summary and discussion of this complex and much-discussed text. (For further discussion, see Hebdige 1995: 87–92; Jenkins 1992: 137–51; Lee 1993: 30–9; and Miller 1987: 149–57.) Bourdieu argues that *taste formations are not simply expressions of individual preference but expressions of class affiliation*. Rather than the consequence of an innate or idiosyncratic sensibility, taste is learned. Moreover, the process of cultural education through which taste is acquired is determined by social class so that, by and large, legitimate taste is associated with the bourgeoisie, middle-brow taste with the petite-bourgeoisie and popular taste with the working class. Bourdieu complicates this broad understanding of class by identifying class fractions internal to each category and defined by a range of variables such as social origin, occupation, education and income. Furthermore, in addition to thinking about economic capital in terms of wealth or salary, he introduces the notion of **cultural capital**, by which he means a learned competence in codes of **cultural value**, 'the general information about cultural artifacts absorbed as a by-product of daily life' (Gershuny 2000: 85). By means of these co-ordinates, Bourdieu is able to schematize taste, demonstrating its class-inflected distribution in which industrialists and commercial employers with high levels of economic capital favour hotel holidays, water-skiing and foreign cars; secondary school teachers and artistic producers with high levels of cultural capital favour cycling holidays, Chinese restaurants and champagne; while farmers and unskilled workers with low levels of economic and cultural capital favour public dances, football and potatoes (Bourdieu 1984: 128–9).

In registering only the overdetermination of taste formations according to the distribution of economic and cultural capital, this summary obscures Bourdieu's wider argument that taste preferences are neither simply the consequence of inevitable cultural laws nor the autonomous choice of individuals. His formulation of **habitus** enables him to walk this careful line between determinism and voluntarism. For Bourdieu, *habitus is the set of class-based dispositions, internalized at the level of the body in the processes of early acculturation, which predispose individuals to act in certain ways without being fully conscious of what structures their decisions*. Habitus functions as:

> the mediating link between objective social structures and individual actors and refers to the embodiment in individual actors of systems of social norms, understandings and patterns of behavior, which, while not wholly determining action (as in the objectivist model) do ensure that individuals are more disposed to act in some ways than others. (Painter 2000: 242)

So a preference for polished floorboards over carpet or a favouring of country and western music over classical can be explained with reference to the 'interpretative intermediary structure' of habitus (Lee 1993: 31), the unexamined aesthetic preferences 'evident in the individual's sense of the appropriateness and validity of his taste for cultural goods and practices' (Featherstone 2000: 99). Although Bourdieu emphasizes both the subjective and structural elements of habitus, several scholars have critiqued his representation of the constrained capacity for individual **agency**, arguing that he emphasizes unduly 'the *systematic* overdetermination of people's life options by institutional factors' (Hebdige 1995: 92; see also Jenkins 1992: 149, and Miller 1987: 156).

As might be expected with a work as influential as Bourdieu's, this is far from the only criticism of *Distinction*. Bourdieu has been criticized for assuming universalizing paradigms on the basis of distinctly French data (Bennett *et al.* 1999: 11–12). More recently, the ongoing validity of his observations has been challenged by those who argue that the 1960s framing of his original research enables a connection to be run between class, occupation and cultural value that does not hold true with current organizational relations of class and labour (Hebdige 1995: 92). Indeed, Bourdieu's definition of class, drawing as it does on both economic and occupational criteria, has been criticized as internally incoherent and his whole project compromised by the extent to which class is reified as the singular index to distinction at the expense of other identificatory categories (Bennett *et al.* 1999: 12, 261). Finally, Bourdieu's assessment of different taste formations from a seemingly objective scholarly perspective – for example, his account of working-class taste as based on functionality not **aesthetics** – has been criticized as an unacknowledged reflection of his own class position (Jenkins 1992: 148–9). Rather than limit itself to a class-based analysis or even solely to the cultural work of distinction, the following section thinks more broadly about the manifestations of taste in a specific domestic context.

THINKING ABOUT DOMESTIC TASTE

The specific discussion of domestic taste in this section does not take the form of an ethnographic survey as in Bourdieu's *Distinction* or Bennett *et al.*'s *Accounting for Tastes*. Instead we focus our readings on just a single house which has particular resonance for one of the authors since it is Annamarie's childhood home and, until 2001, her mother's home of nearly 30 years. A former state house in a small New Zealand town but several times extended and renovated, this home is at once representative and idiosyncratic in terms of the taste formations it articulates. We consider it here by way of example, as a model for thinking about the functions of domestic taste and how household objects work to anchor certain meanings or identities (Csikszentmihalyi and Rochberg-Halton 1981: 173–96).

The house has a name, 'Tara'. The modest gate (see Figure 5.1) with its turned wooden spindles and its white on brown lettering seems comic in its allusion to the plantation splendour of the mansion in *Gone with the Wind* but the intended reference – more obscure, more personal – is to a word shared by the first languages of Annamarie's parents, Gujarati and Gaelic. In 1950s London where Annamarie's parents, Anne and Rustom Jagose, were married, an inter-racial relationship could still generate a sense of

Figure 5.1: 'Tara' gate. Photograph by Annamarie Jagose.

Figure 5.2: 'Tara' plate. Photograph by Annamarie Jagose.

suppressed scandal. This New Zealand house, the only house they bought together, some 15 years later, honours this hybridity through the somewhat déclassé tradition of house naming, itself a democratization of the protocols of aristocratic property ownership. The ethnic legibility of this domestic space – legible, that is, to the small interpretative community of Anne, Rustom and their five children – demonstrates how 'the home provides for most people a grounded space for identity work' (Noble 2002: 57). The particular identity work evident here is effected not at the level of architecture but of decorativeness. We will have more to say shortly about the changing sense of **ethnicity** evident in the house's interior decoration, but for now it is important to note that *domestic objects are here, in an unusually explicit way, imbued with the task of not simply conveying but in an important sense constructing a sense of personal identity.*

The way in which the exercise of taste in the interior decoration of the home articulates personal identity is not always as clear as it is in the previous examples. Consider, for

Figure 5.3: Coloured glass. Photograph by Annamarie Jagose.

Figure 5.4: Hat stand. Photograph by Annamarie Jagose.

example, Anne's construction of miniature scenes, small cameos of domestic life, in various spaces about the house. As a small sampling of these there is the collection of coloured glass displayed in the conservatory (Figure 5.3); the hat-stand and picnic hamper in the hallway (Figure 5.4); the pansy-themed display on an occasional table (Figure 5.5) and the candles and brass lamp on the hearth (Figure 5.6). Similar cameos can be seen in some of the **lifestyle** magazines Anne reads. These staged collections of domestic objects are not haphazard – quite some thought went into Anne's assembling the lamp, the illustrated poetry book and the small arrangement of silk flowers on the

Figure 5.5: Electric spirit lamp. Photograph by Annamarie Jagose.

Figure 5.6: Hearth. Photograph by Annamarie Jagose.

basis of their shared pansy motif – but neither do they seem readily legible in terms of the meanings they convey. In part, this is because of the way in which, seldom changing from one year to the next, they emblematize everydayness.

> The objects that surround us, through social codes or strategies of appropriation, have been invested with particular kinds of social meaning or manifest particular cultural categories: they don't just express personal identity, but embody notions of family, ethnicity, and so on. These meanings and categories are embedded in our domestic environment, reabsorbed – as 'ours' – as affective attachment to, and action within, space. This embedding means that that which we produce as a specific entity – this home, this family – returns to us as a cultural form – home, family – experienced in its specificity, and often invisibly. The categories are 'naturalized', becoming part of the everyday environment. (Noble 2002: 58)

Although the description of these decorative touches as 'scenes' or 'cameos' might suggest they are enacted for others, their location primarily in private parts of the house unlikely to be accessed by visitors suggests that the meanings they stage are for Anne herself. By way of these still-life displays, Anne conveys a certain middle-class aesthetic flair, which also gives a sense of the house's complete inhabitation. Living alone in a large five-bedroom house, Anne uses these arrangements of largely decorative household objects to mark the house as homely and code even little-used spaces as part of a functioning domestic economy.

The display of photographs in domestic spaces commonly works to figure a specific collection of people in the cultural form of 'the family' and Anne's many photographic displays work to code the house as a family home even in the literal absence of other family members. These displays are both informal, such as photographs stuck to the door of the fridge (Figure 5.7) and on a notice-board (Figure 5.8), or formal, such as framed professional portraits displayed together on a wall (Figure 5.9).

Figure 5.7: Photos on fridge. Photograph by Annamarie Jagose.

Figure 5.8: Photo board. Photograph by Annamarie Jagose.

79

Figure 5.9: Photo wall. Photograph by Annamarie Jagose.

Although it might seem particularly obvious in relation to photographs, people habitually

> invest a certain amount of their self into material objects as a way of
> managing their sense of place, social position and identity. The attachments
> formed with and the memories stirred by personal belongings may serve in
> some way as an important reminder of our histories and biographies.
> (Lee 1993: 26)

This can be seen in the kind of timeline effected by Anne's display of the formally framed images, which include a colourized photograph of Rustom's parents and his older sister as a child, an oil painting of Rustom, a photograph of Anne and Rustom on their wedding day and a series of studio portraits of the five children in their various graduation costumes. Financial limitations a bar to her own tertiary education, Anne takes great pride in her children, as can be seen in her transformation of their educational capital into a decorative aesthetic for her informal dining area.

The last identity-based theme we want to consider is Anne's domestic representation of her Irish Catholicism. This takes two distinct decorative themes, Irishness and Catholicism being largely figured separately, but we take them together here since there is a consistency connecting them at the level of representation. Displayed on the wall of Anne's bedroom is a white porcelain crucifix with a piece of dried palm that would have been tucked behind it the previous Palm Sunday (Figure 5.10). This display is connected to Anne's participation in the cycles of the ecumenical calendar. Other displays of Catholic iconography include a porcelain statue of the holy family in a custom-built alcove in the entry hall (Figure 5.11) and a small statue of the Sacred Heart of Jesus (Figure 5.12). All three of these objects have been displayed in the Jagose household since Annamarie was a child. More recently, the number of Catholic decorative objects about the house has proliferated to include less consequential, more kitsch items like the painted crockery

Figure 5.10: Crucifix.
Photograph by Annamarie Jagose.

Figure 5.11: Alcove with holy family.
Photograph by Annamarie Jagose.

Figure 5.12: Sacred Heart of Jesus.
Photograph by Annamarie Jagose.

Figure 5.13: Joseph and Mary tealights. Photograph by Annamarie Jagose.

Figure 5.14: Céad mile fáilte plaque. Photograph by Annamarie Jagose.

tealight covers depicting Joseph and Mary that stand on the servery connecting the kitchen with the dining room (Figure 5.13). This increase in religious objects not associated with actual religious practice perhaps indexes a transition in Anne's thinking about Catholicism as less a religious observance than a cultural identity. A similar interpretation can be offered when thinking about the domestic objects in Anne's house that represent her Irish nationality. Acquired on holidays 'home' to Ireland, these tourist objects are all relatively recent additions to the domestic environment. They figure at once a dislocation from and an identification with Ireland. The religious and Irish objects signal Anne's belonging to specific religious and national groups, working on a decorative or aesthetic level to anchor or reflect her identity formations. In addition, this signification of national belonging in the idea of Ireland as 'homeland' highlights the multiple and layered meanings attaching to the imaginary of 'home': in this case, the *domestic* home is made more 'home-like' by reference to a distant *national* and *cultural* home.

Figure 5.15: Prints of Aran islanders. Photograph by Annamarie Jagose.

Figure 5.16: Cottages of Ireland poster. Photograph by Annamarie Jagose.

In looking briefly at some of Anne's practices of interior decoration, we have indicated a number of ways in which taste customizes domestic space. Our analysis has been attentive to the processes by which the space of the home negotiates everyday relations to ideological categories of identity at the individual, familial, religious and national level. Although it is obvious from this example that specific practices of customizing domestic space are highly personalized and individual, nevertheless, at a more general level, the practice of constructing and signifying identity through space customization is one of the defining practices of domestic and suburban life. Indeed, one might even say that these practices produce the cultural imaginaries of 'home' and 'suburb' as much as they produce individualized identity.

Summary

In this chapter we have argued that:

- the suburb consists of both a material, lived environment, and a complex cultural imaginary (which we have called 'suburbia');
- the material suburb is the product of particular historical and economic processes that caused the proliferation of low-density housing developments around major cities after the Second World War in Western industrialized nations;
- the image of suburbia in contemporary cultures is deeply ambivalent, split between dystopianism and utopianism;
- the idea of home as a paradigmatically private space is historical, not natural, and is related to the historical separation of work space from domestic space;
- taste operates as a means of social and cultural distinction, not merely as the aesthetic expression of the personality of the individual;
- the selection and arrangement of decorative items in the domestic home does not only express the elements of the personal identity of the home's occupants (including, for example, ethnicity, religion, gender and class), but is also a means towards constructing this identity.

EXERCISES

1. Do you live, or have you ever lived, in a suburb? Based on your experience of suburban life – or, if you have not lived in a suburb, based on your understanding of the cultural imaginary of suburbia – explain to another student whether you think your view of the suburb and suburbia is more utopian, or more dystopian, and why.

2. In pairs, try the following exercise. On a sheet of paper, take five to ten minutes to sketch a rough map of the suburb or area where you currently live, marking on your map important locations in your own everyday-life world (for example, the location of your home, your local food shop, your cousin's house, the park where you play with your children ... or whatever else is meaningful to you in your local area). Then get together with your partner to compare maps, and discuss what you think each map implies about the ways in which you relate to your local suburb or area in your own everyday life. Consider how your sense of self may be contributed to by your interaction with your local environment, and how this sense might be altered by living in a different environment.

3. Think about the house or apartment where you currently live. How do the decorations and expressions of personal taste displayed in it express and construct the identities of the person or people who live there? How does taste customize domestic space where you live?

4. Think of an article of clothing, homeware or something similar that you think epitomizes 'bad taste'. Now think of an example illustrating what 'good taste' means to you. Can you explain these opinions with reference to the idea of **cultural capital**? Try asking yourself what kinds of cultural knowledge or training you need to possess in order to understand your chosen 'good-taste' object as tasteful; then consider what exactly it is that makes you consider your 'bad-taste' object to be un-tasteful. Do you think your choices relate in any way to class positions, as Bourdieu would argue?

REFERENCES

BENNETT, T. *et al*. 1999: *Accounting for Tastes: Australian Everyday Cultures*. Cambridge: Cambridge University Press.

BOURDIEU, P. 1984: *Distinction: A Social Critique of the Judgement of Taste*. Richard Nice (trans.), Cambridge, MA: Harvard University Press.

CSIKSZENTMIHALYI, M and ROCHBERG-HALTON, E. 1981: *The Meanings of Things: Domestic Symbols and the Self*. Cambridge: Cambridge University Press.

FEATHERSTONE, M. 2000: Lifestyle and consumer culture. In Lee, M.J. (ed.), *The Consumer Society Reader*. Cambridge, MA: Blackwell, 92–105.

GERSHUNY, J. 2000: *Changing Times: Work and Leisure in Postindustrialist Society*. Oxford: Oxford University Press.

HEALY, C. 1994: Introduction. In Ferber, S., Healy, C. and McAuliffe, C. (eds), *Beasts of Suburbia: Reinterpreting Cultures in Australian Suburbs*. Melbourne: Melbourne University Press.

HEBDIGE, D. 1995: The impossible object: towards a sociology of the sublime. In Carter, E. *et al*. (eds), *Cultural Remix: Theories of Politics and the Popular*. London: Lawrence & Wishart.

JACKSON, K.T. 1985: *Crabgrass Frontier: The Suburbanization of the United States*. New York and Oxford: Oxford University Press.

JENKINS, R. 1992: *Pierre Bourdieu*. London: Routledge.

LEE, M.J. 1993: *Consumer Culture Reborn: The Cultural Politics of Consumption*. London: Routledge.

MILLER, D. 1987: *Material Culture and Mass Consumption*. Oxford: Basil Blackwell.

MUNRO, M. and MADIGAN, R. 1999: Negotiating space in the family home. In *At Home: An Anthropology of Domestic Space*. New York: Syracuse University Press, 107–17.

NOBLE, G. 2002: Comfortable and relaxed: furnishing the home and nation. *Journal of Media and Cultural Studies*. 16:(1) 53–66.

PAINTER, J. 2000: Pierre Bourdieu. In Crang, M. and Thrift, N. (eds), *Thinking Space*. London: Routledge, 239–59.

RYBCZYNSKI, W. 1986: *Home: A Short History of an Idea*. New York: Penguin Books.

SILVERSTONE, R. 1994: *Television and Everyday Life*. London: Routledge.

SILVERSTONE, R. 1997: Introduction. In Silverstone, R. (ed.), *Visions of Suburbia*. London and New York: Routledge.

FURTHER READING

FERBER, S., HEALY, C. and McAULIFFE, C. (eds) 1994: *Beasts of Suburbia: Reinterpreting Cultures in Australian Suburbs*. Melbourne: Melbourne University Press.

FISHMAN, R. 1987: *Bourgeois Utopias: The Rise and Fall of Suburbia*. New York: Basic Books.

HANNIGAN, J. 1998: *Fantasy City: Pleasure and Profit in the Postmodern Metropolis*. London and New York: Routledge.

JOHNSON, L.C. (ed.) 1994: *Suburban Dreaming: An Interdisciplinary Approach to Australian Cities*. Geelong: Deakin University Press.

KAPFERER, J. 1996: A fortunate style of life: the accumulation of symbolic capital in suburbia. In *Being All Equal: Identity, Difference and Australian Cultural Practice*. Oxford and Washington, DC: Berg.

ROSS, A. 1999: Main street is better than alright. In *The Celebration Chronicles. Life, Liberty and the Pursuit of Property Values in Disney's New Town*. New York: Ballantine.

SILVERSTONE, R. 1997: *Visions of Suburbia*. London and New York: Routledge.

Chapter Six

EVERYDAY WORK

Greg Noble

INTRODUCTION

In a well-publicized incident in July 2002, an *Australia Post* employee at a Melbourne call centre was disciplined and had her pay reduced when she refused to remove personal items from her desk (Williams and Ede 2002: 7). Despite this being a common **practice** (Figure 6.1) the coverage sparked a flurry of letters to the editor: some were outraged at the actions of *Australia Post*, others bemoaned the loss of a strong work ethic in Australia. Apart from raising a raft of important issues – management practices and industrial relations, productivity, work satisfaction, the role of personal **identity** at work, the values we hold around work, and so on – this incident reflects the complex relations between home and work, leisure and labour, in the contemporary world.

Discussions of everyday life often make the mistake of assuming that everyday life equates with home and family life, or leisure. However, for most adults work is something that consumes much of our daily activity, most days of the week. Moreover, when we look at it closely, we realize that work is also an important arena for social

Figure 6.1: A workstation decorated with personal photographs, ornaments and non-standard screen-saver. Photograph by Fran Martin.

interaction and cultural values beyond the formal requirements of the working contract. You yourself have probably had some experience of the world of work – perhaps working in a store, food outlet or other business – to help you get through your college study. Think about the things that you do at work, apart from selling or making things or providing services. Do you spend time *avoiding* work? Do you gossip, have you made friends there (or enemies!) or met romantic partners, for example? We shouldn't dismiss these as trivial: a major ethnographic study of scientists working in a laboratory came to the conclusion that scientific discovery was fuelled as much by the petty conflicts of the working environment than the grand claims about the objective pursuit of knowledge (Latour and Woolgar 1986). It may be that these elements of social interaction make the job pleasant, and therefore enhance your performance; they at least may best be understood as saying something about you as a person. Work is also a key place for gaining a sense of self-worth and identity: assuming that many of you are studying to gain a good job in the future, how important will work be to your sense of who you are?

While **cultural studies** has often ignored the world of work, leaving it to the more established disciplines like sociology and psychology, the fact that we spend so much of our lives in and at work suggests it is an important area for the study of everyday life. It is in three overlapping areas – questions of ***subject$_i$v$_i$ty***, the *spatial construction of everyday domains* and the *cultural meanings* that pervade our worlds – that cultural analysis has some important insights to offer.

WHAT IS WORK?

This may seem like a rather silly question. After all, in one sense we all *know* what work is. Yet, as this book has already made clear, some of our most taken-for-granted ideas are indeed very hard to pin down. When we ask people what they think work is – as I ask college students every year in a course I teach – they come up with some predictable but varied answers:

1. work is what you get paid to do;
2. work is what you are made to do;
3. work is something you do outside the home;
4. work is boring (in contrast to leisure, which is fun).

If you consult any substantial dictionary you'll find many definitions of work to choose from. Each of these ideas contains some truth, but each, on its own, is inadequate and misleading. While gaining an income is a central feature of the world of work, there are in fact many things we work at for which we don't get paid: housework, voluntary work, and school or college work (indeed, in general you *pay* for the privilege of studying at college!). On the other hand, there are activities that become work *because* someone gets paid for them – like sex work, compared with sex between partners. However, if sex between partners involved an element of compulsion, then it could *feel* like work.

Indeed, compulsion is a common theme in the way people understand work, both because we have to work to earn a living, and because most workplaces involve forms of supervision that can feel oppressive (we'll return to this later). Yet many of us are lucky enough to experience a great deal of choice and autonomy in work, so compulsion on its own is an inadequate way of defining work. Similarly, while many people express a degree of boredom or tedium in their work, the idea that work is drudgery is not the experience for all workers, all the time. Even though work is often described in opposition to leisure, in fact work can be enjoyable for many. Work is also often described in contrast to home, but the increasing incidence of home-related work – such as telecommuting, home offices, outworking and domestic service – indicates that this isn't a reliable criterion for defining the realm of work either (Figures 6.2 and 6.3).

The point of this is not just to underline the difficult semantic problem of defining work, but to highlight the fact that work is not always clearly distinguished from non-working activity. We can also point out that work has many different forms: part-time work and full-time work can be very different, as can urban and rural work, managerial and factory work, owning a business and working for one, working in a small business and in a large corporation, and so on. Furthermore, work changes historically and socially: what is considered work in one place or at one time is not necessarily the same in another time or place. In other words, work is not a singular category, but covers

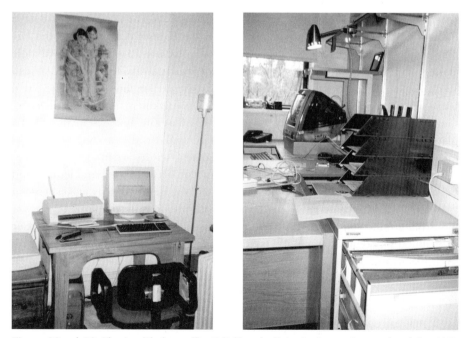

Figures 6.2 and 6.3: The rise of the home office (6.2) blurs the distinction between home and workplace (6.3). Photographs by Fran Martin.

many different types of activities, in various forms. This is discussed in great length in the existing literature on the sociology of work (Hall 1994): the point for us here is to recognize that *work is a cultural* **construct** *dependent on the society in which it is defined and the situation in which it is enacted; that is, it is shaped by the various* **d*i*scourses**, *practices and institutions through which work is made meaningful.*

Perhaps the key element in the **construction** of work as a cultural category is the way it has been placed in opposition to the ideas of home and leisure, as we have seen in the previous chapter. The emergence of **capitalism** in **modern** European society brought about the increasing separation of work and home for many people, particularly in cities, as more people worked in institutions such as factories, and fewer were occupied in home-based productive activity. As we suggested above, home and work have never been completely separate in practice, but as ideas they have been fundamental as a binary opposition in Western cultural systems. This tendency towards the separation of home and work spaces was the foundation of the perception of distinct and separate spheres – of public versus private life – which is still with us today, and which echoes through a whole series of other cultural oppositions (Game and Pringle 1983). As work increasingly became a place in which people's time, their labour-power and the products of that labour are owned and directed by someone else, the home increasingly became perceived as the 'haven in a heartless world' (Lasch 1977), a space of 'free time' and autonomy away from the pressures of the workaday world. As work increasingly became seen as a masculine world of (industrial) **production**, home became identified as feminine, and as the centre of **consumption**. With the development of the large department store in the industrialized West of the late nineteenth century, which was largely staffed by women and frequented by (middle **class**) women, consumption was increasingly identified as a female practice (Corrigan 1997; Reekie 1993). In sharp contrast to work, where your time is someone else's, home also becomes aligned with leisure, in which your time is your own. Of course, these distinctions are highly questionable – for the housewife, home is anything but a place of free time, removed from compulsion and drudgery – but as cultural categories, notions of work as compulsion and home as leisure are fundamental to the Western world. Indeed, it may be that the distinction between work and leisure, and the resultant division between the working day and the weekend, only makes sense in a modern society as it emerges from the institutionalization of the temporal rhythms of industrial production. Such a distinction doesn't make sense in a hunter-gatherer or agricultural society where temporal patterns and productive activity depend more on the rhythms of the day and the season, and the immediate demands of providing sustenance (Sahlins 1972).

So I want to stress again that we are talking here about the divisions between work and home and work and leisure as *social constructions*. Before we can explore the cultural dimensions of work in everyday life any further, however, we must take a detour via the sociology of work in modern society.

MARXISM AND THE DEGRADATION OF LABOUR

The socially and historically specific nature of work, which I have just emphasized, is a key point in the **Marxist** analysis of the labour process in the capitalist mode of production, perhaps the key critical approach in the sociology of work. Marx's starting point in the mid-nineteenth century in analysing labour as socially necessary productive activity is to turn to the philosophy of Hegel. Hegel's achievement, Marx argues, is in showing how, through labour, humans not only transform nature to produce our means of subsistence, but in doing this, *we also produce ourselves as human beings* (Marx 1978: 112). *The essence of ourselves as human is realized through our labour,* whereby we objectify our selves and satisfy our needs, create new needs and develop our capacities as human beings which are the bases for our sociality and our individuality, and therefore our freedom as humans (Sayers 1989).

It is useful to return to this philosophy of labour because our idea of work as drudgery and as a form of enslavement is so entrenched we often can't see work in its entirety. From the perspective of the philosophy of labour we can see that human labour is not only about self-sustenance, but about realizing ourselves as human beings – a view that allows us to see work as always historically specific, and hence as *potentially fulfilling and liberating* as well as being a source of alienation. Think about different types of work available to people. There are many jobs where the overwhelming experience may be of drudgery and routine, of being compelled to do something from which you gain little satisfaction. On the other hand, there are many jobs in which people can experience a very strong sense of satisfaction and self-expression.

Marx picks up these ideas – that work is the way we realize ourselves, and that labour is always historically specific – to show that the problem with work is not the fact that we have to do it, but rather the social and economic contexts that shape the work we have to do. In a capitalist society, Marx showed, the worker sells their labour-power to the capitalist, and therein the contemporary problem of **alienated labour** lies. In selling our labour-power, social relations are reduced to the laws of **commodity** exchange: we lose control of our labour; we lose control of the product of our labour; and in the growing division of labour that accompanies factory production in particular, work becomes routinized, the repetition of mindless disconnected tasks divorced from the creative aspects of the process (Grint 1991: 92).

There ensues a struggle over the realization of that labour-power and the **surplus value** it creates in products, as the worker tries to maximize his or her wages while the capitalist tries to maximize profit. The capitalist, or the management that is created, tries to maximize profit by controlling the labour process through increasing coercion and **surveillance**. Braverman (1974) demonstrates how Marx's analysis of the labour process is still relevant to the highly **technologized** late twentieth century and beyond. Braverman argues that technological change is simply one part of the process whereby capital attempts to control the labour process. By separating the labour process from the worker's skills, by separating conception from execution, and by removing knowledge from the workforce, work becomes degraded and de-skilled in a capitalist labour market largely because it becomes so routinized.

The Marxist analysis, and Braverman's development of it, has often been criticized for being too simplistic and mechanistic. It does, however, contain key insights that are still useful today (Willis 1988). I don't want to rehearse these debates again here, or indeed to supplant the Marxist analysis – rather, I think we can usefully augment the Marxist analysis with insights drawn from the cultural analysis of everyday life. Such a cultural analysis would focus on the ways in which the social construction of work is achieved through everyday practices. An understanding of the subjective dimensions of work – questions of identity, and so on – can expand our understanding of the structural features of the labour process emphasized in the Marxist approach. A crucial step in opening up these questions is an examination of the relationship between **gender** and work.

THE GENDER OF WORK

Some of the most powerful criticisms of the Marxist approach to work came from the developing **feminist** movements of the 1970s and 1980s. Many feminist scholars pointed out that as important as the Marxist focus on class is in understanding the nature of work and relations of production, gender is also a vitally important aspect. Many criticisms were made: the Marxist emphasis on (factory) production, it was argued, obscured other areas of work, paid and unpaid – such as domestic service – and reproduced the cultural equation of masculine/work and feminine/home, hence ignoring the particular experience and location of women (Wajcman 1991). Other feminists pointed out that processes of industrialization historically depended heavily on the higher rates of exploitation of women (Tilly and Scott 1978), a fact left under-theorized in the classical Marxist analysis. Indeed, capitalism continues to rely heavily on the unpaid labour of women in the home to sustain profit levels in industry: women, for example, do much of the labour of consumption that was once performed by paid labour (Game and Pringle 1983).

The increasing number of women returning to the world of paid employment in the late twentieth century made it very hard to ignore the gender in the labour force and to sustain the idea that work was a 'man's world', while studies began to reveal the depths of what has become known as the **gendered division of labour**. Research showed that there were many aspects to this division: many jobs that were typically seen as 'men's work' or 'women's work'; women were less likely to make it up the promotion and management ladders; women received lower pay even when doing the same job; women were more likely to be part-time or casual, and have their careers interrupted by child-rearing, and so on (Wajcman 1991). Despite the feminist critique of this situation, cultural assumptions about what women should and shouldn't do prevailed, requiring organized social protest and legislative change. Even today, many jobs are still seen as being 'natural' for women, such as nursing and teaching. This is despite the evidence of substantial historical change in employment patterns for women: some occupations, like clerical work, were once the sole preserve of men, even though they are now much more likely to be performed by women (on lower pay and with less status) (Crompton and Jones 1984). Computer programming was once performed by women who were no more than secretaries; as it became more important with computerization, men entered the field, and the status and pay increased (Wajcman 1991). Significantly, the very idea of skill – what gets valued as being difficult and requiring training – is very much a gendered idea: women's work is often seen to be a 'natural expression' of **femininity**, and hence not skilled – for example, sewing or nursing – while what is seen as highly skilled tends to be the domain of men – such as medicine. Cockburn (1983) traces the function of gendered ideas of skill and the use of technology in the workplace, and their relation to work hierarchies and industrial conflict.

Even today, years after the emergence of feminist movements that challenged these stereotypes, many such assumptions about 'women's work' versus 'men's work' are still held, suggesting that gender continues to play an important part in women's educational and occupational choices, and their experience in workplaces. Advertisements for workplace technologies such as computers have tended to rely on **sexist** images of dumb but sexy female secretaries, and powerful-looking men in suits (Pringle 1988). Similarly, conservative representations of the nuclear family still feature in advertisements for home computers (Noble 1999). The issue of gender is not only important, then, from a sociological perspective: it also allows us to begin thinking about the role of cultural values and meanings in the way work is conceived and practised.

WORK AS A SPATIAL DOMAIN

It is important to stress that home and work are not just ideas, but institutionalized spaces that have to be created and recreated through social practices. As Nippert-Eng (1996) demonstrates, the boundaries between work and home are socially constructed and must be constantly maintained. Different environments function in different ways as 'territories of self'; in the workplace, institutional imperatives frame conventions for self-presentation, but we can also shape our environment through our own use of objects and practices. Nippert-Eng details many aspects of this 'boundary work' in her analysis of employees in a research laboratory. These employees draw on various objects and practices to give each space a sense of being home or work. The workplace is often defined as a place through specialized workplace objects – from work-specific items such as the tools of one's job, computers and filing cabinets, through to things as banal as coffee cups, keys and calendars. Nippert-Eng cites the example of having different work and home address books as a way of identifying and separating these different 'territories' (Figures 6.4–6.7). Employees also develop specific activities that define their work practices – routines, breaks, forms of workplace interaction.

Figure 6.4: 'Home things' on a bedside table: novels, toys and a shot-glass of sentimental value, and a novelty alarm clock. Photograph by Fran Martin.

Figure 6.5: 'Work things' on a window ledge at the office: pens, tape, floppy disks, post-it's, tea for tea breaks. Photograph by Fran Martin.

Once we create these distinct spheres, we have to have ways of moving between them, little rituals for helping us make the shift: the cup of coffee first thing at work to get us into the right frame of mind, changing clothes to help us relax when we return home, and so on. All these seemingly trivial practices help us negotiate the spaces that we call work and home. Think about the things you do to help 'get in the mood' for working, or that help construct a special sense of being at work. Nippert-Eng suggests, however, that not all people negotiate the relation between home and work in the same way, and she distinguishes between **tactics** for segmenting and integrating home and work. 'Segmenters' are those

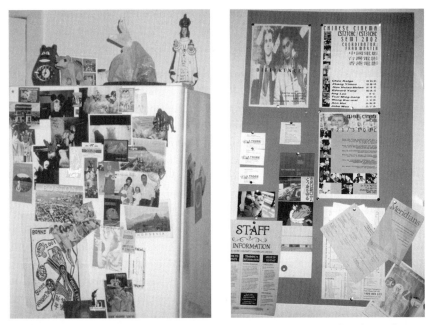

Figures 6.6 and 6.7: Home decoration (refrigerator with personal photos, postcards and artworks) versus work decoration (office notice-board with work-related notices – but note the personal pet photo). Photographs by Fran Martin.

who prefer to draw sharp distinctions between home and work, while 'integrators' are those who happily blur this boundary. Most of us employ both kinds of tactic.

Employers might also have expectations about the kinds of objects and practices you engage in at work that symbolize the right work attitude. A particular kind of clothing – whether this be a special uniform or simply a standard of formal dress – might represent to your employer and to customers that you are geared up to work, or have a professional or diligent approach. Signs may be put up at work to constantly remind us of appropriate behaviours. Even the **aesthetics** of the workplace – the paint used on the walls, the colour and design of technologies, furniture and so on, all remind us in a way to stay 'professional' and to not be distracted by non-work aspects.

These seemingly trivial examples have important consequences for the conduct of work. As the example of the *Australia Post* worker shows, we transgress the boundaries between home and work by introducing aspects of our private selves into work contexts, and this could be taken to mean that we don't take work seriously enough. For the *Australia Post* manager who penalized the employee, her photos and football poster were obviously too great a transgression of the discipline and attitude needed at work. Presumably the logic is that if you are thinking too much about your home and social life, then you aren't doing your job. Some workplaces, such as call centres, are specifically organized to reduce the amount of space each employee has and the amount of social interaction that can occur: these strategies increase the number of employees that can fit into the working space and decrease the amount of time spent off-task. We'll return to the issue of control of the work space below: suffice it to say that the way we 'fill' the work space has significant social and economic dimensions.

There is another way of looking at all this, though. Research conducted in the late 1990s into people's relationships with their computers in a university workplace showed that employees often went to great lengths to introduce personal items into their workplace or to reshape the work items, such as computers, that exist at work (Noble and Lupton 1998). As computers become increasingly pervasive in workplaces, they become more central to the ways we negotiate the category of work. Some employees went to great lengths to master their new technology, becoming informal experts because they saw their status as competent professionals at stake. They put enormous effort into reconfiguring the computer, learning how to install new software, labelling the hard drive, redesigning the interface, and so on. Other employees went out of their way to 'domesticate' the technology, making the workplace and the computer familiar by introducing meanings and uses that are more likely to come from the home or social life. Many interviewees engaged in acts of **appropriation**, taking back and claiming as theirs items that may otherwise have represented a form of control over them: employees personalized their computers through decoration and redesigning the screen; others gave the hard drive a personal name. Some used the computer to 'gossip'. On the other hand, more employees were using their computer to do work in non-work time, because the computer made this easier. Either way, at stake here is the re-negotiation of the spaces of work and home. This is particularly significant in an era when the division between home and work is becoming less clear: computerization means work is increasingly encroaching into the home and private life. 'Domesticating' working life through acts of appropriation is one way of evening up this balance, or at least making the work space less alienating and more habitable.

At issue here is more than just the creation of discrete spaces; our senses of **identity** are also at stake.

SUBJECT TO WORK

Work has always been central to our sense of identity: who we are, what we do, where we belong. When we meet people at parties, for example, often the first question we ask is 'What do you do?' It is our way of finding some connection, of identifying something about the person we are talking to that defines them, at least in part. Some suggest that work is becoming less central while consumption practices are becoming of greater import. Certainly gone are the days when, especially for men, work was the major if not the only source of personal identity, but it's probably truer to say that the relation between work and identity has become more complex. Rather than get caught up in the debate over whether work or leisure is more important to our sense of self, we can simply recognize, drawing from the philosophy of labour we've already outlined, that both domains – as 'territories of the self' – involve elements of the processes of self-realization, the creation of ourselves as human beings. Indeed, one anthropologist has revitalized Hegel's insights by applying them to the world of consumption (Miller 1987). As cultural analyses of everyday life have demonstrated, the formation of **subjectivity** is an ongoing process operating across all practices and institutions.

We have already seen how gender identities have an important part to play in the experience of work and the structure of the workplace. Some exponents of the Marxist approach have also shown how worker identities are interwoven in the conduct of daily life at the workplace. For example, Burawoy (1979) shows that workplace 'games' to see who can do the most work and who knows the technology best are ostensibly aimed at alleviating boredom but also involve status and competence – crucial to employees' sense of self. Here, however, workers' identities are seen as functional for managerial control. On the other hand, de Certeau's insights into *la perruque* – workers' appropriations of the employer's time and materials for their own purposes – suggest the ways in which workers' identities are a form of **resistance** to the powerful (1984: 25–8). If we recognize that work is a social domain and not just a place where commodities are produced, the question of subjectivity at work becomes more complex than the reduction to the effects of control or resistance would suggest. As we have seen in the example of the university, within the workplace competing subjectivities are at play: the desire to make work homely is at odds with the desire to appear professional and competent. In either case, what is at stake is the way we see and present ourselves.

For some companies – like *Australia Post* – this could be problematic, but it is probably true that employers generally encourage the interplay between workers' personalities from social life and the world of work. In the service and retail industries, du Gay (1996) argues, new articulations of the relation between work and consumption have created complex work identities that can complicate the relation between work and leisure (pp. 4–6). This is partly because many new areas of employment, particularly in service and retail, increasingly draw on people's personalities in their performance of their work. In her study of airline attendants, Hochschild (1983) shows how they are trained to carry out 'emotion work' to give customers a sense of personal service and comfort. The overlap between personal and public demeanour might be especially true for the professional for whom the 'career' is a 'project of the self' that lies partly outside the context of a specific job, and relates to a larger, reflexive process of self-management (Grey 1994). The self at work draws from aspects of personality outside the workplace: employees are expected, for example, to have a certain 'character' to fit into the business. Psychological testing of employees developed in the twentieth century as a way of ensuring workers are integrated into the workplace, 'governing the soul' (Rose 1990). Current management discourses – such as those around excellence and corporate culture – continually encourage employees to identify with the enterprise, to make a personal investment in the organization (du Gay 1996: 54). The company cannot guarantee, however, how employees will respond to these imperatives: if the line between work and home, private and public self is often transgressed in exploitative ways, it can also be the source of employee resentment. Questions of subjectivity always return to relations of **power** and **resistance**.

DISCIPLINE AND POWER

In the work of people like du Gay and Rose, analysis of the relation between work and subjectivity focuses on the extension of managerial control into the 'soul' of the employee, drawing on the work of Foucault. Another line of Foucauldian analysis has approached the question from the perspective of administration. Based on Foucault's (1979) use of Bentham's model of the Panopticon as an example of modern **disciplinary power** (see Chapter 3), Foucault argues that administrative techniques in modern institutions involve observation, normalizing judgement and examination that produce systems of constant **surveillance**. This surveillance functions to produce 'docile bodies': bodies that have been trained to fit the logic of administration such that self-discipline replaces coercive control. As we saw in Chapter 3, for Foucault, power is integrative rather than coercive. Zuboff (1988) elaborates Foucault's model to talk of the new 'information panopticon' in the contemporary **postindustrial** economy, in which information technologies extend managerial control and produce an 'anticipatory conformity' amongst employees. She looks at both the technological capacity for surveillance (through software that measures keyboard strokes), and the hierarchical and individuated organization of the modern office (the separation of workers and the all-seeing position of the supervisor) (see also Lyon 1994). This line of analysis could equally be applied to the call centre, the 'hi-tech sweatshop', where employees are constantly monitored. On the one hand their physical location is highly controlled – they are often segregated from other workers to minimize non-work activity; on the other, technology constantly measures their efficiency – their time taking a call, going to the toilet, the success of their call, and so on – information that is fed back to their supervisors (Horin 1998: 6). At some call centres, employees are required to raise their hand to go to the toilet; others are set up like a classroom (Williams and Ede 2002: 7).

While most workplaces aren't this oppressive, many do draw on forms of spatial organization and technological monitoring to ensure high levels of productivity. But they also draw on techniques for harnessing the employee's personality to the workplace to ensure commitment and loyalty. The analyses based on Foucault's examination of how subjectivities are managed through disciplinary practices present a notion of power that has implications for the ways in which employees operate as 'free individuals' (Knights and Willmott 1989). A sense of professional competence is part of a 'self-disciplining' that *confirms an identity as a productive worker*, but that also *reproduces the power relations that exploit the worker*. The Foucauldian approach provides a strong theoretical analysis of the interweaving of subjectivity and power, and a basis for understanding how, particularly in occupations involving 'responsible autonomy', internalized self-discipline explains worker cooperation (Sosteric 1996). Even seemingly democratic processes like total quality management and team working – designed to give employees a say in the production process – function to produce more pervasive forms of surveillance and control that shift the onus of responsibility onto the shoulders of the most vulnerable (Sewell and Wilkinson 1992).

Power, as Foucault (1980: 142) proposes but never follows up, always produces resistance – a point he shares with Marxist and feminist perspectives. We've already seen in de Certeau's discussion of *la perruque* how resistance plays an important role at work: **tactics** is what de Certeau calls those practices deployed by the powerless that undermine the logic of the institution (see also Chapter 3). We can see instances of this resistance in contemporary working life, even with the new technologies Zuboff and others have shown to be capable of greater forms of surveillance: recent data suggests that 30 per cent of office e-mail in Australia contains gossip, jokes or other 'unproductive' messages (Croucher 2001: 7). It is perhaps easy to see why bosses are now developing high technology to catch their 'cyberslackers' (Campbell 2000: 11). We could suggest that placing 'too many' personal items might also be construed as a form of resistance, as a way of evading the control of others over the spaces in which we live and work. Yet, as I've argued above, the complex dimensions of everyday working life mean we can't simply reduce these examples to the interplay of control and resistance, as important as this is. At stake here are a range of issues – the creation of social spaces, cultural meanings, our sense of self and the different subjectivities we inhabit – in the ways we manage and give shape and meaning to our worlds.

Summary

In this chapter, we have argued that:

- work is a central domain of everyday life, not something outside it;
- work can't be easily and objectively defined, because it is a cultural construct dependent on the situation in which it is enacted – that is, it is shaped by various local and specific discourses, practices and institutions;
- Marxism provides a key approach to analysing the philosophical and socio-structural dimensions of work;
- feminist perspectives demonstrate that our meanings and practices of work are highly gendered;
- work as a spatialized domain culturally defined against home and leisure is signified through particular types of practices and objects;
- work is a key site for the formation of subjectivity – not as a single source of identity, but in the ways we try to shape the various aspects of our sense of self, and the ways these aspects are in turn shaped by the workplace as an institution;
- work is structured by the practices whereby employers seek to control employees' labour, either by shaping the spaces in which we work or by harnessing aspects of employees' personalities – processes that we attempt to resist or negotiate.

EXERCISES

1. Make a list of all the things you do at work that aren't necessarily part of your job description, or things that you do that are more socially orientated than work-related. How much time do you spend doing these? Why do you do them? Do they contribute to or detract from your performing of the job? How many of them may help the completion of your job? (If you don't have a job, think about one, such as working in retail, where these issues might be important.)

2. How is your workplace (either in a paid job or even your desk at home) marked as a 'working space' via objects and practices? What special things do you do, or have, that help you make the transition from home to work, or from work to home? Are you a 'segmenter' or 'integrator'? What expectations can you think of held by specific objects and practices at the place of work you know best?

3. Think about different types of work you have done. Can you think of examples in which the overwhelming sense is of drudgery, routine and compulsion? Can you think of particular things you've worked at that have contributed to a strong sense of personal satisfaction – an essay, an artifact you've made or a service you've performed? How have these been 'work'? Were they paid? Did you see these as expressing or shaping your sense of self?

4. Make a list of jobs that are typically viewed as 'women's work' or 'men's work'. Are they still seen this way? Do they have to be? Are they jobs that can't be performed by the other gender? Why have they become so gendered?

5. How has your labour been directed or controlled in workplaces you have experienced? What roles have the following features played in this: spatial organization, direct supervision by a manager, technology, self-discipline? How have these been effective (or not)? How did they make you feel? Why?

REFERENCES

BRAVERMAN, H. 1974: *Labor and Monopoly Capital*. New York: Monthly Review Press.

BURAWOY, M. 1979: *Manufacturing Consent*. Chicago: University of Chicago Press.

CAMPBELL, M. 2000: Rude awakening for workers loafing on the Net. *The Australian*, 19 January, 11.

COCKBURN, C. 1983: *Brothers*. London: Pluto Press.

CORRIGAN, P. 1997: *The Sociology of Consumption*. London: Sage.

CROMPTON, R. and JONES, G. 1984: *White Collar Proletariat*. London: Macmillan.

CROUCHER, J. 2001: Number crunch. *Sydney Morning Herald Good Weekend*, 22 September, 7.

DE CERTEAU, M. 1984: *The Practice of Everyday Life*. Rendall, S. (trans.), Berkeley: University of California Press.

DU GAY, P. 1996: *Consumption and Identity at Work*. London: Sage.

FOUCAULT, M. 1979: *Discipline and Punish*. Sheridan, A. (trans.), Harmondsworth: Penguin.

FOUCAULT, M. 1980: Power and strategies. In Gordon, C. (ed.), *Power/Knowledge*. New York: Pantheon, 134–45.

GAME, R. and PRINGLE, A. 1983: *Gender at Work*. Sydney: Allen & Unwin.

GREY, C. 1994: Career as a project of the self and labor process discipline. *Sociology* 28(2), 479–97.

GRINT, K. 1991: *The Sociology of Work: An Introduction*. Cambridge: Polity Press.

HALL, R. 1994: *Sociology of Work: Perspective, Analyses and Issues*. Thousand Oaks, CA: Pine Forge Press.

HOCHSCHILD, A. 1983: *The Managed Heart*. Berkeley: University of California Press.

HORIN, A. 1998: Working the phones. *Sydney Morning Herald, Spectrum*, 19 September, 6.

KNIGHTS, D. and WILLMOTT, H. 1989: Power and subjectivity at work. *Sociology* 23(4), 535–58.

LASCH, C. 1977: *Haven in a Heartless World – The Family Besieged*. New York: Basic Books.

LATOUR, B. and WOOLGAR, S. 1986: *Laboratory Life*. Princeton: Princeton University Press.

LYON, D. 1994: *The Electronic Eye*. Minneapolis: University of Minnesota Press.

MARX, K. 1978: The economic and philosophic manuscripts of 1844. In Tucker, R. (ed.), *The Marx-Engels Reader*. New York: Norton, 66–125.

MILLER, D. 1987: *Material Culture and Mass Consumption*. Oxford: Blackwell.

NIPPERT-ENG, C.E. 1996: *Home and Work: Negotiating Boundaries Through Everyday Life*. Chicago, IL: University of Chicago Press, 1996.

NOBLE, G. 1999: Domesticating technology. *Australian Journal of Communication* 26(2), 55–74.

NOBLE, G. and LUPTON, D. 1998: Consuming work: computers, subjectivity and appropriation in the university workplace. *The Sociological Review*, 46(4), 803–27.

PRINGLE, R. 1988: *Secretaries Talk: Sexuality, Power and Work*. St Leonards, Sydney: Allen & Unwin.

REEKIE, G. 1993: *Temptations: Sex, Selling and the Department Store*. St Leonards, Sydney: Allen & Unwin.

ROSE, N. 1990: *Governing the Soul*. London: Routledge.

SAHLINS, M. 1972: *Stone Age Economics*. London: Tavistock.

SAYERS, S. 1989: Work, leisure and human needs. In Winnifrith, T. and Barrett, C. (eds), *The Philosophy of Leisure*. Basingstoke: Macmillan, 34–53.

SEWELL, G. and WILKINSON, B. 1992: 'Someone to watch over me': surveillance, discipline and the just-in-time labor process. *Sociology* 26(2), 271–89.

SOSTERIC, M. 1996: Subjectivity and the labor process. *Work, Employment and Society*, 10(2), 297–318.

TILLY, W. and SCOTT, J. 1978: *Women, Work and the Family*. New York: Holt, Rhinehart & Winston.

WAJCMAN, J. 1991: *Feminism Confronts Technology*. Sydney: Allen & Unwin.

WILLIAMS, J. and EDE, C. 2002: This is the happy snap that cost an office worker $3000. *Daily Telegraph*, 16 July, 7.

WILLIS, E. 1988: Introduction. In Willis, E. (ed.), *Technology and the Labor Process*. Sydney: Allen & Unwin, 1–13.

ZUBOFF, S. 1988: *In The Age of the Smart Machine*. Oxford: Heinemann.

FURTHER READING

ADKINS, L. 2002: *Revisions: Gender and Sexuality in Late Modernity*. Philadelphia, PA: Open University.

BREHM, J. and GATES, S. 1997: *Working, Shirking, and Sabotage: Bureaucratic Response to a Democratic Public*. Ann Arbor: University of Michigan Press.

CONSTABLE, N. 1997: *Maid to Order in Hong Kong: Stories of Filipina Workers*. Ithaca, NY: Cornell University Press.

GIDDENS, A. 1996: Work and economic life. *Introduction to Sociology*. New York: W. W. Norton.

HESSE-BIBER, S. and CARTER, G.L. 2000: *Working Women in America: Split Dreams*. New York: Oxford University Press.

JERMIER, J.M., KNIGHTS, D. and NORD, W.R. (eds) 1994: *Resistance and Power in Organizations*. London; New York: Routledge.

LYON, D and ZUREIK, E. (eds) 1996: *Computers, Surveillance, and Privacy*. Minneapolis: University of Minnesota Press.

McDOWELL, L. 1995: Body work: heterosexual gender performances in city workplaces. In Bell, D. and Valentine, G. (eds), *Mapping Desire: Geographies of Sexualities*. London and New York: Routledge.

MEILAENDER, G.C. (ed.) 2000: *Working: Its Meaning and its Limits*. Notre Dame, IN: University of Notre Dame Press.

MOE, K.S. (ed.) 2003: *Women, Family, and Work: Writings on the Economics of Gender*. London: Blackwell.

OGASAWARA, Y. 1998: *Office Ladies and Salaried Men: Power, Gender, and Work in Japanese Companies*. Berkeley: University of California Press.

RANTALAIHO, L. and HEISKANEN, T. (eds) 1997: *Gendered Practices in Working Life*. New York: St Martin's Press.

SCHLOSSER, E. 2001: *Fast Food Nation*. New York: Houghton Mifflin.

Introduction to section

3

Everyday life and commodity culture

Fran Martin

WHAT THIS SECTION AIMS TO DO

In the previous section we analysed how everyday life is conditioned and shaped by the architectural, imagined and social spaces in which it takes place: those of the city, the suburb, the home and the workplace. In this section, our primary focus shifts from *space and place* to *time and history*. Our main aim in this section is to give you the sense that, today, we inhabit a very particular historical moment within the development of **capitalist culture**, and to show you that an understanding of this fact is vital to the analysis of everyday life in contemporary cultures. The three chapters that comprise this section examine:

- how the recent rise of a **discourse** on *lifestyle* encourages us to imagine our everyday lives as exercises in self-fashioning through **consumption**;
- how a complex interplay of **power**, **resistance** and **incorporation** can be seen in the familiar activity of *shopping*, understood as an everyday **practice** circumscribed by the conditions of **commodity culture**; and finally
- how *fashion* works as a complex social system that both sustains the logic of built-in obsolescence that is so central to **commodity culture**; and also enables consumers to exercise a degree of **agency** in forging personal **identities**.

The key concepts covered in these chapters include:

- **capitalism**;
- consumption;
- commodity culture;
- **identity** formation;
- power and resistance in commodity culture.

In this Introduction, we will briefly historicize the rise and development of industrial capitalism in the **modern** and **postmodern** periods, and introduce some key terms and

103

theoretical tools that we hope will be useful to you in working through the chapters that follow. we begin with some historical and definitional work that will help us sort out what exactly it is we refer to when we talk about 'commodity culture'.

SO WHAT IS 'COMMODITY CULTURE'?

The starting point for thinking critically about the kinds of commodity culture that we find in modern, capitalist societies is the work of Karl Marx, and his account and critique of culture under capitalist relations of **production** (1906). Marx gives us a highly complex and very productive analysis of the distinctive forms of economy and culture that arise with the emergence of **capitalist** economies in **modern** societies. Capitalism is the economic system that is now globally dominant, in which the **surplus value** created by the labour of workers is taken as profit by capitalist classes that control the means of production. For Marx, the kinds of culture found in modern, capitalist societies are distinctive because of the distinctive ways in which the relationship between workers and the things they produce – the products of their labour – are structured. These relationships are in turn productive of altered social relations in society as a whole. Marx's theory contrasts the **use-value** of an object and the human need that the object will fulfil, on the one hand, with the **exchange-value** of an object and the **commodity** form, on the other. He proposes that every commodity contains these two aspects: use-value and exchange-value, but importantly, *a commodity is an object whose exchange-value dominates its use-value*. In practical terms, *commodities are things that were not produced to satisfy a human need in their producer, but were produced specifically in order to be exchanged, their value abstracted in monetary form*. For example, in today's commodity culture, a sweater you see in a shop window is not valued primarily according to how warm it can keep a human body; instead it is valued primarily by the amount of currency it can be exchanged for on the market. Instead of being worth 'two winters' worth of daytime warmth', say, it is worth $60. This is how the owners of the clothing company that manufactured the sweater think about it, and this $60 price – which no doubt includes a healthy profit for them – is really the reason they made the sweater in the first place. The sweater is a commodity.

We saw above that in capitalism the goods that workers produce are not for the use of the workers themselves; rather, these goods are sold on the market for the profit of their employers. To get goods, then, workers have to buy them: hence, *workers become consumers*. A consumer is a **subject** in a capitalist society defined by her or his practices of **consumption**. Arguably, all subjects in capitalist societies are defined by our positioning as consumers or potential consumers. *Denied the chance, in industrial and* ***postindustrial*** *societies, to find meaningful identity in the activity of production, workers begin to seek identity in the activity of consumption*. Very importantly for our purposes, consumption is always a cultural as well as an economic phenomenon.

HISTORICIZING THE RISE OF COMMODITY CULTURE

I wrote earlier that the capitalist cultures we inhabit today are specifically the product of **modernity**: that period of world history since about the eighteenth century. But now I want to draw attention to a finer distinction made by many commentators, *within* that rather lengthy time period of 'modernity' in general. Specifically, I want to discuss cultures of consumption that many argue take on particular forms from somewhere about the middle of the twentieth century onwards. Many historians of the rise of commodity culture point to a period within Western cultures between the late 1950s – after the end of the Second World War – and the early 1960s, in which a radical change occurred in the character of consumption. This moment is sometimes called 'the moment of mass consumption'. Alternatively, in his path-breaking book *Everyday Life in the Modern World* (1971), Henri Lefebvre analyses this as the moment that produced in France what he calls 'the bureaucratic society of controlled consumption' – a term that implies a society defined by the characteristics of:

- relative affluence;
- increased leisure and prominent leisure cultures;
- the centrality of consumption;
- industrialization; and
- technologization. (pp. 60–4)

This postwar period was indeed one of increased affluence for North American society and many European societies, but what distinguishes the character of consumption after this moment from consumption prior to it more specifically is the *new relative affluence of working people*. This was the first time that economic conditions allowed working people, rather than just the upper classes, to *consume on the basis of desire rather than need alone*. The period witnessed, for example, a leap in the number of working-**class** households that could afford televisions, refrigerators, cars, overseas holidays and similar commodities that in earlier periods were the preserve of the upper classes alone.

This same postwar period is also the period that is often characterized as the genesis of **postmodernity**: the historical period in industrialized societies since the conclusion of the Second World War in the mid-twentieth century. Socially, postmodernity is characterized by:

- the rise of the mass market;
- increased automation;
- increased travel; and
- the rise of mass communication and media.

Postmodernity is linked to a particular form of economic organization: a period within the global organization of capitalism that is known as **advanced** or late **capitalism**. As Celia Lury shows in her book, *Consumer Culture*, it's possible to list the features that characterize consumption within **advanced capitalism** in distinctive ways. Lury

(1996: 29–36) proposes that among other things, contemporary cultures of consumption are characterized by:

- the availability of an unprecedentedly large *number* and *range* of consumer goods;
- the tendency for more and more aspects of human interaction to be made available through the market (the privatization of education, health insurance and health care; the **commodification** of leisure practices like holidays);
- the expansion of shopping as a *distinctive leisure pursuit* (there is more on this Chapter 8);
- the rise of *more and more different forms of shopping* (for example, giant malls, mail order and internet shopping, second-hand shopping);
- the political organization of consumers (in consumer protection bodies, and so forth);
- more and more ways to borrow money (credit cards, hire purchase, and so forth);
- the growing importance and sophistication of forms of packaging and display;
- the pervasiveness of advertising in everyday life;
- the emergence of 'consumer crimes' (such as credit card fraud);
- the emergence of consumer illnesses (such as kleptomania).

In sum, the main point to understand here is that *the forms of commodity culture that are so familiar to us today are the product of a very particular historical moment: advanced capitalism. Things haven't always been as they are today: the forms of culture we're thinking about in this chapter are historically specific and particular, and different from cultural forms in the past.*

COMMODITY CULTURE AND IDENTITY

We wrote above that practices of consumption always have a *cultural* as well as an *economic* aspect. That is, consumption is not only about a particular, historically delimited *type of economic organization* (late capitalism); consumption is also about the *cultural activity of embodied social subjects.* We also wrote that the relationship between people and commodities has become increasingly central to our lives. The aspect of that relationship that we're most interested in, in what follows, is how our relationship with commodities produces a sense of **identity** for us. Commodities are not bought for their practical use-value alone. In today's consumer culture, the products we consume also do the **ideological** work of *helping us define and signify who we are*, so that our sense of personal identity consolidates in part through our relationship with the symbolic world of **consumption.** Annamarie Jagose has much more to say about this relationship in Chapter 7 on 'The invention of lifestyle'. For now, there are just a couple of important points to note. First, it's crucial to realize that we're not necessarily arguing that commodities somehow 'delude' us into finding ourselves in places where we aren't. Rather, we think we *really do*, inevitably, 'express ourselves' through commodities. We think they *really do* help us to imagine what kind of life it is that we have, or what life we want. And we think they *really do* provide us with a sense of ourselves. In other words, we think that *we can look at our 'identities' in contemporary culture as worked out, in large part,* *through our relationships with the commodities that we exchange, use and possess.* Maybe that sounds slightly strange to you. If it does, that may be because the way of thinking about identity that we've just outlined touches on a *paradox* that's central to the way we tend to define personal identity today. It's the first of three paradoxes we want to raise in relation to commodity culture and identity. We'll leave you with a brief statement of these three paradoxes as food for thought as you begin working your way through the chapters that follow.

Paradox 1: how do we understand personal identity?

- Is identity unique, autonomous and independent? That is, are we who we are regardless of our possessions? (This is a way of thinking about the individual subject that's central to the very influential **individualist**, humanist tradition.)
- Or is identity defined through the exchange, possession and use of goods? (This is an idea that the following chapters may lead you to consider.)

Paradox 2: how can commodity culture sell us 'individuality'?

- Evidently, commodity culture successfully sells us 'individuality' and 'distinction' very successfully.
- But it somehow manages to do so through products that are *mass-produced* with *standardized* design.

The third paradox we want to discuss concerns *critical approaches* to individual subjects within commodity culture. As such, this third point is particularly relevant and important to us as we begin thinking about commodity culture. Very, very broadly, and inevitably, rather crudely, we'd suggest that **cultural studies** approaches to the individual subject within commodity culture can be divided into two main camps or tendencies (you may recall we raised a related point in the Introduction, about the tension between **agency** and restraint in everyday life).

1. Some theorists – and these are often but not always scholars (including Henri Lefebvre, Theodor Adorno, Max Horkheimer and Jean Baudrillard) who draw more strongly on the history of **Marxist** scholarship on capitalist culture – argue that *individual subjects within commodity culture are manipulated by it, are robbed of individual freedom, are essentially dupes of the capitalist system.*
2. Other theorists, on the contrary, (including both Michel de Certeau and John Fiske) emphasize the opportunities afforded by contemporary commodity cultures for individual subjects to elaborate **agency** and productive pleasures.

Thus, we arrive at Paradox 3: how should we think of individual subjects within consumer culture?

- As manipulated by this culture; robbed of individual freedoms; as dupes of the capitalist system?
- Or as finding new kinds of pleasure and **agency** in consumer culture?

As you will discover as you read the three chapters that follow, much current critical thinking about everyday life and commodity culture is marked by the intricate and at times irresolvable tensions indexed in these central paradoxes.

REFERENCES

LEFEBVRE, H. 1971: *Everyday Life in the Modern World*. Rabinovitch, S. (trans.), London: Penguin Press.

LURY, C. 1996: *Consumer Culture*. Cambridge: Polity.

MARX, K. 1906: *Capital: A Critique of Political Economy*. Moore, S. and Aveling, E. (trans.), Chicago: C.H. Kerr.

Chapter Seven

THE INVENTION OF ☐ LIFESTYLE

Annamarie Jagose

Think about the word '**lifestyle**', a term encountered commonly in everyday life today. What does it mean, exactly? In newspapers or magazines, articles concerned with interior decorating, gardening, cooking and dining out are often organized into sections under the rubric of lifestyle. *Diabetic Lifestyle* is an online monthly magazine for diabetics and their families and friends. Groups of people as diverse as homosexuals and ferals are sometimes referred to as having 'alternative lifestyles'. A five-acre piece of land complete with house, swimming pool and stables on the outskirts of a city is described by a real estate agent as a 'lifestyle block'. A 1980s tabloid television programme that showcased celebrity homes was called *Lifestyles of the Rich and Famous*. Martha Stewart, a high-profile American media personality who has made her name advising on matters of domestic style, has been described as a 'lifestyle guru', a 'lifestyle queen' and a 'lifestyle evangelist'. The term 'lifestyle' is a common one, although a consideration of its everyday uses indicates that it has a general rather than a precise definitional ambit. A multivalent concept, lifestyle draws promiscuously on a range of concepts such as **taste**, income, health status, diet, aspiration, **subculture** and leisure in order to represent everyday life in advanced capitalist **cultures** as an accretion of *personal style achieved primarily through* **consumption**. This chapter will survey critical thinking on lifestyle with a particular focus on consumption as a **practice** of **identity**-making. Taking the concept of lifestyle as its central focus, it will analyse relations between **commodity** objects and **consumer** identity.

LIFESTYLE AND CONSUMPTION

In one of the earliest sustained considerations of lifestyle as a critical category, Michael Sobel (1981) undertakes an interdisciplinary review of the term's use, complaining that 'there is almost no agreement either empirically or conceptually as to what constitutes a lifestyle' (p. 2). As a counter to this situation, he proposes a working definition for lifestyle:

> Almost all sociologists will agree that lifestyle may be defined as 'a distinctive, and therefore recognizable, mode of living'. To this definition the condition of expressiveness (alternative choice) is attached. [...] It is also reasonable to require that lifestyle be eminently observable or deducible from observation. [...] Thus, lifestyle consists of expressive behaviors that are observable. (p. 28)

In Sobel's definition, lifestyle is a way of life chosen by the individual over other possible options, and recognizable as such to others. While a useful beginning, this definition is still fairly vague in terms of specifying what expressive behaviours might constitute a lifestyle and how specific modes of living acquire recognizable profiles.

Max Weber, an early German sociologist, is often credited with focusing critical attention on lifestyle, although he does not use that exact term. Making an important distinction between groups defined on the basis of class affiliation and groups defined on the basis of status, Weber (1966) observes that 'with some over-simplification, one might thus say that "classes" are stratified according to their relations to the **production** and acquisition of goods; whereas "status groups" are stratified according to the principles of their consumption of goods as represented by special "styles of life"' (p. 27). Although Weber assumes a **Marxist** model with its privileging of class as an analytic tool, he understands that lifestyles – or, as he puts it, 'styles of life' – are important since, in so far as they distinguish status from class, they evidence *a system of social distinction based on consumption rather than production*. That is, by foregrounding the concept of 'styles of life', Weber argues that an individual's social value and the demarcations of the social order more generally are not only derived from the capitalist production of material objects, but also from the everyday ways in which those objects are used.

The **cultural studies** approach to lifestyle has followed Weber's lead in drawing attention to the ways in which lifestyles are articulated as recognizable modes of living through the everyday practices of consumption. That is, lifestyle is legible through the frames of meaning enabled by consumer goods and the stylized self-presentation achieved by the individual's material and affective investment in commodity culture.

> 'Lifestyle' is a term which is used to refer to the new consumer sensibility [...] characteristic of modern consumption; through lifestyle, consumers are seen to bring a more stylized awareness or sensitivity to the processes of consumption. As a mode of consumption, or attitude to consuming, it refers to the ways in which people seek to display their individuality and their sense of style through the choice of a particular range of goods and their subsequent customizing or personalizing of these goods. (Lury 1996: 80)

This chapter will have more to say about lifestyle as a staging of individuality and style through consumption, but first it is necessary to provide a context for Lury's implicit historicizing of lifestyle as a category associated with the new and the **modern**.

LIFESTYLE AND MODERNITY

The identification of lifestyle is a specifically modern phenomenon, and modernity and the rise of **mass culture** are its defining context. Lifestyles emerge as complex processes of self-presentation and social differentiation in modern societies in which industrialization, urbanization and secularization have reconfigured traditional structures of social order and hierarchy. Anthony Giddens (1991) draws attention to this modern character of lifestyle when he argues that lifestyles emerge as **technologies** for fashioning identity outside the more stable classificatory frameworks of traditional cultures:

> Lifestyle is not a term which has much applicability to traditional cultures, because it implies choice within a plurality of possible options, and is 'adopted' rather than 'handed down'. Lifestyles are routinized practices, the routines incorporated into habits of dress, eating, modes of acting and favored milieux for encountering others; but the routines followed are reflexively open to change in the light of the mobile nature of self-identity. Each of the small decisions a person makes every day – what to wear what to eat, how to conduct himself [*sic*] at work, whom to meet with later in the evening – contributes to such routines. All social choices (as well as larger and more consequential ones) are decisions not only about how to act but who to be. The more post-traditional the settings in which an individual moves, the more lifestyle concerns the very core of self-identity, its making and remaking. (p. 81)

Lifestyles, then, are only possible in modernity, in the absence or breakdown of traditional knowledge systems or social orders that determine the individual's place and value in the wider culture. Indeed, given their crucial function in the production and performance of the individual's sense of self, lifestyles might usefully be considered as **tactical** compensation for such an absence or breakdown, as ways in which the material artifacts of mass culture are used to articulate an individual's identity. After all, as Giddens reminds us, the routinized practices that constitute lifestyles are 'not only about how to act but who to be'.

The rise of mass consumption – commonly dated to the late 1950s (Bocock 1993; Storey 1996) – saw to it that almost everyone, regardless of income level or employment status, had some relation to consumer culture. Post-1960s, the character of mass consumption altered significantly with the transition from Fordist to post-Fordist production/consumption cycles; a transition in which a centralized, standardized mass production that allowed little consumer choice was largely superseded by an increasingly flexible, specialized mass production that, through market segmentation, both serviced and solicited a proliferation of diverse consumption practices. This post-Fordist landscape of production and consumption – or we could say of consumption and production since the cycle is mutually rather than unidirectionally generative – is familiar to us in our everyday lives. One only needs to pause a minute in the breakfast cereal aisle of the supermarket to see everyday evidence of flexible production, diversified commodities and individualized consumption. You have a choice between Kellogg's Cornflakes and Sanitarium Cornflakes or, for something different, Kellogg's Crunchy Nut Cornflakes. Or there's Uncle Toby's Weeties if you feel like a wheatflake rather than a cornflake. For a more compact block of wheatflakes, you could try Sanitarium's classic Weet-Bix (now also available in oat bran and hi-bran variations on the standard) or Uncle Toby's Vita-Brits (which come in organic as well). Kellogg's also offers Cocopops, Rice Bubbles, Crispix, Frosties, Froot Loops and Honey Smacks. Perhaps it seems as if not much stands or falls on the purchase of one breakfast cereal over another. In and of itself, it is of course true that the choosing of Vita-Brits over Weet-Bix or cocoa over plain Crispix is not constitutive of identity. Such a decision, however, is only one small tessellation in the mosaic of consumption, one micro-choice among the innumerable aesthetic judgements through which consumption congeals as personalized lifestyle (Figures 7.1–7.4).

Consumption here does not refer to the purchase of only material goods but also services such as having one's house cleaned, and leisure activities such as going to the movies. Knitted up by a myriad of consumer decisions, lifestyles are constituted by the emergence in modernity of what Chaney (1996) calls 'new expectations for the control

Figures 7.1–7.4: Courtesy Sanitarium Health Food Company. Registered trademark of Australasian Conference Association Ltd.

and use of time in personally meaningful ways' (p. 15). Chaney's reference here to the use of time reminds us to think of consumption in the broad sense as both an expenditure of money and an expenditure of time. Time, no less than money, defines the practices of consumption that constitute lifestyle. For the development of modern consumer culture defines time and money as counter-weighted economies, as can be seen in the common formulation 'cash rich, time poor'. Although in the early twentieth century the rise of industrialization and mass production, coupled with a sharp delineation between work and leisure, was widely expected to generate democratic free time, in fact it produced the situation with which we are familiar today in which, as the saying goes, time is money. 'Consumer culture emerged in the often unacknowledged social decision to direct industrial innovation toward producing unlimited quantities of goods rather than leisure. This 'decision' meant a culture of work and spend. And time was transformed into money on and off the job' (Cross 1993: 5). Even though we more commonly think of our consumption patterns and hence our lifestyles as defined by our access to money, there is a crucial way in which they are equally defined by our access to time. Although this fact goes under-recognized in most critical discussions of consumption, it implicitly structures many everyday understandings of autonomy or compulsion:

> It is not surprising then if many people think to themselves in the morning –
> once they are capable of thinking anything at all – 'What shall I (or must I)
> do today? How shall I (or must I) spend my time today?' Far fewer, we may
> suppose, wake up and think 'What shall I spend today? What must I buy
> today?' (Steedman 2001: 1)

LIFESTYLE AND THE FORMATION OF IDENTITY

Earlier I suggested that lifestyles are produced through everyday practices of consumption. In this sense it can be seen that the individual's intense investment in commodity culture is explicable to the degree that his or her identity, the ongoing production of his or her sense of self, is negotiated in large part through consumption. Although he goes on to problematize the idea that individuals freely choose their identities through a selective interface with the world of consumer goods, Mike Featherstone (2000) gives a good account of lifestyle's common formulation:

> Rather than unreflectively adopting a lifestyle, through tradition or habit,
> the new heroes of consumer culture make lifestyle a life project and display
> their individuality and sense of style in the particularity of the assemblage of
> goods, clothes, practices, experiences, appearance and bodily dispositions
> they design together into a lifestyle. The modern individual within consumer
> culture is made conscious that he [*sic*] speaks not only with his clothes, but
> with his home, furnishings, decoration, car and other activities which are to
> be read and classified in terms of the presence and absence of taste. (p. 95)

Featherstone's figure of the modern individual 'speaking' through commodities suggests how in the **construction** of lifestyle – and, by corollary, identity – consumer goods are drawn into circuits of meaning in excess of their materiality or instrumentality. In order to think practically about how this might work, let's take Featherstone's citing of 'decoration' as an example.

Like many other popular lifestyle publications, *Inside/Out*, an Australian design and decorating magazine, implicitly assumes that personal identity finds its expression through commodities. Whether it is profiling Natalie Bloom, founder of Bloom cosmetics, in her inner-city mid-century modern interior (*Inside/Out*, March 2002) or celebrity chef Maggie Beer in her rustic farmhouse in the countryside (*Inside/Out*, April 2002), *Inside/Out* draws on the common connection between consumption and identity. No surprise, then, that the uber-modern, jetsetting Bloom is photographed contemplatively 'in a rare quiet moment swinging in her favourite seat, a Bubble chair by Finnish designer Eero Aarnio' (*Inside/Out*, March 2002) while at Beer's place the featured seat is a traditional, dark wooden rocking chair. In terms of their functionality, both seats are very similar in that they combine sitting with the possibility for restful movement. In terms of style and the meanings such style puts into circulation, however, the two chairs have nothing in common, the transparent plastic and modern sleekness of the former contrasting dramatically with the solid, traditional lines of the latter. Of course, the chairs are only a small aspect of the respective profiles on Bloom and Beer but, in foregrounding the stylistic rather than the utilitarian, they productively demonstrate the ways in which *consumption practices are legible as processes of self-fashioning*.

Another everyday framing of the signifying link between consumption and identity formation can be seen, perhaps unsurprisingly, in the **discourse** of advertising, where frequently the desirability of the product is indexed to its ability to confer its attributes on the consumer. In this context, consider the recent slogans used to launch a car, the latest model Rover 75: 'The only choice is the colour. Rover 75 Connoisseur. A class of its own'. Here the campaign to establish the Rover 75 as a leader in the luxury car market hinges on a **strategy** designed to frame the choosing of the Rover 75 as evidence of good judgement, an act of discernment prefigured in the very name of the car, Connoisseur. In buying the Rover 75 Connoisseur one demonstrates one's own connoisseurship. Although the connotative connections between product and consumer attribute are not usually as literally asserted as they are here, the same logic governs the marketing – and, to a certain extent, the purchasing – of all branded commodities.

BRANDED LIFESTYLES

The phenomenal rise of the brand in the 1980s provides a useful way of thinking about how practices of consumption congeal as lifestyles and articulate identity. The brand – think Nike, Disney, Benetton – is a corporate logo that functions as a condensation of a range of complex meanings and values. These meanings and values are not intrinsic to the branded product, but are conferred on the product through the process of branding. Rather than promoting the product or even promoting the meanings metonymically attached to the product, brand marketing promotes the brand itself: in many ways, the brand *is* the product. Tommy Hilfiger is a good instance of this transcendence of brand over product. A globally recognized brand, Hilfiger does not manufacture anything: its extensive range of products is instead made under licence by other companies (Klein 2000: 26). Hilfiger then is pure brand. Or think of Nike, its ubiquitous swoosh promising so much more than just athletic footwear, a promise articulated most fully in the worldwide proliferation of Niketown, Nike's flagship store and brand showcase. Organized as an immersion experience and sampling the architectural logics of the museum, the theme park, the nightclub and the superstore, each Niketown maintains a consistent branding strategy that associates the Nike brand with a sporting ethos of hard work and sweet victory that is at once aspirational and no-nonsense: Just Do It. A new product line of Nike's, Nike ID, which allows the online customizing of a particular style of shoe in terms of materials, colour and the specification of a brief text at the back of the shoe, acknowledges the ambiguous relation between brand name and personal identity: 'Nike ID is all about you' (Figure 7.5).

In some cases, certain lifestyle celebrities take on the cultural force of a brand. The American lifestyle adviser Martha Stewart is a good example. A suburban caterer in the 1970s, by the 1990s Martha Stewart had evolved into a brand identity, and her business, Martha Stewart Living Omnimedia, was a hybridized marketing and media venture that managed her syndicated newspaper columns, the publication of her monthly magazine, *Martha Stewart Living*, and her lifestyle books, merchandising tie-ins with Kmart, and the production of her television programmes. 'Remember', Stewart is alleged to have told her assistants on more than one occasion, 'I'm not Martha Stewart the person any more.

Figure 7.5: The Nike ID sneaker can be customized with personalized text; as the slogan says; 'Nike ID is all about you'. Copyright Nike, Inc., 2002. Nike and the swoosh design marks are registered trademarks of Nike, Inc. All rights reserved. Courtesy Nike, Inc.

I'm Martha Stewart the lifestyle' (Byron 2002: 17). High-profile British cooks Jamie Oliver and Nigella Lawson can also be considered lifestyle celebrities, their television programmes, cookbooks and merchandising outreach negotiating an apparently seamless transition between their own lives and the lifestyles they promote. So Oliver releases *Cookin'*, his CD compilation of his favourite music to cook by (the final track by his own band, Scarlet Division) and promotes a Royal Worcester oven-to-tableware range with names derived from the 'mockney' taglines popularized on his television shows. Both Oliver and Lawson star in their own successful television cooking show series, organized around the conceit of their everyday lives. In lifestyle terms, the scenes of Lawson dropping her children, Cosima and Bruno, at school before popping in to the local butcher are just as instructional as those in which she demonstrates how to bare-handedly separate an egg. Shot predominantly in their own homes, Oliver's *Naked Chef* series and Lawson's *Nigella Bites* produce life as lifestyle.

The elaborate marketing processes by which a brand comes to denote not a product but a style, a personality, an attitude, a worldview, a fantasy, a set of values, is often described as lifestyle branding, the annexation to a brand of a whole way of life.

> Lifestyle merchandisers, Ralph Lauren and Calvin Klein, do not sell commodities. They produce and circulate the labels that connote a desirable lifestyle, available through the purchase of up-scale commodities bearing Calvin Klein or Ralph Lauren labels. One wears not a dress but a Ralph Lauren, and thereby participates in the nostalgia his ads promote. In buying and wearing a Ralph Lauren or a Calvin Klein, we are actually consuming a simulatory image [...].

> In late-capitalist consumption, social, cultural values have become the signifier for product characteristics, which in turn are the signifier for exchange value. However, in the case of the consumption of lifestyle, social, cultural values are imagistically simulated and circulated as signifiers. The simulation of social, cultural values is much more powerful than the social, cultural values themselves. Decontextualized, the image of social, cultural values can then be juxtaposed with the image and sign of product characteristics to connote a particular lifestyle. Addressees respond to images emotionally and immediately, connecting social, cultural values with product characteristics. In other words, lifestyle based upon social, cultural simulation is perceived as constructed by product characteristics. The consumption of these product characteristics would then be visually constituted for the consumer and present to others the possession of a lifestyle. (Lowe 1995: 66–7)

In describing the image-based circulation of values as simulatory, Lowe borrows his vocabulary from French philosopher Jean Baudrillard's **postmodern** account of commodity culture.

BAUDRILLARD AND COMMODITY CULTURE

As an explanation of what impels consumer society, Baudrillard rejects the notion that consumption is structured by consumer need. He argues instead for 'a logic of desire' (Poster 1988: 44) in which commodities assume the value of a sign, the meanings of which rely not on the material consumer object itself but on the existence of other commodities that constitute a system of signs across which deferred meaning ceaselessly plays. One of Baudrillard's examples of a consumer object is a washing machine, which, he observes, functions on both a denotative and a connotative level. At the level of **denotation**, the washing machine's meaning and value is determined by its utility, its capacity to clean clothes. At the level of **connotation**, however, the washing machine puts into circulation meanings that are not determined by its function. Baudrillard suggests 'comfort' and 'prestige' might be two such meanings; we could add others, say, 'modern', 'reliable' and 'luxury'. All sorts of other consumer objects might equally convey 'prestige', for instance, and it is this substitutability that constitutes a **semiotic** field of interconnected consumer objects, generating desire not for any particular object, but as a definitionally *insatiable affect* that characterizes consumer society. As Baudrillard writes:

> This evanescence and mobility reaches a point where it becomes impossible to determine the specific objectivity of needs [...]. The flight from one signifier to another is no more than the surface reality of a desire, which is insatiable because it is founded on a lack. And this desire, which can never be satisfied, signifies itself locally in a succession of objects and needs. (Poster 1988: 45)

Motivated by desires that can, by definition, never be satisfied, Baudrillard's consumer inhabits a postmodern culture in which the sign has won out over the consumer object.

In later work, Baudrillard further refines his thinking about the nature of the relation between the sign and the consumer object. Where he initially argued for the precedence of the sign over the object, increasingly he insists that there is *no distinction to be made between them, no logic that can distinguish between the object and its representation*. In order to extrapolate this counter-intuitive logic, Baudrillard introduces the notion of **simulation**, a term he uses to describe a commodity culture in which the mass media discourses of advertising and marketing conflate the real with the representational, creating a self-contained system of meaning in which signs refer only to themselves. A simulation is not the same as a fake or a lie. It is not an untruth beneath which is obscured something true or real. Rather, simulation refuses that structuring difference. As Baudrillard puts it, 'simulation threatens the difference between "true" and "false", between "real" and "imaginary"' (Poster 1988: 168). What does this mean for our thinking about lifestyle? As the quotation from Donald Lowe above suggests, Baudrillard's concept of simulation takes to the extreme the idea that identities are constructed through practices of consumption. For simulation focuses our attention on not the *material value* but the *semiotic value* of the consumer object, implying that identity formation is yet another simulacrum produced through the free play of the sign.

117

LIFESTYLE: OPPRESSIVE OR ENABLING?

For Baudrillard, the social practice of consumption that is integral to lifestyle is not so much a strategy through which consumers articulate their own self-fashionings as a mechanism for annexing consumers to the oppressive manipulation of meaning orchestrated through the discourses of advertising and the mass media. Consumers, then, are merely the means for establishing and maintaining the differences between commodities according to the requirements of capital and a regulatory social order. Objects, according to Baudrillard,

> undertake the policing of social meanings, and the significations they engender are controlled. Their proliferation, simultaneously arbitrary and coherent, is the best vehicle for a social order, equally arbitrary and coherent, to materialize itself effectively under the sign of affluence. (Poster 1988: 17)

This idea that consumption is a technology of social control, that it is the practice through which individuals are corrupted by repressive **ideological** formations, has a long intellectual history and can be seen in the work of classic social theory thinkers such as Karl Marx, Herbert Marcuse and Theodor Adorno, as well as in various more recent declensions. 'Today, to assuage the horrors, to overcome the loneliness of modernity, people flock to malls where "proto-communities" of strangers seek clothes, cultural products and techno-gadgets that promise gratification or at least recognition through possession' (Langman 1992: 74). Such accounts tend to represent the consumer as without **agency**, powerless in the face of corporate manipulation, and consumption as a misguided attempt to evade the alienation and inauthenticity it actually secures.

Contemporary anti-consumerism activists such as Naomi Klein and Kalle Lasn emphasize the inauthentic, dehumanizing aspect of commodity culture. Lasn, founder of the anti-corporate adbusters movement, argues that the choices articulated through lifestyle consumption are more properly compulsions:

> Do you feel as if you're in a cult? Probably not. The atmosphere is quite un-Moonielike. We're free to roam and recreate. No one seems to be forcing us to do anything we don't want to do [...]. By consensus, cult members speak a kind of corporate Esperanto: words and ideas sucked up from TV and advertising. We wear uniforms – not white robes but, let's say, Tommy Hilfiger jackets or Airwalk sneakers (it depends on our particular subset). We have been recruited into roles and behavior patterns we did not consciously choose. (Lasn 1999: 53)

Lasn calls for the 'demarketing' (p. 150) of our bodies and lives, a call that resonates with Klein's call for 'no logo'. Where Lasn compares commodity culture to a cult, Klein characterizes consumer desire as 'deep longing for the seductions of fake' (Klein 2000: 159). Both Lasn and Klein productively foreground the social, economic and political inequities that structure **globalized** consumption, the very inequities that underlie lifestyle's choice and self-fashioning: for example, sweatshop third-world working conditions for the manufacture of first-world commodities; the iconic borrowing of the insignia of disenfranchised subcultures for mass-media advertising campaigns; the ecological plundering of non-renewable resources in the manufacture of consumer objects (Figures 7.6–7.8).

Figure 7.6: Courtesy www.adbusters.org.

Figure 7.7: Courtesy www.adbusters.org.

119

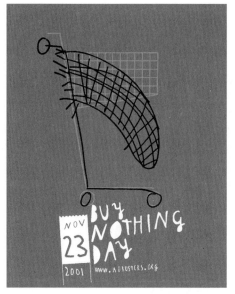

Figure 7.8: Courtesy www.adbusters.org.

In focusing on the oppressive aspects of commodity culture, these accounts usefully counter the voluntarist fantasy of the consumer who fashions his or her identity according to whim. Alternatively, wanting to contest the representation of the consumer as a malleable dupe, recent theorists have tended to foreground consumption as a site of pleasure, agency and autonomy. It is important not to oversimplify consumption, to see it as a homogenous activity that might finally be defined as either oppressive or pleasurable, either an **overdetermined** serfdom or an exercise of free will. Any theory of lifestyle must be able to encompass its exploitative and its enabling aspects, a point Tim Edwards (2000) makes when he describes consumer culture as structured not only by desire but also by hunger (p. 191). For instance, it is vital that any theory of lifestyle is able to describe both those with **cultural capital** and disposable incomes and those whose access to consumption might be severely limited by material or other structural constraints. In thinking about how **race** overdetermines the **interpellative** force of commodity culture, Susan Willis (1995) identifies the ways in which the construction of identity through consumption is not only limited by economic factors: 'Can we conceive of mass culture as black culture? Or is mass culture by its very definition white culture with a few blacks in it?' (p. 143). The possibility here of a specifically black consumption returns us again to the deeply ambiguous character of lifestyle and the practices of consumption that support it. For even as they are recuperated for **capitalism** as niche markets, certain individuals and interest groups – for example, the eco-consumer who makes purchasing decisions based on environmental politics or the gay consumer backed by the so-called pink dollar – articulate through consumption not only a lifestyle, but a lifestyle based on a dissident cultural **politics**.

This raises the possibility that lifestyles and the personal identities they house are not only secured through a negotiation of consumerism but perhaps also at times by a **resistance** to and even an outright rejection of consumerism.

> Some of us may and do, from time to time, seek identity by browsing in front of shop windows, purchasing goods and internalizing their images. These may prove disappointing or may provide considerable support to our ego-ideals and identities. At other times, however, our identities may be built around resistance to consumption and consumerism and the subversion of the symbolism carried by objects. Defying the slogans of advertisers and sneering at the propaganda of commodities may be a sound enough base for constructing an ego-ideal as the worship of the shopping mall.
> (Gabriel and Lang 1995: 98)

The processes of self-fashioning articulated through lifestyle, then, are neither simply pleasurable and empowering nor merely oppressive and dehumanizing. They are not determined in advance but are context specific. Above all, they are incomplete and ongoing, situational and improvisory, impelled by the promise of satisfaction and haunted by the possibility of inadequacy.

Summary

In this chapter, we have argued that:

- lifestyles are modern systems of social distinction based on practices of mass consumption;

- patterns of consumption are crucial aspects of the processes of self-fashioning since consumer goods play an important role in the articulation of individuality, style and subjectivity;

- consumer goods assume meanings in excess of their materiality or instrumentality;

- the corporate brand usefully exemplifies the way in which consumer goods act as bearers of complex systems of meaning, ethics and value;

- most acts of consumption can best be understood in terms of desire rather than need;

- although sometimes characterized as a capitalist trap or an opportunity for free-wheeling self-expression, consumption is neither simply oppressive nor simply liberating.

EXERCISES

1. Do you consider that you have a lifestyle? How would you define it? Has it changed over the last five years? If you don't consider that you have a lifestyle, why not?

2. Using this chapter and its references as a guide, identify a number of pro- and anti-consumerist arguments. Use these to organise a class debate around the proposition 'You only need a lifestyle if you don't have a life.'

3. Identify a specific consumer object – for instance, Volkswagen's new Beetle or a Nokia 8890 mobile phone – and write a list of its connotative qualities. Compare lists with a classmate, noting similarities and dissimilarities.

REFERENCES

BOCOCK, R. 1993: *Consumption*. London: Routledge.

BYRON, C. 2002: The making of Martha. *The Weekend Australian Magazine*, April 27–28, 16–19.

CHANEY, D. 1996: *Lifestyles*. London: Routledge.

CROSS, G. 1993: *Time and Money: The Making of Consumer Culture*. London: Routledge.

EDWARDS, T. 2000: *Contradictions of Consumption: Concepts, Practices and Politics in Consumer Society*. Buckingham: Open University Press.

FEATHERSTONE, M. 2000: Lifestyle and consumer culture. In Lee, M.J. (ed.), *The Consumer Society Reader*. Cambridge, MA: Blackwell, 92–105.

GABRIEL, Y. and LANG, T. 1995: *The Unmanageable Consumer: Contemporary Consumption and its Fragmentations*. London: Sage.

GIDDENS, A. 1991: *Modernity and Self-identity: Self and Society in the Late Modern Age*. Cambridge: Polity Press.

Inside/Out, March 2002: Surrey Hills: News Magazines Ltd.

Inside/Out, April 2002: Surrey Hills: News Magazines Ltd.

KLEIN, N. 2000: *No Logo*. London: Flamingo.

LANGMAN, L. 1992: Neon cages: shopping for subjectivity. In Shields, R. (ed.), *Lifestyle Shopping: The Subject of Consumption*. London: Routledge, 40–82.

LASN, K. 1999: *Culture Jam: How to Reverse American's Suicidal Consumer Binge – and Why We Must*. New York: William Morrow & Company.

LOWE, D. 1995: *The Body in Late Capitalist USA*. Durham, NC: Duke University Press.

LURY, C. 1996: *Consumer Culture*. Oxford: Polity Press.

POSTER, M. (ed.) 1988: *Jean Baudrillard: Selected Writings*. Oxford: Polity Press.

SOBEL, M.E. 1981: *Lifestyle and Social Structure: Concepts, Definitions, Analyses*. New York: Academic Press.

STEEDMAN, I. 2001: *Consumption Takes Time: Implications for Economic Theory*. London: Routledge.

STOREY, J. 1996: *Cultural Studies and the Study of Popular Culture: Theories and Methods*. Athens: University of Georgia Press.

WEBER, M. 1966: *Theory of Social and Economic Organization*. New York: Free Press.

WILLIS, S. 1995: I want the black one: being different: is there a place for Afro-American culture in commodity culture? In Carter, E. *et al.* (eds), *Cultural Remix: Theories of Politics and the Popular*. London: Lawrence & Wishart.

FURTHER READING

BIANCHI, M. (ed.) 1998: *The Active Consumer: Novelty and Surprise in Consumer Choice*. London: Routledge.

CLARK, D. 1993: Commodity lesbianism. In Abelove, H. *et al.* (eds), *The Lesbian and Gay Studies Reader*. New York: Routledge, 186–201.

FRANK, T. 1998: *The Conquest of Cool: Business Culture, Counterculture and the Rise of Hip Consumerism*. Chicago: University of Chicago Press.

HEARN, J. and ROSENEIL, S. 1999: *Consuming Cultures: Power and Resistance*. New York: St Martin's Press.

HICKS, D. 1999: *My Kind of Garden*. Suffolk: Garden Art Press.

JACKSON, P. (ed.) 2000: *Commercial Cultures: Economies, Practices, Spaces*. Oxford: Berg.

KEAT R. *et al.* 1994: *The Authority of the Consumer*. London: Routledge.

LEE, M.J. 1993: *Consumer Culture Reborn: The Cultural Politics of Consumption*. London: Routledge.

LEE, M. (ed.) 2000: *The Consumer Society Reader*. Malden, PA: Blackwell.

LODZIAK, C. 2002: *The Myth of Consumerism*. Sterling, VA: Pluto Press.

MILES, S. 2000: *Youth Lifestyles in a Changing World*. Buckingham: Open University Press.

MILLER, D. *et al.* (eds) 1998: *Shopping, Place and Identity*. London: Routledge.

NIVA, M. (ed.) 1997: *Buy this Book: Studies in Advertising and Consumption*. London: Routledge.

SLATER, D.R. 1997: *Consumer Culture and Modernity*. Cambridge: Polity Press.

STEBBINS, R.A. 1997: Lifestyle as a generic concept in ethnographic research. *Quality and Quantity* 31, 347–60.

STOREY, J. 1999: *Cultural Consumption in Everyday Life*. London: Arnold.

Chapter Eight

SHOPPING

Audrey Yue

Film discussed in this chapter:
- *Pretty Woman* (Garry Marshall, 1990).

INTRODUCTION

Shopping is an activity connecting individual action, inter-personal interaction and quotidian experience that increasingly structures and restructures the **practices** of everyday life. Contemporary shopping practices highlight the transformation in our society from **production** to **consumption**, industrial to **postindustrial**, **modern** to **postmodern**. As a practice of consumption, shopping negotiates the **identity** of the self through the act of material acquisition. Shopping is a process of transformation that produces the modern **shopper** as a **subject** of personal gratification and public recognition and representation. This chapter will consider how different kinds of shopping produce different forms of **power, resistance, strategies** and **tactics**, concepts introduced in Section 1 of this book.

The practice of shopping as we know it today evolved against the backdrop of industrialization and the rise of capitalism. When market fairs and commercial bazaars gave way to specialist shops in the West in the nineteenth century, the separation between home and work became more defined. New roles appeared to distinguish owners from employees and shoppers from shop clerks (Kingston 1994: 1–2; Miller 1981). Crafts-persons who no longer had to spend time peddling their wares to potential customers were afforded greater efficiency through the specialization of skills and the integration of tasks. The rise of modern shopping practices was intimately linked with the rise of manufacturing, the standardization of production techniques and the distribution of an increasingly complex and wide range of goods. Originally an activity identified with women from the upper classes, shopping contributed to the emergence of leisure as a distinct and widespread set of cultural practices. It also heralded the democratization of luxury as, by about the mid-nineteenth century, shopping was no longer solely confined to the acquisition of daily necessities.

As a practice of consumption, shopping is both individual and social, both routine and recreational, both anxious and pleasurable. It is an ambiguous experience, a private activity conducted in a public space. The tension between privacy and sociability also produces shopping as both a rational and an impulsive practice, oscillating between a pleasurable social form and necessary maintenance (Lehtonen and Mäenpää 1997: 144). It is a chore when it involves the obligatory acquisition of essential goods for daily living, but a pleasant distraction when conducted as an open-ended activity with no definite tasks. 'Doing the shopping', for example, connotes the regularity of routine, like the routine involved in doing the weekly food and grocery shopping: it is an act that is planned and limited. 'Going shopping', on the other hand, constructs shopping as a leisurely act with no precise plans and destinations. 'Trippism' is a term that refers specifically to the pleasure-seeking aspect of shopping, of going somewhere else, away from home or work duties, to enjoy oneself (Lehtonen and Mäenpää 1997: 148–50). 'Going shopping' is potentially transgressive and excessive, as one may end up spending too much money or too much time. Indeed, 'shopping for' and 'shopping around' refer to two quite distinct practices of shopping (Falk and Campbell 1997: 2–6). While 'shopping for' focuses on the practicality of daily shopping, 'shopping around' or window-shopping is recreational and arguably marginalizes the economic aspect of the activity.

These different practices of shopping constitute the modern shopper as a subject of consumption, as someone who is involved in 'self-construction by a process of acquiring commodities of distinction and difference' (Bauman 1988: 808). In the film *Pretty Woman* (Garry Marshall, 1990), Vivian's (Julia Roberts) transformation from a prostitute to an upper-**class** woman gives us an exemplary dramatization of shopping as a practice that creates identities for individuals as belonging to particular social classes. The first shopping sequence demonstrates shopping as a strategy that regulates class distinctions. Vivian, after being given a large amount of money by Edward (Richard Gere) to buy clothes more suitable for her role as his dinner companion, arrives at a Rodeo Drive boutique only to find that she is asked to leave by a scornful sales assistant who, on seeing Vivian in her prostitute's outfit, deems that she is not worthy to enter the store. Vivian's outfit constitutes her identity as working class, allows her to be read as such by the sales assistant, and prevents her from being able to shop at an elite boutique. The second shopping sequence sees Vivian succeeding in purchasing a dress after a phone intervention from Bernard, the manager of the Beverly Hills Hotel, confirming that Vivian is indeed staying there with Edward. Edward's inability to recognize her that evening at the bar highlights the transformative power of the **tasteful** black cocktail dress Vivian has bought. Clothes signify class, and this makeover sequence shows shopping as a practice that allows Vivian to transcend her working-class appearance. But Vivian's ascent is also enabled by the socially ascribed value of her beauty: 'Those, who, like Vivian, are beautiful [are presumed to] deserve to have the social privileges that allow them to wear the clothes that suit their beauty' (Wartenberg 2000: 318).

Shopping is not simply reducible to the acquisition of things. As the example from *Pretty Woman* shows, beyond the literal act of consumption and economic exchange, it is an act of 'buying an identity'. Far from the glamour strip of Rodeo Drive, this is reflected even

125

in daily shopping, where the shopper expresses a choice mediated by constructions of self, body, taste and social distinction. Vivian's ability to pass as upper class is made possible not only by her stylish new clothes: her physical beauty, enhanced by elite shopping, allows an alternative basis for class aspirations. Shopping not only *expresses* but is *constitutive* of different cultural **ideological** configurations, such as the class configurations dramatized in this film (Douglas 1997). It is always conducted in a relational context where new identifications are produced through the active **appropriation** of the meanings inherent in goods, and new **cultures** are also formed through constantly changing interactions with new spaces of consumption (Shields 1992). Shopping is practised through the regimes of looking, browsing and touching, as well as through intermingling with the **geography** of its diverse environments, such as community flea markets, air-conditioned shopping malls and eclectic arcades.

DEPARTMENT STORES AND SHOPPING MALLS

The shopping mall is the postmodern successor to the modern department store, whose advent in the second half of the nineteenth century radically changed the way commodities were sold. With the invention of railways and horse-drawn buses, the modernization of transportation systems, together with the development of wide urban streets, revolutionized shopping. Manufacturers, distributors and consumers were able to access and patronize bigger stores that retailed a wider assortment of things. Neighbourhood shops that previously made things to specification and sold goods on-premises and through personal price negotiation soon gave way to the novel one-stop department store that stocked standardized, mass-produced commodities in high volumes with a relatively low, fixed and plainly marked price. Stores such as Macy's in New York, The Fair in Chicago and David Jones in Sydney practised rationalization and bureaucratization in their new management techniques and labour relations. They also modernized shopping by selling *consumption as a leisure practice* through their organization of space.

The Bon Marché, a Paris department store established in the late nineteenth century (1869), is an example of 'a mass marketplace for an emerging mass society' (Miller 1981: 53). Occupying 52,800 square metres of surface space, the store was gigantic, with large, naturally lit and spacious open bays that facilitated browsing and allowed the best strategic display of goods. It stocked a vast range of commodities, from dry foods, clothing, furniture, haberdashery, stationery and toys to shoes, kitchen utensils, sports and garden goods, camping wares and toiletries, and it recorded a vast number of sales and shoppers. The increase in the consumption of comfort, leisure and luxury demonstrates how shoppers were seeking their identities from the commodities they were purchasing. The Bon Marché not only celebrated bourgeois culture, with its opulent displays of the bourgeois **lifestyle** that the shopper could lay claim and aspire to, it also popularized bourgeois lifestyle by turning merchandise into mass **consumer** goods at considerably lower prices than were available before (Miller 1981: 2, 167) It

Figure 8.1: Photograph taken in 1928 of the Grands Magasins du Bon Marché department store in Paris.

was an *economic* institution intimately linked with modern commerce and mass society, as well as a *cultural* institution that cultivated consumption as a popular everyday practice.

Consumption was sold through display strategies of seduction and **spectacle**, 'part opera, part theatre, part museum':

> Dazzling and sensuous, the Bon Marché became a permanent fair, an institution, a fantasy world, a spectacle of extraordinary proportions, so that going to the store became an event and an adventure. ... Everywhere merchandise formed a decorative motif conveying an exceptional quality to the goods themselves. Silks cascaded from the walls of the silk gallery, ribbons were strung above the hall of ribbons, umbrellas were draped full blown in a parade of hues and designs. Oriental rugs, rich and textural, hung from balconies for the spectators below. (Miller 1981: 167–8)

These techniques reorganized space and aestheticized selling by introducing a new style of consumption based on spectacle and the activity of *looking*. The juxtaposition of multiple displays showing one **commodity** at a time disorientated the shopper with a phantasmagoria of goods, simultaneously creating the illusion of scarcity and thereby increasing the compulsion to purchase. **Commodity fetishism** is entailed in this process whereby consumer choices are produced in response to a constructed desire, and the commodity is invested with the quasi-magical property of satisfying the consumer's every want while all signs of the real labour that produced the commodity are erased. The visual spectacle of retail makes shopping pleasurable by transforming it into 'a

127

theatre of everyday life' (Shields 1992: 7). Consumer identity is also constructed through an exchange of looks. The novel use of glass and mirrors in the interior of the new department stores added to the intoxicating distraction of the stores by reflecting and multiplying the display, making the shopper more self-aware of her presence in the space, especially when seduced by the sight of her own literal reflection. Such exchanges constitute the shopper as a self-conscious subject of consumption. German philosopher and cultural critic Walter Benjamin's description of the arcades and the figure of the *flâneur* expresses well the new relationship between consumers and commodities:

> Strolling could hardly have assumed the importance it did without the arcades.
>
> The arcades ... are glass-covered, marble-panelled passageways through entire complexes of houses whose proprietors have combined for such speculations. Both sides of these passageways, which are lighted from above, are lined with the most elegant shops, so that such an arcade is a city, even a world, in miniature.
>
> It is in this world that the flâneur is at home. ... [H]e is as much at home among the facades of houses as a citizen is in his four walls. To him the shiny, enamelled signs of businesses are at least as good a wall ornament as an oil painting is to a bourgeois in his salon. The walls are the desks against which he presses his notebooks; news-stands are his libraries and the terraces of cafés are the balconies from which he looks down on his household after this work is done. (Benjamin 1973: 36–37)

For Benjamin, the shopping arcades and the department stores of the nineteenth century epitomized modernity. New strategies of consumption introduce specific **technologies** of looking by fixing the gaze between the shopper and the commodity, on the one hand, and by creating a series of distracted and interrupted looks that are potentially resistant to shopping, on the other. Although strolling, browsing and window-shopping are considered acceptable practices because department stores are socially accessible and there is no time limit on how long one can spend in them, these spatial and spectatorial regimes also saw the emergence of modern modes of **surveillance** characterized by 'correct' and 'incorrect' practices of shopping. While the shopper's implicit process of self-monitoring is sanctioned as a culturally 'correct' practice, along with the rise of department stores kleptomania and shoplifting surfaced as new, indicatively modern problems.

Modern department stores and shoplifting are two closely linked institutions. Pathologized as a form of urban sickness afflicting people who are not in full control of their senses, shoplifting was first diagnosed as 'monomania', a term coined by C.C.H. Marc to describe a compulsive and obsessive urge to steal (Miller 1981: 198). In 1883, the term 'department store theft' was used to forge a link between impulsive stealing and department stores (p. 200). Because the majority of the new wave of thefts were committed in these stores, kleptomania was further theorized as a disease shaped by socially created conditions such as the store's seductive attractions, which allegedly tempted people to steal. The discovery that most of the shoplifters were well-to-do women who took things that were of little or no consequence provoked the debate further. Linked to pathological sexual disorders, pregnancy, menopause and menstruation, kleptomania was later diagnosed as a 'female disease'. Elaine S. Abelson (1989) argues that such a medical **discourse** was used to maintain class and **gender** boundaries because shoplifting middle-class women were a threat to the prevailing social mores: 'The individual became the focus; the crime was lost. Neither the excesses of the institutions nor consumer capitalism were indicted. The fault lay within the women themselves' (p. 12).

Although shoplifting has become an everyday practice in a world inundated by the temptation and desire to own things, the **sexist** ideology that constructs and reproduces the stereotype of the female kleptomaniac remains strong. Cecilia Fredriksson (1997) problematizes this approach by questioning the relationship between women and modernity in her study of EPA, a Swedish chain store in the 1940s. In one interview, a woman who grew up in the country remembers how shocked her mother was when she visited the EPA with a friend who was caught stealing a lamp. Fredriksson suggests that women were unable to cope with the demands of modernity: 'even the most trustworthy person could be transformed into a common thief' (p. 121). She extends this argument by profiling another type of female shoplifter at the EPA. The 'shop-rat' was a female bag-thief who could not resist the temptations of an anonymous crowd of women and their handbags. Unlike the professional pickpockets who were usually young boys and, it was thought, could be rehabilitated, shop-rats were 'amateur criminals who could not keep their hands to themselves' (p. 121). They strolled around, showed no interest in the displays, and robbed other women who were too distracted by the array of goods on offer to look after their own handbags. Because female thieves resisted the pattern of modern female consumption, they were regarded as kleptomaniacs or shop-rats who threatened the safety of others in public spaces.

Theorists such as William Kowinski (1985), Anne Friedberg (1993) and Margaret Morse (1990) have problematized the **utopian** claim that department stores and arcades are truly 'public' spaces. Their studies on contemporary shopping malls show how a privatized public space is ideologically constructed to maximize the effectiveness of consumption. Reproducing the enclosed interior of the arcade and taking the form of a multi-storeyed department store, the mall is the ultimate expression of an artificial urban environment. Chadstone Shopping Centre (CSC), one of Australia's biggest regional shopping malls, located in the affluent south-eastern suburbs of Melbourne, provides a useful example here, one that also offers broader insights into the 'mall cultures' of many contemporary Western and East Asian societies. Built in 1960 as the state of Victoria's first free-standing shopping complex, its recent expansion leaves the centre with over 400 retail shops, five department stores, three supermarkets, 60 eating establishments, a 16-screen cinema megaplex, a bowling alley and, in future, even a university, servicing a suburban population of 650,000 people and 250,000 dwellings (Gandel Retail Trust 2002). Bordered on all sides by multi-level car parks, sited safely away from the major arterial roads, temperature-controlled all year round, and with tree-lined atriums separating the shared pedestrian walkways from the shops, CSC is, like other generic malls the world over, a private space where anonymous individuals sharing similar demographics gather together in a controlled version of a street (Morse 1990: 198). Protected from the public by a subtle but panoptic form of surveillance and control, the mall's governance includes unobtrusive plainclothes detectives, security guards and video cameras, and the corporate strategies of management planners.

CSC's spatial organization provides the basis for a critique of how the cultural activity of 'malling' has become a primary topos of *postmodern consumption*. Postmodern consumption is characterized by practices that merge leisure and consumption activities. Fully integrated with services such as banks, barbers, dry cleaners and optometrists, spruikers (people who stand outside a particular shop calling to passers-by to encourage them to enter) complement the theme park design and add to the carnival-like atmosphere. Shoppers can sip their lattés next to the Laura Ashley shop or pick up some sushi opposite the Made In Japan homeware store. The artificiality of the environment encourages distraction whilst effectively furthering the mall's commercial objectives.

Morse's concept of 'nonspace' highlights the state of distraction. The nonspace is a dislocated space in between public and private, interior and exterior, artificial and natural, individual and communal (1990: 207). The mall's **aesthetics** of consumption reflect this ambiguity, encouraging what Friedberg has called 'a perpetual mode of *flânerie* [strolling]' (1993: 112). Kowinski calls this the 'zombie effect' of the mall, where the shopper experiences a sense of floating for hours induced by the over-stimulation of the senses, and becomes contradictorily excited, relaxed and confused all at once (1985: 339). These spatial strategies of selling use the experience of dislocation to promote an environment of distraction that is conducive to consumption. Intoxicated by its phantasmagoria, the shopper is lulled into the potential of purchase. The promotion of CSC in a local *Melbourne Shopping Guide* pamphlet supports this. Listed in the contents page under the heading 'Destinations' is an advertisement for the shopping centre, with the tagline, 'When not in Rome, go to Chadstone' (*Melbourne Shopping Guide* 2002: 2, 26). Branded as the 'Fashion Capital of Australia', CSC's marketing strategy further manipulates the experience of dislocation through fashion tourism. It encourages shoppers to 'take a trip to Chadstone' and uses the idea of shopping-as-travel to anchor the pleasure of trippism. The shopper, transported but confined, exercises consumer power by internalizing the strategies of travelling, looking and having. The purchase of the 'Italian' and 'international labels' advertised fulfils the promise of arrival by imbuing the local shopper with a cosmopolitan and global identity.

The cultural activity of malling also produces resistant practices of consumption. Meaghan Morris reclaims the female shopper through the figure of the pedestrian and a discussion of the tactics of walking (1998). Her focus on the allegorical figure of the woman-walker (women who do not drive to shopping centres) shows how walking reconstitutes subject positions and relations. Morris's account recognizes that, unlike the myth of the generic mall, different shopping centres produce different histories and subjectivities of place. Non-consuming loiterers such as 'mall rats' and 'mall jammers' appropriate the shopping centre in tactical ways that are also constitutive of subjecthood. 'Hanging out' at the shopping mall has become almost a rite of passage for suburban teenagers, who view the space as both convenient (near to home whilst also apart from the confines of domestic space) and safe (compared to the dimly lit streets at night). At CSC, teenagers in different school uniforms gather during weekday afternoons at a huge bus interchange outside the Coles supermarket located next to the Hoyts cinema megaplex and the Kmart chain store. Lingering to chat and form friendships, they jostle for space with supermarket trolleys and discount-store shoppers, and re-appropriate the transit function of the bus interchange. School uniforms and fashion styles are used to mark out territorial boundaries and difference from rival groups. 'Dressing up' on the weekends and hanging out outside certain shops while not necessarily making purchases in them also dissolves the distinction between having and being, and constitutes an important process of self-cultivation. Although mall rats and mall jammers are considered a nuisance by mall governors and shop owners, they rarely disrupt the flow of consumer traffic. Jack Katz writes that shoplifting teenagers who engage in deviant activities in shopping centres do so as a form of competition amongst themselves (1988: 56). Because teenage shoplifting is viewed by the teenagers themselves as a kind of sporting event, where being able to steal is likened to success in a difficult task, and those who are caught are often first-time offenders, mall authorities have tended to treat this deviancy indulgently rather than as criminal, with most offenders being let off lightly with a slight reprimand. Nonetheless, as well as the increased mobilization of surveillance devices, mall strategies aimed at deterring loiterers have included the installation of more pedestrian rails (to prevent skateboarding) and fewer benches. Despite these measures, young people, the homeless, the unemployed and elderly pensioners continue to use shopping centres as meeting places, shelters and spaces of non-consumptive sociability.

Department stores and shopping malls are modern and postmodern institutions, respectively, that express the topos of consumption. Their spatial practices constitute the shopper as a mass consumer as well as subject of consumption. Shopping is thus an ambivalent practice that is both private and public, both pleasurable and necessary. The following section extends this argument by examining how supermarket and market shopping produce different identities for different shoppers.

SUPERMARKET AND MARKET CULTURES

Like lifestyle and leisure shopping in department stores and malls, the routine grocery shopping trip is a practice that transforms retail culture into consumer culture and imbues the consumer with different identities. This section will analyse how the modern supermarket and the neighbourhood produce market constitute different subjectivities for the shopper. The organizational geography of the sites, their spatial practices and the strategies of display will all be examined.

The recent expansion of supermarkets and megamarts has impacted upon the patterns of everyday consumption. The growth of self-service, the availability of new and global foods and the use of electronic retailing have radically changed the practice of grocery shopping. The once reliable and popular neighbourhood store, with its eclectic assortment of food products, idiosyncratic display and personalized service, has given way to the superstore characterized by high volume, low prices, large variety of goods, and free and ample parking (Seth and Randall 1999).

First used as a term in the 1930s, the supermarket emerged alongside the development of mass-production technologies such as the cash register, the automobile, packing, refrigeration and mass communications (Michman and Greco 1995: 75). In countries such as Britain and America, an industrial working class with a regular wage provided a regular demand for mass-produced goods while an emergent middle class produced a demand for a wider variety of goods. The concept of the supermarket, typified by large-scale retailing and standardized, mass-produced consumer goods arose in such a context. As one of the first large-scale retail institutions, the supermarket relies on practices such as impulse buying, the promotion of competitive national brands and customer self-service. Stores such as Tesco, Safeway, Sainsbury's, Food Lion, Coles and Wellcome, in Britain, the USA, Australia, Hong Kong and Taiwan have become as generic as the products they retail.

The supermarket uses spatial strategies organized around the site to promote and enhance the art of food trade. Like the department store and the mall, the supermarket is usually abutted by a large, underground, multi-storeyed and usually crammed car park that enables consumers not only to park but to purchase in bulk their weekly grocery shop, aided by the close proximity to the car park of a coin-operated trolley-hire system. Indeed, the availability of the automobile in the last 30 years has enabled the rapid rise and success of the supermarket, which relies on a wide group of consumers from a large catchment area and their ability to purchase in large quantities. Unlike the neighbourhood store where one walks, almost daily, to purchase single items such as milk, eggs and bread, contemporary supermarket consumers, more often than not, drive to the store and shop weekly. In-store services such as banking, key cutting and dry cleaning also function as necessary ancillaries to the time-poor postmodern shopper who will make the weekly trip to (not necessarily the nearest but) the biggest and most serviced one-stop supermarket within a reasonable 15-minute drive of home.

As a large-scale store with narrow aisles stocking a huge assortment of food and non-food products, the supermarket is organized, like the department store, to maximize the use of its space in order to attract the attention of shoppers with strong product loyalty, as they walk quickly along the aisles and glance only fleetingly at the thousands of separate items on display. Despite the supermarket's strategy of distributing mass standardized products and producing homogenous choices, new and global food varieties now proliferate there. The postmodern supermarket shopper can choose from seven varieties of rice, five types of potato and a dozen different kinds of bread. Generic and specific practices of consumption are evident in the store's strategies of display. At the fresh produce section, for example, big, waxed, genetically modified, mass-farmed apples take up two-thirds of the display aisle while on the refrigerated shelves next to it sit half a dozen or so specially packed trays of vacuum-sealed organic apples. These two different strategies of apple display produce two practices of apple consumption: a homogenized practice characterized by a preference for mass merchandising and a competitive price appeal (cheap and worm-free apples), and a specific lifestyle practice marked by differentiation and a possible awareness of movements such as food environmentalism and health food fads. Although organic apples are available at the local organic produce store or market, organic buying in the supermarket offers the shopper a convenient mix of choice structured around costs and varieties (organic/non-organic; food/non-food products). These strategies of fruit differentiation produce the mass consumer as the same but slightly different, structured by hierarchies in taste and class.

Time is also a factor to consider for the supermarket shopper who desires convenience. Open between 18 and 24 hours seven days a week, the supermarket caters to more and more workers of irregular and night shifts, essay-cramming students in search of a snack, and double-income families who are too busy and too tired to jostle with the crowd to shop at the end of the working week. Its longer opening hours and the lower cost of its products offer flexibility to different lifestyles and compete with other food institutions such as the 7–11 or other franchise convenience stores, the health food shop and the delicatessen. New supermarket departments such as florists, delis, bakeries and gourmet foods not only service new consumer needs but produce new identities for the shopper who selects both mass-produced and speciality items.

Resistant practices in the supermarket vary. Magazine-reading while standing at the checkout queue is a common tactic to while away the monotony of the wait despite the efficiency of barcode scanners and the popularity of the 8-items-or-less express checkout lane. The display of magazines at the checkout section is a common strategy engineered by the supermarket and geared toward impulse buying. For a shopper who reads the magazines and returns them to the shelf before s/he reaches the checkout register, the practice of magazine-reading without the need to purchase tactically subverts this strategy by allowing the shopper to consume through the pleasure of catching up on the latest entertainment gossip or the most innovative home improvement techniques, without making a purchase. Unlike shoplifting, magazine-reading without purchase is an acceptable and tolerated practice within the organizational logic of the store. For the shopper, such a practice can be seen as resistant because consumption is realized without the **hegemony** of purchase. A similar but not-so-accepted practice is that of sampling the fresh produce such as dates, nuts and grapes without purchase. Again, the supermarket's strategy of displaying fresh produce maximizes customer self-service: large trays of neatly stacked fruits and vegetables are organized as spectacles to tempt the shopper's visual and tactile senses. But not packaging the products, and allowing the shopper to touch and choose the quantity s/he desires, also enables the shopper to resist; in this instance, tactical consumption ensues in the practice of eating, or 'trying it out', without purchase (and potentially without even the intention to purchase).

Another tactical appropriation of supermarket shopping is evident in the Safeway supermarket in the northern Melbourne suburb of Preston in Australia, where I live. In the past 12 months, Preston has become, because of its progressive migrant service and interpreting provisions and amenities, and because of its already emerging Islamic community, the main suburb in Australia to resettle recently arrived asylum-seekers of Muslim backgrounds who have been granted temporary protection visas. At the Safeway supermarket, groups of fully veiled hijab-wearing Muslim women gather, sometimes with their families, to shop, usually after 10 at night. Mona Abaza (2001) has recently written that shopping malls in Egypt allow veiled Muslim women access to public space and a new identity based on consumption. Although Abaza's analysis is based upon a study of the new rich Muslim middle class in their home countries such as Egypt, Saudi Arabia and Malaysia, her conclusion can also be extended to the Safeway in Preston, where supermarket shopping paradoxically provides a new and alienated community with a space of safety against the post-September 11th backdrop of a notably more racist, anti-Muslim, neo-conservative Australia. Rather than the hegemonic strategies of the supermarket producing a mass of homogenized consumers who are assimilated with similar tastes, actual practices of supermarket shopping here point to just the opposite. As a temporary space of safety couched in discourses of domesticity and food provision, the supermarket, with its security surveillance, becomes one of the few public spaces accessible to these women and their families, who are made to feel increasingly unsafe by recent racist violence. Hanging around in the supermarket allows these Muslim women to legitimately gather together in public to socialize and catch up on each other's lives. Supermarket shopping produces a public autonomy that is relatively free from racist harassment, and an individual subjectivity to negotiate the processes of migration and transition. Such a practice also illustrates and extends Humphrey's argument that economic consumption produces economic citizenship through consumer rights (1998: 157); economic citizenship here is also an assertion of cultural citizenship – of cultural rights and the right to belong. While the supermarket, with its large, chain-store generic and sanitized appeal provides no specific sense of community, Safeway in Preston, like the shopping malls for Muslim women in Egypt, has become a tactical place of emerging community.

Another consumer culture that is challenging the supermarket in the production of a neighbourhood and a community is the produce market. Produce markets in Europe, the USA, Australia, New Zealand and East Asia are usually located in residential suburbs to serve the needs of the local community. They were established when needed, much like Sydney's Haymarket and Paddy's Market, which were rebuilt in 1869 to cater to an expanding working class, and Melbourne's Queen Victoria Market in 1878 to serve the northern suburbs (Kingston 1994: 46). Kingston reveals that in the period before the First World War, the middle classes shopped at city department stores and suburban stores while produce markets served the needs of the working classes (1994: 45) The period of postwar European migration in Australia saw produce markets transform into a multicultural and cosmopolitan mix of aromas and produce. In recent years, the pursuit of lifestyle shopping and the gentrification of inner-city suburbs have led to the rise of market shopping as an alternative popular practice amongst the middle class.

Produce markets now sell a diverse range of food and non-food commodities to cater to their disparate demographics, including meat, fish, clothing, jewellery and sundries such as party supplies, gifts, tobacco and homewares. Kingston suggests that market shoppers 'want to shop not only for their immediate requirements in fresh food and groceries, but also for other articles – clothing, shoes, household items, toys' (1994: 46). Because markets are characterized by single stalls or shops run by individual vendors and hawkers, the range of commodities available is more eclectic and idiosyncratic than that found in the supermarket. Examples might include Polish delis, Filipino-owned grocery stalls, factory-seconds soap shops, cheese and continental cake stands, second-hand garden supplies and local community organic produce co-operatives. Markets thus offer a greater and more individualized range of commodities compared to the homogenized and standardized mass-produced stock of the supermarket. Clearly, the market's spatial logic and its heterogeneous commodities suggest that market shopping is characterized by practices that give the market shopper a different identity, one perhaps that is more localized and communal than that produced by supermarket shopping (Figures 8.2 and 8.3).

Unlike car-reliant supermarket shopping, contemporary market shopping is characterized more by walking and strolling, suggesting that market shopping is less formal and, indeed, more leisurely. Night markets, street stalls, bazaars and fairs epitomize the logic of these practice, which are also enabled by the market's organizational geography of open display stalls and shops that are located next to the footpaths or on the streets. Unlike the chore of supermarket shopping, market shopping merges routine with leisure. Narrow aisles, high shelves and coin-operated trolleys are discarded in favour of haphazardly arranged table stands, mobile container stalls and sometimes even stools and ground mats. Shoppers usually bring their own trolleys or shopping bags and boxes, encouraging an atmosphere of DIY and non-uniformity. Prices are usually flexibly handwritten and haggling is acceptable, especially

Figures 8.2 and 8.3: Photographs taken in a produce and sundries market in Melbourne, Australia. Photographs by Audrey Yue, courtesy Centreway Management, Preston, Melbourne, Australia.

at closing times when vendors, who are eager to clear supplies, offer bulk discounts. In many markets, customer self-service is minimal. Personalized service ensures that shoppers can look forward to a chat with the traders or the spontaneous carnivalesque busking of street performers. As Humphrey asserts, retail cultures are transformed into consumer cultures through interaction (1998: 5).

Usually branding themselves as community markets, produce markets emphasize the freshness of their produce and their close relationship to the local economy. The postcard advertisement (Figure 8.4) highlights these. The slogan 'Enjoy the FRESHNESS' suggests that this enhances market shopping as a daily activity for some and a lifestyle weekend practice for others. As a daily activity, market shopping continues a tradition common before the advent of the supermarket and the technological advance of refrigeration. This is invoked through the denotative reference in the ad to 'generations of families'. This also anchors market shopping as a desirable family practice. As a Saturday-morning practice, market shopping adds to a lifestyle motivated by the desires for nutrition, health and an authenticity that, unlike the sanitized environment of the supermarket, the carnival of the market claims to provide.

Figure 8.4: Postcard advertisement for Preston Market, Melbourne, Australia. Courtesy Centreway Management, Preston, Melbourne, Australia.

The appeal of the market is further anchored through the promotion of a cosmopolitan range of fish, vegetables, delicacies and groceries 'from around the world'.

The market brings the global to the local through its status as a site for the community. Shoppers and vendors usually live in the neighbourhood. For a minimal charge, free-standing stall membership is open to anyone who offers a service or a product desired by the community, ranging from craftwork to massage and tarot-reading. Participation is organic and grassroots-based. The transience of the stalls adds to the dynamism of a communal space that is constantly evolving, reflecting the ever-changing identities of the neighbourhood as it adapts to the global movement of people, ideas and tastes.

Summary

In this chapter we have argued that:

- shopping is a practice of consumption that produces different identities for different consumers;

- shopping is both strategic and tactical;

- modern and postmodern spaces engineer strategies that demand conformity as well as engendering practices meaningful to the consumer;

- shopping produces the shopper as a self-conscious agent of consumption;

- shopping is a practice of consumption that produces 'consumer rights';

- shopping has become a terrain for engaging with civic responsibility, cultural rights, collective identity and common good/s.

EXERCISES

1. Use an example from second-hand shopping cultures such as vintage clothing boutiques, opportunity stores and 'cash converters' to consider the relationship between identity, commodity, taste, value and class.

2. Take a field trip to your local shopping mall, and list and discuss some examples of resistant practices in relation to the politics of gender, age and class.

3. Compare and contrast the spatial organization of a bakery at a produce market, and the bakery department of a supermarket. Discuss how their displays exemplify strategies of control and produce tactics of resistance.

REFERENCES

ABAZA, M. 2001: Shopping malls, consumer culture and the reshaping of public space in Egypt. *Theory, Culture and Society* 18(5), 97–122.

ABELSON, E.S. 1989: *When Ladies Go A-Thieving: Middle-Class Shoplifters in the Victorian Department Store*. Oxford: Oxford University Press.

BAUMAN, Z. 1988: Sociology and postmodernity. *Sociological Review* 36(4), 790–813.

BENJAMIN, W. 1973: *Charles Baudelaire: A Lyric Poet in the Era of High Capitalism*. Harry Zohn (trans.), London: Verso.

DOUGLAS, M. 1997: In defence of shopping. In Falk, P. and Campbell, C. (eds), *The Shopping Experience*. London: Sage, 1–14.

FALK, P. and CAMPBELL, C. (eds) 1997: *The Shopping Experience*. London: Sage.

FREDRIKSSON, C. 1997: The making of a Swedish department store culture. In Falk, P. and Campbell, C. (eds), *The Shopping Experience*. London: Sage, 111–36.

FRIEDBERG, A. 1993: *Window Shopping: Cinema and the Postmodern*. Berkeley, University of California Press.

GANDEL RETAIL TRUST 2002: *Chadstone: The Fashion Capital* (21/11/02), <http://www.gandel.com.au/dir143/gandel.nsf/ChadstoneWeb?Open?> accessed 15 January 2003.

HUMPHREY, K. 1998: *Shelf Life: Supermarkets and the Changing Cultures of Consumption*. Melbourne: Cambridge University Press.

KATZ, J. 1988: *Seductions of Crime: Moral and Sensual Attractions in Doing Evil*. New York: Basic Books.

KINGSTON, B. 1994: *Basket, Bag and Trolley: A History of Shopping in Australia*. Melbourne: Oxford University Press.

KOWINSKI, W.S. 1985: *The Malling of America: An Inside Look at the Great Consumer Paradise*. New York: William Morrow.

LEHTONEN, T. and MÄENPÄÄ, P. 1997: Shopping in the East Centre Mall. In Falk, P. and Campbell, C. (eds), *The Shopping Experience*. London: Sage, 136–65.

Melbourne Shopping Guide 2002. Melbourne: Visa.

MICHMAN, R.D. and GRECO, A.J. 1995: *Retailing Triumphs and Blunders: Victims of Competition in the New Age of Marketing Management*. London: Quorum.

MILLER, M.B. 1981: *The Bon Marché: Bourgeois Culture and the Department Store, 1860–1920*. Princeton: Princeton University Press.

MORRIS, M. 1998: *Too Soon Too Late*, Minneapolis: Indiana University Press.

MORSE, M. 1990: An ontology of everyday distraction: the freeway, the mall and television. In Mellencamp, P. (ed.), *Logics of Television: Essays in Cultural Criticism*. Bloomington: Indiana University Press, 193–221.

SETH, A. and RANDALL, G. 1999: *The Grocers: The Rise and Rise of the Supermarket Chains*. London: Kogan Page.

SHIELDS, R. (ed.) 1992: *Lifestyle Shopping: The Subject of Consumption*. London, Routledge.

WARTENBERG, T.E. 2000: Shopping esprit: *Pretty Woman*'s deflection of social criticism. In Desser, D. and Jowett, G.S. (eds), *Hollywood Goes Shopping*. Minneapolis, University of Minnesota Press, 309–29.

FURTHER READING

BOWLBY, R. 2000: *Carried Away: The Invention of Modern Shopping*. London: Faber.

COHEN, L. 1998: From town center to shopping center: the reconfiguration of community marketplaces in postwar America. In Horowitz, R. and Mohun, A. (eds), *His and Hers: Gender, Consumption and Technology*. Charlottesville: University Press of Virginia.

HALTER, M. 2000: *Shopping for Identity: The Marketing of Ethnicity*. New York: Schocken Books.

HORNE, S. 2002: *Charity Shops: Retailing, Consumption and Society*. London: Routledge.

HOROWITZ, R. and MOHUN, A. (eds) 1998: *His and Hers: Gender, Consumption and Technology*. Charlottesville, University Press of Virginia.

KRAUCAUER, S. 1995: *The Mass Ornament: Weimar Essays*. Levin, TY. (trans.), Cambridge: Harvard University Press.

MILLER, D. 2001: *The Dialectics of Shopping*. Chicago: University of Chicago Press.

MILLER, D. 1998: *A Theory Of Shopping*. Cambridge: Polity Press.

NIXON, S. 1996: *Hard Looks: Masculinities, Spectatorships and Contemporary Consumption*. New York: St Martin's Press.

RAPPAPORT, E.D. 2000: *Shopping for Pleasure: Women in the Making of London's West End*. Princeton, NJ: Princeton University Press.

SATTERTHWAITE, A. 2001: *Going Shopping: Consumer Choices and Community Consequences*. New Haven: Yale University Press.

WRIGLEY, N. 2002: *Reading Retail: A Geographical Perspective on Retailing and Consumption Spaces*. London: Arnold.

FASHION $\square$

Annamarie Jagose

> If there is no copying, how are you going to have fashion?
>
> Coco Chanel

Like many of the forms of everyday life, fashion seems too trivial to warrant serious consideration. It is frivolous, fleeting and superficially concerned with appearance. Yet precisely to the extent that it seems an unworthy subject for critical attention, fashion functions as a productive site for thinking about the ambiguity of everyday life. Like other commodities, clothes offer a dynamic field for studying the interface between culturally available **commodity** forms and the **construction** of a sense of self. This is because clothes are not simply material objects of practical use, but also acquire meanings and values that transfer to the **consumer** within a fashion system. This crucial difference between clothes and fashion has been defined by the French structuralist Roland Barthes (1983) in the following quasi-mathematical formula:

> Fashion can in fact be defined by the relation of two rhythms: a rhythm of dilapidation (d), constituted by the natural replacement time of a garment or wardrobe, on the exclusive level of material needs; and a rhythm of purchase (p), constituted by the time which separates two purchases of the same garment or wardrobe. (Real) Fashion, we might say, is p/d. If $d = p$, if the garment is replaced as soon as it is worn out, there is no Fashion; if $d > p$, if the garment is worn beyond its natural replacement time, there is pauperization; if $p > d$, if a person buys more than he wears, there is Fashion, and the more the rhythm of purchase exceeds the rhythm of dilapidation, the stronger the submission to Fashion. (pp. 297–8)

Valued far in excess of their utility function, clothes are a significant part of the consumer's negotiation of personal and group **identity**. This chapter will discuss fashion as a way of thinking about *the everyday tension between social control and personal* **agency**.

Imagine a fast-motion, time-release film of the interior of your wardrobe over the last decade. As certain items of clothing appear or disappear, as colour palettes and patterns change, as hemlines and waistlines rise and fall, as you trace variations on a theme – the V-neck, the roll-neck and the boat-neck or pale denim, overdyed denim and dirty denim – as you glimpse that almost-forgotten shirt with the button-down collar, those steel-capped boots, those cargo pants, that fluoro T-shirt, those leather slides, you are witnessing a record of your own interface with the fashion system. In my own imagined wardrobe documentary, Levi's 501s are replaced by Levi's Engineered jeans; pleat-fronted, narrow-legged pants give way to flat-fronted bootcuts; skirts that were once mini evolve into below-the-knee A-lines. Why is it unthinkable to wear three-quarter length trousers one season and desirable the next? Do fashion transformations evidence slavish conformity or individual style? In short, where does fashion come from?

THE 'TRICKLE-DOWN' EFFECT

Thorstein Veblen, a *fin-de-siècle* American sociologist, argues that fashion is a mark of social differentiation that originates with the upper strata of society and is gradually taken up by the lower classes through processes of emulation. This model of fashion's downward diffusion has become known as the 'trickle-down' effect and, though much modified and contested, still prominently informs contemporary academic and popular understandings of the social forces assumed to motivate changes in the fashion cycle. In his investigation of the modes of self-presentation of the upper or, as he puts it, the leisure **class**, Veblen (1899) identifies leisure not simply as free time but as itself a status symbol, 'an evidence of pecuniary ability to afford a life of idleness' (p. 43). Since leisure 'does not commonly leave a material product' (p. 45), Veblen argues that members of the leisure class rely on **spectacular** displays of **consumption** as public demonstrations of their wealth:

> The basis on which good repute in any highly organized industrial
> community ultimately rests is pecuniary strength; and the means of showing
> pecuniary strength, and so of gaining or retaining a good name, are leisure
> and a conspicuous consumption of goods. (p. 84)

Veblen takes fashion as an exemplary illustration of his argument not only because clothing is a visible and publicly available sign of wealth and standing, but also because fashion's seasonal transformations require a level of consumption that is, in functional terms, extremely wasteful. Assuming that 'each class envies and emulates the class next above it in the social scale', Veblen identifies the leisure class as defining 'all canons of reputability and decency' (pp. 104–5). For Veblen, then, fashion's main function is one of differentiation. Most obviously, fashion differentiates between upper and lower classes. However, as the leisure class expands due to the social mobility enabled by late nineteenth-century industrialization, Veblen argues that fashion equally becomes the mechanism for making increasingly fine-tuned differentiations between members of the leisure class – for example, between those who are both wealthy and well born and those who are only wealthy or only well born (pp. 76–7).

> Since the wealthy leisure class has grown so large, or the contact of the leisure-class individual with members of his own class has grown so wide, as to constitute a human environment sufficient for the honorific purpose, there arises a tendency to exclude the baser elements of the population from the scheme even as spectators whose applause or mortification should be sought. The result of all this is a refinement of methods, a resort to subtler contrivances, and a spiritualization of the scheme of symbolism in dress. And as this upper leisure class sets the pace in all matters of decency, the result for the rest of society also is a gradual amelioration of the scheme of dress. (p. 187)

It is important to note here that Veblen is making two related points. *First, fashion is used to mark hierarchical social distinctions between individuals. Second, through the trickle-down process of emulation, the fashions of the leisure class determine the fashions of society in general.*

Although Veblen offers a number of different explanations for the constant changes in what constitutes the fashionable (pp. 173–7), it is Georg Simmel (1971) who explicitly and causally connects the processes of differentiation and emulation – that is, the downward diffusion of fashion – with the necessity for change in fashion.

> Social forms, apparel, aesthetic judgement, the whole style of human expression, are constantly transformed by fashion, in such a way, however, that fashion – i.e., the latest fashion – in all these things affects only the upper classes. Just as soon as the lower classes begin to copy their style, thereby crossing the line of demarcation the upper classes have drawn and destroying the uniformity of their coherence, the upper classes turn away from this style and adopt a new one, which in its turn differentiates them from the masses; and thus the game goes merrily on. Naturally the lower classes look and strive towards the upper, and they encounter the least resistance in those fields which are subject to the whims of fashion; for it is here that mere external imitation is most readily applied. (p. 219)

In Simmel's account, it is precisely the lower classes' imitation of the upper classes' style that causes the fashionable to become unfashionable, generating a fresh need for a new form of fashion. By its very nature, 'as fashion spreads, it gradually goes to its doom' (p. 302).

While Veblen's and Simmel's arguments were worked out in the specific cultural and historical contexts of late nineteenth- to early twentieth-century America, the basic form of the 'trickle-down' effect they describe has been used to account for the contemporary downward diffusion of the styles originating from the fashion houses of such famous designers as Christian Lacroix, Donna Karan and Jean Paul Gaultier. In this scheme, fashions originate in designer collections launched at spectacular, high-profile shows. They are picked up by the celebrities and socialites who attend these shows. Fashion journalists and commercial buyers further facilitate the downward dissemination of particular fashions, which are taken up by early and then late fashion adapters. High-street designers modify aspects of the fashion for everyday wear and at the point when the ready-to-wear market is saturated with the look it is no longer fashionable. Take, for example, the fashion trajectory of Vivienne Westwood's deconstructed bra:

> Vivienne Westwood created the idea of a bra to be worn as outerwear, showing it originally over the top of dresses. Designer Jean Paul Gaultier took this concept and produced conical-shaped bra-top dresses much favoured by the pop star Madonna. The idea eventually filtered down to the high street in a much more conservative form, however, the basic shape and design of the bra-dress remained. (Bohdanowicz and Clamp 1994: 93)

This 'trickle-down' understanding of fashion can easily be seen in women's magazines, which represent themselves as brokering the latest designer fashions to a mass readership: 'The new silhouette for winter', 'Trends for spring/summer 2001', 'Key trends for the season' and 'The return of the fringe' (*Marie Claire* 2001: 8). Frequently such magazines will juxtapose photographs and descriptions of the latest season's catwalk fashions with versions of the same look available from high-street designers. *Vogue*, for example, runs a regular Index section in which admirers of a cowl-neck sweater from Fendi are directed to a similar but cheaper and widely accessible item from the Nautica Jeans Company, and readers who like the latest look of Ralph Lauren's jodhpurs are encouraged to consider the knock-off Riley riding pants available through Bloomingdale's (*Vogue* 2001: 437–8). *Marie Claire* runs a comparable section, where cheaper alternatives to the catwalk fashions are suggested to enable readers to create 'this winter's look' by mixing and matching (Figure 9.1).

Not just the fashion industry but the forms of social organization have changed radically in the century or so since Veblen and Simmel were writing. Nevertheless, for now we can note the following general characteristics of the 'trickle-down' theory.

- It represents fashion as reproducing relations of social inequity.
- It is attentive only to those relations of stylistic influence that can be traced from upper to lower social levels.
- It represents class and/or wealth as the defining category for analyses of social stratification.
- It assumes that it is natural for people to look up to and imitate those above them on the social scale.

THE 'TRICKLE-UP' EFFECT

Attempts have been made to revise the 'trickle-down' theory. For example, various scholars have argued that class and wealth are not the only grounds for social distinction: 'Groups must be defined not only in terms of hierarchical social status but also in terms of status difference established by sex, age, and **ethnicity**' (McCracken 1988: 102–3). A

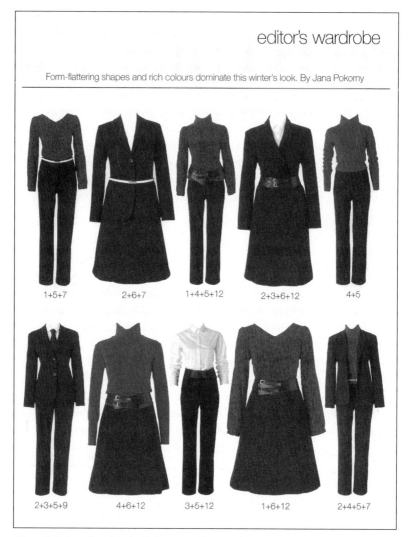

editor's wardrobe

Form-flattering shapes and rich colours dominate this winter's look. By Jana Pokorny

1+5+7	2+6+7	1+4+5+12	2+3+6+12	4+5
2+3+5+9	4+6+12	3+5+12	1+6+12	2+4+5+7

Figure 9.1: Page from Marie Claire Australia, *March 2001, 141. Photographs by Jason Ell, courtesy* Marie Claire, Australia.

critical model that counters the 'trickle-down' effect more substantially, reversing many of its assumptions, is – perhaps unsurprisingly – the 'trickle-up' effect. In this model, fashion is generated by **subcultural** groups or stylish individuals whose innovations are picked up and disseminated more broadly by fashion manufacturers and designers. The upward diffusion of fashion is not strictly a new phenomenon. Veblen himself noted in passing the fashion for men of the leisure class to be clean-shaven, but since this style formation came from below – 'a transient and unadvised mimicry of the fashion imposed upon body servants' (Veblen 1899: 186) – he assumed it would be short-lived. Nevertheless, the 'trickle-up' effect has been largely a post-1960s development enabled by cultural developments as various as the decline of *haute couture* and the fragmentation of the fashion markets, the baby-boom-led rise of youth culture, the transnational flow of commodity items and the **globalized** reach of mass media.

Since the 1960s, the 'bottom-up' model, in which new styles emerge in lower-status groups and are later adopted by higher-status groups, has explained an important segment of fashion phenomena. In this model, age replaces social status as the variable that conveys prestige to the social innovator. Styles that emerge from lower socioeconomic groups are often generated by adolescents and young adults who belong to subcultures or 'style tribes' with distinctive modes of dress that attract attention and eventually lead to imitation at other age and socioeconomic levels. New styles also emerge from subcultures within middle-class strata, such as artistic and gay communities (Crane 2000: 14).

The 'trickle-up' theory not only disputes the notion that wealth and high-class status are the most important factors in determining fashion but proliferates the possible cultural sites where fashions might originate. In recent years, for instance, it has been possible to trace the mainstreaming of various niche styles from the oversized gold jewellery and Adidas sneakers of the black rapper to the wide-legged jeans of the skateboarder, from the piercings of the neo-tribal modern primitive pursuing programmes of body modification to the early 1990s 'lesbian chic' look. So established is the notion of the 'trickle-up' effect that industries which depend on keeping abreast of the increasingly quick revolutions of the fashion cycle now draw on the expertise of coolhunters, people whose job it is to detect nascent trends at street level and feed that information back into the mechanisms of mass **production**. Baysie Wightman, a coolhunter working for Converse in the early 1990s who noticed that the cool kids on the street were turning against the expensive, hi-tech, multi-coloured basketball sneakers, has been credited with bringing back the 1970s classic Converse One Star. Dee Dee Gordon, a contact of Wightman's, went one step further and initiated the backless One Star sneaker-sandal after she noticed a Los Angeles street style which had 'white teen-age girls dressing up like *cholos*, Mexican gangsters, in tight white tank tops known as "wife beaters", with a bra strap hanging out, and long shorts and tube socks and shower sandals' (Gladwell 1997: 78). Hanging out at skateboard parks, malls, bars and nightclubs, the coolhunter tracks fashions almost at the moment of their formation and the speed of the 'trickle-up' effect is raised to the second power.

> The sneakers of Nike and Reebok used to come out yearly. Now a new style comes out every season. Apparel designers used to have an eighteen-month lead time between concept and sale. Now they're reducing that to a year, or even six months, in order to react faster to new ideas from the street. The paradox, of course, is that the better the coolhunters become at bringing the mainstream close to the cutting edge, the more elusive the cutting edge becomes. (Gladwell 1997: 78)

This paradox is at the heart of fashion: trickle up or trickle down, *the process of becoming fashionable is always the beginning of the end of fashionability.*

145

NETWORK OF INFLUENCES

There are aspects of fashion diffusion that cannot adequately be explained by either the 'trickle-up' or 'trickle-down' theories. Why do some fashions – catwalk or subcultural – fail to appeal to a wider population and never take off? Might there be more complicated ways of mapping the diffusion of certain fashions than the 'trickle-up' or 'trickle-down' theories imply? It is not only that the stages of the fashion cycle from innovation to obsolescence are getting faster and faster but that the cycle can no longer be thought of as singular and self-contained. Let's look, for example, at the fashion career of the Doc Marten boot. Now Famous for its air-cushioned sole, the Doc Marten was originally designed in 1946 by Dr Klaus Maerten in Germany as corrective footwear, and was initially particularly popular with older women. In 1959, the exclusive licence was acquired by Bill Griggs of the Griggs Boot Making Partnership in Northamptonshire and in 1960, Griggs began manufacturing the Dr. Martins AirWair boots in Britain aimed at the working man (Brydon 1998, 10).

Fig. 9.2: Doc Martens classic boot. Courtesy Doc Martens.

Not considered a fashion item at all, by the late 1960s it had become the boot of choice for skinheads, now emerging as a visible subculture in urban centres, who took as one of their sartorial prototypes the white working-class man (Hebdige 1979: 55–6). In the 1970s, the Doc Martens' status as a fashion item grew more widespread, being worn particularly as streetwear by middle-class youth. In the 1980s in New Zealand, I myself acquired a pair in cherry red which, despite the fact that they had been bought for me by my mother, signalled my membership in a lesbian subculture that made a fashion statement of the blurring of the vestiary codes of **gender**. In London in the mid-1990s, on my way home to Melbourne with several elegant pairs of Italian shoes in my suitcase, the connection between lesbianism and the Doc Marten still made enough nostalgic claim on me for me to visit recreationally one of the vast Doctor Marten Stores where

I saw that the label had expanded to include clothing and accessories while the Doc Marten itself has morphed into dozens and dozens of fantastic styles:

> Docs themselves now come in 150 different styles and in a range of colors, textures, patterns, including gold and silver lamé, paisley, gingham, flowers, pastels, velveteen, glitter black, silver or lilac, lace, tartan, nubuck red, mustard, eggplant, cobalt blue or lime green ... There are desert boots and beatle boots and corporate shoes that, while still possessing the patented sole, are more suitable to wear with a business suit ... There are mary janes with thick soles, or in gold and silver lamé with rainbow coloured laces, or in red, black, or white patent leather. (Brydon 1998: 11)

Fig. 9.3: Doc Martens open-toed sandal. Courtesy Doc Martens.

Fig. 9.4: Doc Martens high boot. Courtesy Doc Martens.

Fig. 9.5: Doc Martens graffiti-style boot. Courtesy Doc Martens.

Neither the 'trickle-up' nor the 'trickle-down' effect satisfactorily describes this process. The subcultural **appropriation** of what was originally orthopaedic footwear complicates the seemingly straightforward up/down directionality of either model and might, at best, be conceptualized as a horizontal diffusion of fashion. While the middle-class acquisition of the Doc Marten as street style could be described as 'trickle up', the lesbian (and latterly, gay) resignification of the boot requires again a more sophisticated analytic model, since the relation between skinhead and homosexual subcultures is impossible to calculate with any straightforward recourse to hierarchy. And if the massive variations now available point to the democratization of the Doc Marten as style, it is far from clear what original sartorial code, if any, is being cited. It is not simply that fashion drifts either from high to low or from low to high. The trajectories of fashion diffusion are more complicated and less predictable than those unidirectional models suggest.

The networks of fashion diffusion are too complex to be described by the simple gravitational forces of down or up. Any attentive study of fashion diffusion will show that fashions do not simply descend or ascend before becoming extinct at the limits of their trajectory. Rather, fashion cycles intersect with other fashion cycles, forever being tweaked here or hijacked there, snuffed out almost at the moment of their inception or resignified and recycled, until the precise lines of influence and imitation are illegible in an endlessly complex capillary cross-hatching. Indeed, so complicated are the infinite and unanticipated relays of certain fashions and their evolutionary modifications that it is not always possible to track with any certainty the exact relations of causality that structure their transmission.

> When rappers rap about Versace it's no wonder that hip-hop designers are doing not only hooded cashmere sweaters or shirts of Egyptian cotton, but also nylon puff jackets trimmed with fur. As to who is determining what in the movement up and down, the stylistic currents are such, and the semiotic flow, that it's easy to be misled. (Blau 1999: 156)

With their interpretative confidence about the unidirectionality and predictability of fashion diffusion, both the trickle-down and the trickle-up theories oversimplify the actual vagaries of fashion.

Moreover, both theories implicitly assume that fashion is singular and coherent, some bounded phenomenon that begins at the high or low end and travels inexorably in the opposite direction. However, the same globalized **technologies** of media and communication that have sped up the cycles of change connecting this season's designer fashion with the mass market have also *proliferated the number of styles that might be considered fashionable at any one time*. As fashion theorist Elizabeth Wilson (1993) writes: 'Our culture of global mass media feeds us so much information that a massive cultural eclecticism is the only possible response' (p. 6). This eclecticism is often associated with the post-Fordist fragmentation and flexibility that are the hallmarks of **postmodernism**. The fragmentation and proliferation of fashion can be seen on the street, in the store's new season's lines and perhaps most clearly in the fashion media, where dozens of contradictory looks are equally touted as the new fashion. Take, for example, *Vogue Australia*'s 2001 showcasing of trends from the latest European designer collections. On the one hand, the current look emphasizes strength and boldness: 'The signature looks of the spring/summer '02 international collections revealed a depth of creativity and originality, from graphic prints and textures to bold ethnic and folkloric details. The verdict? Strong looks for strong women' (p. 128). On the other hand, the look foregrounds wispiness and dreaminess: 'Swirly prints, wispy dresses and ethnic-inspired accessories turn 70s hippie style into the dreamiest look of the season' (p. 180). As this fashion editorial makes clear, different styles – even conflicting, contradictory styles – can be simultaneously in fashion. Although everything is not fashionable, *late-capitalist fashionability takes many forms*. It does not have a clear, single profile but articulates itself through a stylistic pluralism that has no overarching coherence.

RETHINKING FASHION

If the 'trickle-down' effect is associated with an oppressive reproduction of the superiority of the upper class, equally the 'trickle-up' effect is frequently critiqued as a conservative capitalist recuperation of alternative **ideologies**. In this respect, both models represent fashion as a single **hegemonic** force dedicated to maintaining the status quo. However, it is not necessary to characterize fashion in this overdetermined manner. It might be more useful to think about fashion as a set of interrelated effects produced haphazardly by the cultural work of disparate groups such as producers and consumers, marketers and the mass market, capitalists and activists, designers and subcultures, scholars and media commentators. This approach enables us to think about fashion less as a coherent project with a fixed social agenda than as a *multivocal field where dominant and **resistant** discourses are both maintained and resisted, reinforced and contested*. A strength of this approach is that it prevents us from thinking about fashion as an entity separate from the critical discourses that analyse it. After all, the fashion industry, like the advertising industry, is necessarily highly attuned to the shifts and changes in value that constitute its fashion cycles. Fashion, then, is not outside the interpretative circuits that contextualize it but an important constitutive aspect of them.

Ben Stiller's film *Zoolander* (2000) provides a way of thinking about this self-reflexive quality of fashion. *Zoolander* satirizes the world of catwalk fashion and the male model. Starring Stiller as Derek Zoolander, an impossibly stupid male supermodel, the film pokes fun at the vacuity of the fashion industry. One of *Zoolander*'s story lines centres around a conspiracy to assassinate the prime minister of Malaysia, a conspiracy hatched by a clutch of fashion designers determined to maintain the offshore sweatshop conditions that ensure their profits. Much of the film's humour comes from the ways in which it incorporates situations, locations and celebrities from the fashion world into its

149

mise-en-scène. For instance, the leader of the corrupt fashion designers is a caricature of Karl Lagerfeld; there are cameo appearances by actual fashion designers such as Tom Ford and Stella McCartney, and several scenes were shot at real-life fashion awards. But the *Zoolander* joke doesn't stop there. A recent real-life *Vogue* photo-shoot of the Parisian *haute couture* shows by celebrity American photographer Annie Leibovitz used the unlikely Ben Stiller as a model. In shot after shot, beside the Seine or in front of the Eiffel Tower, dwarfed by professional female models in Chanel or Lacroix, Stiller creases his forehead into one of the gormless looks that are Derek Zoolander's signature catwalk expression. *Zoolander* is not the only textual reference for Leibovitz's photographs, since they equally draw on classic fashion photography, one citing a 1960s Melvin Sokolosky photograph, another a more recent 1980s Helmut Newton image. Both tribute and spoof, the *Vogue* spread exemplifies the way in which fashion is a reactive force, maintaining itself through constant transformation. As Herbert Blau (1999) argues, 'It becomes apparent that mainstream fashion is soon inhabited by appearances that were one thought to be sources of a strategic overthrow, or for the transient moment outside, or below, the pale of established codes' (p. 145). The incredible resilience of fashion as a system can be traced not to its omnipotence but to its adaptability, its flexible annexation of an infinite and unpredictable range of cultural material.

FASHION AS DISTINCTION OR FASHION AS DEMOCRATIZATION

More recently, fashion scholarship has been interested less in the mechanisms of 'trickle down' or 'trickle up' than in identifying and analysing the fashion motivations of the consumer:

> Because of the enormous complexity of diffusion processes on a societal level in the late twentieth century, attention has shifted away from the process of diffusion itself to an analysis of the responses to clothing by consumers and to the role of clothes in the construction of personal identity. The concept of 'reception' endows the consumer with a greater level of agency than was the case in the older diffusion models, the consumer now actively making selections rather than passively responding to what is available. (Crane 2000: 236)

If you think about the various reasons that attract you as a consumer to one item of clothing over another, you might start to see how reception studies of fashion tend to complicate the central concept of distinction on which both the 'trickle-down' and the 'trickle-up' models rely. For while we might wear certain fashions in order to distinguish ourselves from some groups of people and affiliate ourselves with others, the concept of distinction does not fully describe our fashion choices: 'Fashion is not just about categorizing and ranking material culture; it is also about the manipulation of desire, pleasure and the play of the imagination (Finkelstein 1996: 37). We are not, of course, in full, conscious possession of the manifold reasons why we choose one pair of sunglasses over another or this shirt rather than that. All the same, let me try and unravel the motivations behind my last fashion purchase, a pair of black, elastic-topped Minnie Cooper shoes with cream detailing. Loosely speaking, distinction was part of the purchase logic since Minnie Coopers are a New Zealand design object seldom seen in Australia where I live. A far more over-riding consideration for me, however, was the shoes' novelty since they were an anchor style of the new autumn collection. Then there were considerations of the comfort and quality that I associate with the brand. But looking back, my main feeling on buying the shoes was an intense pleasure, for the money to buy the shoes was given to me as a birthday present by friends.

The work of French philosopher Gilles Lipovetsky could explain some of the structuring experiences of my shoe purchase. Lipovetsky considers the dynamics of social distinction inadequate to the task of explaining how fashion works. He downplays the role of distinction in the process of mass consumption, arguing that factors such as personal autonomy, **individualism**, utilitarianism, pleasure and choice are more important: 'Consumption, by and large, is no longer an activity governed by the quest for social recognition; it is undertaken in an effort to achieve well-being, functionality, pleasure for its own sake' (Lipovetsky 1994: 145). Rather than see fashion as a form of social control or even a form of social contest, Lipovetsky argues for a **utopian** reading of fashion as a training ground for democracy:

> On the occasion of each shift in fashion, there is a feeling, however tenuous, of subjective freedom, of liberation from past habits ... In a society of individuals committed to personal autonomy, it is clear why what is new offers such a lively attraction: it is experienced as an instrument of personal 'liberation', as an experiment to be undertaken, an experience to be lived, a little adventure of the self. The consecration of the new and modern individualism go hand in hand; novelty is in phase with the aspiration to individual autonomy. If consummate fashion is shored up by the logic of capitalism, it is equally sustained by cultural values that find their apotheosis in the democratic state. (p. 154–5)

Lipovetsky's characterization of fashion as a democratizing force associated with novelty, change and liberation is far removed from Veblen's and Simmel's understanding of fashion as a mechanism for maintaining and reproducing social hierarchies. It is less important to side with one theorist over another than to understand that an apparently insignificant and superficial phenomenon such as fashion is intimately tied to the workings of **power** and **ideology** that structure our everyday lives.

Summary

In this chapter, we have argued that:

- though seemingly trivial, the practices of fashion demonstrate the everyday tension between social control and personal agency;
- fashion theorists have represented fashion as central to both the reproduction of relations of social inequity ('trickle-down' theory) and the recuperation of resistant ideologies ('trickle-up' effect);
- recent cultural shifts – such as market fragmentation, mass media and globalization – mean that more complicated models are required for thinking about fashion diffusion;
- some commentators characterize fashion as committed to maintaining the social quo while others see it as a potentially liberatory force associated with democracy and social transformation;
- fashion does not have a fixed social agenda but is a set of flexible, unstable effects that is taken up and used to meet the various, sometimes contradictory, requirements of different interest groups.

EXERCISES

1. List the last three items of clothing you bought for yourself. For each item, identify what considerations influenced your purchase. Your friends? Fashion magazines? Price? Brand?

2. If you were a coolhunter, what current fashion trend would you identify as future directed? What reasons can you give for your assessment?

3. Make a list of the brands of different clothes you know and rank them in order of desirability. Explain the logic of your ordering system.

REFERENCES

BARTHES, R. 1983: *The Fashion System*. Ward, M. and Howard, R. (trans.), New York: Hill & Wang.

BLAU, H. 1999: *Nothing in Itself: Complexions of Fashion*. Bloomington: Indiana University Press.

BOHDANOWICZ, J. and CLAMP, L. 1994: *Fashion Marketing*. London and New York: Routledge.

BRYDON, A. 1998: Sensible shoes. In Brydon, A. and Niessen, S. (eds), *Consuming Fashion: Adorning the Transnational Body*. Oxford: Berg.

CRANE, D. 2000: *Fashion and its Social Agendas: Class, Gender, and Identity in Clothing*. Chicago and London: University of Chicago Press.

FINKELSTEIN, J. 1996: *After a Fashion*. Melbourne: Melbourne University Press.

GLADWELL, M. 1997: The coolhunt. *The New Yorker*, 17 March, 78–88.

HEBDIGE, D. 1979: *Subculture: The Meaning of Style*. London: Methuen.

LIPOVETSKY, G. 1994: *The Empire of Fashion: Dressing Modern Democracy*. Porter, C. (trans.), Princeton: Princeton University Press.

Marie Claire, March 2001: Melbourne: Murdoch Magazines.

McCRACKEN, G. 1988: *Culture and Consumption: New Approaches to the Symbolic Character of Consumer Goods and Activities*. Bloomington: Indiana University Press.

SIMMEL, G. 1971: Fashion. In Levine, D.N. (ed.), *On Individuality and Social Forms*. Chicago and London: University of Chicago Press, 294–323.

VEBLEN, T. 1899: *The Theory of the Leisure Class: An Economic Study of Institutions*. New York: Macmillan.

Vogue, October 2001: New York: Condé Nast Publications.

Vogue Australia, March 2001: Greenwich, New South Wales: Condé Nast Publications.

WILSON, E. 1993: Fashion and the postmodern body. In Ash, J. and Wilson, E. (eds), *Chic Thrills: A Fashion Reader*. Berkeley: University of California Press.

FURTHER READING

COLE, S. 2000: *Don We Now Our Gay Apparel: Gay Men's Dress in the Twentieth Century*. Oxford: Berg.

DE LA HAYE, A. and WILSON, E. (eds) 2000: *Defining Dress: Dress as Object, Meaning and Identity*. New York: Manchester University Press.

ENTWHISTLE, J. 2000: *The Fashioned Body: Fashion, Dress, and Modern Social Theory*. Malden: Polity Press.

EWING, E. 1992: *History of Twentieth-Century Fashion*. Latham: Barnes & Noble.

FUSS, D. 1992: Fashion and the homospectatorial look. *Critical Inquiry* 18 (Summer), 713–37.

HOLLANDER, A. 1994: *Sex and Suits*. New York: Knopf.

JOHNSON, K. and LENNON, S. (eds) 1999: *Appearance and Power*. Oxford: Berg.

POLHEMUS, T. 1994: *Streetstyle: From Sidewalk to Catwalk*. London: Thames & Hudson.

Introduction to section 4

Everyday practices

Fran Martin

WHAT THIS SECTION AIMS TO DO

In Section 3 of this book, we introduced you to the idea that contemporary, **postindustrialized** cultures can be characterized as examples of **commodity culture**: a form of culture produced by particular histories and specific forms of economic and social organization. In this final section, we build on that work to consider in detail three sets of cultural **practices** that are an integral part of our everyday lives in commodity culture today, and that take particular, distinctive forms as a result of their realization within that cultural context. The forms of cultural practice we examine in Section 4 should be seen always in relation to their crucial, defining context as aspects of, and responses to, contemporary commodity culture. The three chapters that comprise this section examine:

- how the seemingly banal and unremarkable everyday life practices of *food and eating* are in fact imbued with complex cultural meanings, which may either shore up dominant systems of **power** or, alternatively, express and enact **resistance** to those systems; this chapter also examines in detail the ways in which everyday food practices construct and express notions of ethnic **identity**, or **ethnicity**;
- how our quotidian interactions with domestic *technology* – especially the telephone – both shape and express current forms of cultural power; our complex relationships with domestic technologies are conceived as a form of cultural practice that consists, more specifically, in the technology's **production**, regulation, representation and **consumption**, and the ways in which the technology contributes to the **construction** of **identity**;
- how our relationships with modes of everyday travel – by way of cars, bicycles, public transport, and the electronic routes of telematics – enable us to elaborate and express complex forms of cultural **identity**; the regulation of mobility by the **strategies** of institutional **power** is also examined, and it is suggested that our various modes of mobility today indicate the cultural and economic configurations of a world more than ever transnationally inter-connected.

The key concepts covered in these chapters include:

- cultural practice;
- strategies and **tactics** (revisited after our introduction in Section 1);
- **technoculture** and technology as culture;
- cultural practice and/as identity formation;
- travel and mobility as pervasive states of being in today's quotidian cultures.

But what is 'practice', exactly? Surely it means something more specific than just 'the ways people do things'. How have other scholars of society and culture thought and written about cultural practice? And indeed, how should we understand the relationship between the academic and intellectual pursuits of writing and 'theory', on the one hand – what we're doing in this book, and what you'll be doing too, more than likely, in assessment tasks as part of the course for which you're reading the book – and, on the other hand, the everyday life pursuits of eating, using technology and getting around: the forms of cultural 'practice' that we analyse in this section? How can we theorize practice, and how does 'doing theory' *relate* (or not) to everyday life practice? These are the questions we will address in the remainder of this Introduction.

THEORIES OF PRACTICE

There exists in the social sciences – especially sociology and anthropology – a large and complex body of work known as 'practice theory', which investigates intricate conceptual questions including that of the relationship between objectivism and subjectivism, and how social scientists ought to think about their own work of analysing society in the light of the differences between these approaches. Although this work certainly informs our own theorization of cultural practice, we will not cover this work in any great detail, as our aim is not to give an account of these complex debates in the social sciences but rather to offer you a basic introduction to the idea of practice as it is employed in contemporary **cultural studies** approaches to everyday life. (If you are interested in further pursuing practice theory in the social sciences, please refer to the references cited at the end of this Introduction.) For our purposes here, we will define a cultural practice as: *a meaningful activity performed habitually by a social **subject** or group of social subjects in a particular historical and cultural context, which as a result is subject to and responds to a specific network of power relations.* To elucidate just what we mean by that, we turn below to some of the most influential theorists of social practice: Pierre Bourdieu and Michel de Certeau.

Probably the most influential theorist of social practice in recent decades has been the French sociologist Pierre Bourdieu, especially in his two books, *Outline of a Theory of Practice* (1977; originally published in French as *Esquisse d'une théorie de la pratique, précédé de trois études d'ethnologie Kabyle* in 1972) and *The Logic of Practice* (1989; originally published in French as *Le sens pratique* in 1980). In those books Bourdieu elaborates a theory of social practice which proposes that practice is inherently and

155

definitively linked with the **habitus**: a concept you have already read about in Chapter 5. Recall from that chapter that habitus refers to those dispositions (for example, **taste**) that are internalized in the individual subject as part of the process of his or her socialization and that express – usually unconsciously – aspects of the system of power relations into which the subject is socialized (for Bourdieu, in our contemporary societies these power relations are primarily those of **class**). Bourdieu (1977) refers to the systems of power relations that organize societies, simply, as structures (pp. 78–87). For Bourdieu, practice involves both the reproduction of the cultural relations that support the existing structures; and negotiation by social subjects with the conditions of their subjection to these structures – for example, in negotiations around **cultural capital** (as subjects try to accumulate it, exchange it, display it and evaluate it in their everyday interactions with others). Most importantly, Bourdieu holds that practice is activity that is produced out of, and to a large extent determined by, the subject's habitus; that is to say, Bourdieu's conception of practice emphasizes the ways in which quotidian cultural activity tends to reflect, express, shore up and reproduce existing power relations (1977: 78–87). He writes in summary: 'In short, the habitus, the product of history, produces individual and collective practices, and hence history, in accordance with the schemes engendered by history' (1977: 82). The enclosing circularity of the argument is obvious here: history – which takes on its distinctive forms as a result of the shaping force of structures of power – produces the habitus, which socializes individuals into particular kinds of practices, which then reproduce the same structures of power that inform them. Thus, *the existing social system and its power structures reproduce themselves unconsciously by means of the cultural practices of the socialized individual*.

In distinction to this emphasis in Bourdieu's writing on the circularity and dogged self-reproduction of the social system and its structures of power is the work of Michel de Certeau: another theorist whose work you have already encountered (in Chapter 2), and whose book *The Practice of Everyday Life* (1984; originally published in French as *Arts de faire* in 1974) represents another key work in the theorization of everyday life practice. In elaborating his own theory of practice, de Certeau draws in important ways both on Bourdieu and on French historian and philosopher Michel Foucault's book *Discipline and Punish: The Birth of the Prison* (1977; originally published in French as *Surveiller et punir; naissance de la prison* in 1975). However, de Certeau criticizes the tendency of both Bourdieu and Foucault to emphasize the ruses of **power** – which de Certeau calls **strategies** – at the expense of a serious consideration of cultural practices that are not in the service of **hegemony**, and that may even be construed as *counter-hegemonic*. You will recall from Chapter 2 that de Certeau refers to such 'minor' practices – enacted every day by social subjects in our negotiations with the structures of power that shape our everyday lives – as **tactics**. For de Certeau, the 'practices' analysed by Bourdieu correspond not to *all* practices enacted by real social subjects, but only to the **strategies** by which power reproduces itself through social practice (1984: 52).

Similarly, de Certeau argues that following Foucault's analysis of the procedures associated with technologies of power, such as the prison:

> It remains to be asked how we should consider other, equally infinitesimal, procedures, which have not been 'privileged' by history but are nevertheless active in innumerable ways in the openings of established technological networks. This is particularly the case of procedures that do not enjoy the precondition, associated with all those studied by Foucault, of having their own place (*un lieu propre*) on which the panoptic machinery can operate. These techniques, which are also operational, but initially deprived of what gives others their force, are the 'tactics' which I have suggested might furnish a formal index of the ordinary practices of consumption. (1984: 49)

In other words, in distinction to both Foucault and Bourdieu, de Certeau wants to emphasize those cultural practices which, while they must of necessity negotiate with the entrenched power relations that shape society, nevertheless do not merely reflect and reproduce those power relations, but also contest and struggle against them.

The three chapters that follow proceed from a set of conceptual starting points derived from the work of these key theorists of cultural practice. We might schematize these starting points as follows.

- There can be no cultural practice 'outside of' or independent from existing social power relations (for example, the power relations of class inequality that structure contemporary commodity cultures; or the power relations that structure discourses on **race** and ethnicity in a particular social context).
- However, it does not follow that *all* cultural practices are necessarily doomed to reflect and reproduce existing power relations: some forms of cultural practice may also *contest* and *resist* them.

PRACTICES OF THEORY

Finally, a brief note on a more complex set of questions raised by the activity of *theorizing practice*. While their conceptualization of cultural practice vis-à-vis power differs significantly, both de Certeau and Bourdieu underscore the importance of seeing 'theory' – academic inquiry into society and culture – not as separate from social practice but as *itself* a form of social practice. For example, Bourdieu, grappling with the idea of *objectivism* inherent in the model of classical anthropology, commences his *Outline of a Theory of Practice* with the thought-provoking observation that:

> The practical privilege in which all scientific activity arises never more subtly governs that activity (insofar as science presupposes not only an epistemological break but also a social separation) than when, unrecognized as privilege, it leads to an implicit theory of practice which is the corollary of neglect of the social conditions in which science is possible. (1977: 1)

Bourdieu is criticizing the tendency for social science (and perhaps academic inquiry more broadly) to assume the substantive differentiation of its *own* practice – what we have called 'the practice of theory' – from the cultural practices of the 'ordinary people' – that is, non-academics – which are its object of analysis. In presuming this radical distinction between the two forms of practice (the practice of theory and the practice of everyday life), Bourdieu contends, the theorist effectively *erases* the social and cultural context of her own work: a context that in reality is informed, no less than the context of the 'ordinary' cultural practices she studies, by structures of power. (We might, for example, follow Bourdieu's suggestion and consider the degree of social privilege that may, in part, be what has enabled the theorist to amass particular (academic) forms of **cultural capital** – a social privilege which may then, in turn, be strengthened and reproduced through her possession of these forms of knowledge.) It seems to us that Bourdieu's observations here on the status of academic inquiry *as* cultural practice, and his critique of the **ideology** of scientific objectivism, find an echo in cultural studies' self-conscious engagement with the practices and **politics** of our own everyday lives. As you work your way through the following three chapters, it might be interesting to bear in mind that if, in this book as a whole, we eschew the objectification of the everyday life practices of others *qua* 'others' and try instead to gain a productive critical distance on *our own* everyday lives in contemporary commodity cultures, then our own practices of cultural analysis should not be seen as substantively separate from the rest of our everyday life practices (eating, using the telephone, travelling). What will it mean, then, to conceptualize our own academic pursuits as a form of everyday life practice – something that is inherently a part of, and not separate from, our daily struggle to make sense of our lives and our selves in the context of those power relations that structure our early twenty-first-century commodity cultures?

REFERENCES

BOURDIEU, P. 1977: *Outline of a Theory of Practice*. Nice, R. (trans.), Cambridge: Cambridge University Press.

BOURDIEU, P. 1989: *The Logic of Practice*. Nice, R. (trans.), Cambridge: Polity Press.

DE CERTEAU, M. 1984: *The Practice of Everyday Life*. Rendell, S. (trans.), Berkeley: University of California Press.

FOUCAULT, M. 1977: *Discipline and Punish: The Birth of the Prison*. Sheridan, A. (trans.), New York: Pantheon Books.

Chapter Ten

EATING ☐

Audrey Yue

Film discussed in this chapter:
- *Autumn Moon* (Clara Law, 1992).

INTRODUCTION

Eating is central to the sustenance of daily life. We eat to stay alive, yet it is a task we often take for granted because the everydayness of eating aligns it with the perfunctory. Eating demonstrates the relations between the human body and **identity**. Through eating, individuals are incorporated into networks of **production** and exchange; individuals also incorporate themselves with the meanings associated with food. Eating is a **practice** of **consumption** that produces new meanings. Cultural shifts are reflected in historical changes in the consumption of food, where meanings are constructed through the development of new taxonomies, the articulation of satisfaction or dissatisfaction with food, and the **resistance** to advertising or medical messages. In other words, the food **consumer** uses food and practices of eating to express different cultural meanings. Central here is the issue of **power** as both acceptance and resistance. Making sense of eating and food thus requires an understanding of a variety of social, cultural and historical contexts, as well as how subjects construct their own identities, life histories, and their views of themselves and their bodies.

EATING AND FOOD AS AMBIVALENT PRACTICES OF POWER AND RESISTANCE

Scholarship on food and eating has emerged as an important field of study as the increased emphasis on media and urban **culture** continues to fuel interest in food-related matters such as **taste**, skill, authenticity, **lifestyle** and health. Whilst studies in anthropology, sociology and history focus on eating and food as categories and classifications, recent developments in **cultural studies** stress the relationship of food and eating to individual, local and global identities.

> As individuals, we eat into culture, continually oscillating between primary, natural and necessary acts, as simultaneously, we consume and ingest our identities. The mouth machine takes in, but it also spits out. While in some cases there is a direct equation between eating and being, in mundane ways we also shift the lines that connect what we eat with who we are. Rather than simply confirming who we are, eating conjoins us in a network of the edible and inedible, the human and non-human, the animate and inanimate. In these actions, the individual is constantly connecting, disconnecting and reconnecting with different aspects of individual and social life.
>
> Elspeth Probyn, *Carnal Appetites: Food, Sex, Identities,* p. 17.

Eating is an act of orality. The pleasure of swallowing can be associated with the pleasure of speaking. These pleasures suggest that eating is not simply a mere act of the ingestion or incorporation of food: eating constitutes who we are as we become what we eat when food crosses the frontier between the world and the self, the outside and the inside. Eating also reconstitutes who we are to those around us when food links us to other people, other products and other desires. As feminist cultural theorist Elspeth Probyn (2000) asserts, *eating is an act of consumption that expresses identity.* What we eat not only shapes who we are, but who we are is also continually reshaped by food. This way of thinking about the relationship between eating and food to identity reflects Michel de Certeau's thesis on consumption as a practice that exposes power relations.

According to de Certeau (1984), eating, like reading, walking or shopping, is a system of practice. *To practice is not simply to use and apply; rather, a practice is an act of doing that also affords the opportunity to evade the regulatory strategies of official power* (see the Introduction to this section). Eating is a system of practice that enables the food consumer to produce meanings about themselves and the world around them in a way that may be different from those 'official' or original meanings intended by the producer. It is an act of consumption that opens up the gap between the two competing forces of **strategies** and **tactics** (see Chapter 3 and the Introduction to this section). As a practice of consumption, eating can be a tactic utilized by food consumers to retaliate against the strategies of food producers.

Russian formalist Mikhail Bakhtin provides an example of such top-down and bottom-up contestations in his study on *Rabelais and His World* (1984). Examining the divide between the Church and pagan folk cultures in the Middle Ages, he shows how feasting functions as a practice that exposes the struggles between official Christianity and local pagan rites. During this period, two different practices of feasting existed side by side. The Church carried out its official feasts, which emphasized rank, privilege and ritual; the local pagans conducted their unofficial celebrations with public and inclusive marketplace banquets. With given names like 'feast of the ass' and 'feast of fools', marketplace feasting displayed parodic practices of swallowing, drunken orgies and gluttony (p. 5). These celebrations used food to express life, death, suffering, triumph and renewal, reflecting the collective labour of work and the victory of the people over the world. Here, Bakhtin shows how eating is tactical because it is **resistant**. Marketplace feasting resisted the strategies of the Church through the democratic, carnival-like participation of the people. It was an inclusive occasion for conversation, producing a form of speech that was frank and popular. Popular speech helped to undermine the authority of the Church. Feasting also celebrated the ambivalent victory of suffering. While food nourishes and regenerates life (creative), the act of devouring also destroys life (destructive). Bakhtin's study shows clearly how the practices of eating and food could resist the power hierarchy that separated official Church and unofficial pagan culture. As a tactic of resistance, eating is an ambivalent practice that gains its meaning from its positioning within a given cultural system.

EATING AND FOOD AS CULTURAL SYSTEMS

> Eating, in fact, serves not only to maintain the biological machinery of the body, but to make concrete one of the specific modes of relation between a person and the world, thus forming one of the fundamental landmarks in space-time. ... Every food practice directly depends on a network of impulses (likes and dislikes) with respect to smells, colors, and forms, as well as to consistency types; this geography is as strongly culturalized as the representations of health and good table manners and thus is just as historicized. In the long term, of all these exclusions and choices, the food that is reserved, authorized, and preferred is the place of a silent piling up of an entire stratification of orders and counterorders that stem at the same time from an ethnohistory, a biology, a climatology, and a regional economy, from a cultural invention and a personal experience. Its choice depends on an addition of positive and negative factors, themselves dependent on objective determinations of time and space, on the creative diversity of human groups and individuals, on the indecipherable contingency of individual microhistories.
>
> From 'Plat du jour', in Michel de Certeau, Luce Giard and Pierre Mayol, *The Practice of Everyday Life. Volume 2: Living and Cooking*, pp. 183–5.

Practices of eating and food reveal the **hegemonic construction** of culture in a given society. Examining food as a cultural system, anthropologist Claude Levi-Strauss (1970) explores a wide of range of practices surrounding eating, including the choice and mix of ingredients, methods of preparation, ways of consumption and elimination, styles of table manners and compatibility of types of food to different social class. He suggests that the transformation of 'raw' to 'cooked' food exposes a cultural system ordered by a logic of perceived quality – what is edible or inedible, which types of food require preparation, and when food becomes rotten. The cultural values of exclusion, appropriateness and incompatibility reveal how a society uses language to establish a sense of the internal coherence of its structure. The anthropology of food reveals a cultural order in its analysis of eating as social practice. Such an approach recognizes that *'taste' is culturally shaped and socially controlled*.

Taste has both physical and social meanings. Despite slight variations, all palates are attuned to identifying common flavours such as sweetness, sourness, saltiness and bitterness. Taste is also culturally derived from constructed preferences and our social habits of consumption. According to sociologist Pierre Bourdieu (1984), taste as a more general social phenomenon classifies different groups according to different **class** and functions as a form of social distinction (see Chapter 5). The consumption of certain types of food by the upper class, for example, shows how this class uses taste in food, just as it uses taste in music, art or clothes, to differentiate itself from the lower classes. As the lower classes seek to emulate the former, the upper class changes its tastes again and again, thus preserving differences in status. Taste in food thus reveals the hegemony of class. Changing tastes in food also reflect the changing patterns of consumption through migration, inter-generational differences and cross-cultural co-existence.

Not only do different tastes in food express differences in class, regions and inter-cultures, French philosopher Roland Barthes (1961/1997) suggests that the whole world and its social environment is present in and signified by food. Food is a sign that produces meanings about the values of power and difference. Mary Douglas (1975/1997) applies this metaphor of food as a vehicle for communication in her study of British food and the calendar constitution of the meal. The calendar of eating reveals how meals are ordered through a scale of importance through the day (breakfast to supper), the week (e.g. Sunday dinner), the year (e.g. Christmas, fasting days) and life-cycle series (e.g. funeral or christening). This analysis reveals that the meal is a physical event that classifies social and cultural boundaries, highlighting not only what constitutes food, but how and where we eat it.

Jack Goody (1982) criticizes a Levi-Straussian approach for failing to consider social relations and individual differences. Using a political economy approach, Goody argues that a cultural study of food and eating must also involve the micro-level of the household and a macro-level such as the formation of the state structure. A tax on food and food services, for example, will impact upon the budget of a household and alter consumption patterns. Sidney Mintz (1989) takes a similar approach by making history central to his analysis of the materiality of food. Using sugar as a key example, he shows how it functions in the West as a metaphor for the social relations between the producers of sugar (the owners of plantations cultivated by African slavery and indentured labour) and the consumers of the **commodity**. The increase in sugar consumption from the nineteenth century to the present day reflects the history of colonialism and the attendant emergence of **capitalism** and leisure in the West.

Clearly, food and eating are never just food and eating, and their significances are never solely nutritional. The practices of food and eating are tied to relationships of power and resistance, of inclusion and exclusion, as well as cultural ideas about classification (including food and non-food, the edible and the inedible), the human body and the meaning of health. From fusion food, designer food, foot and mouth disease and salmonella outbreaks to the World Vision images of hunger, trade wars and campaigns against multinational corporations, the complex web of practices around eating and food create food networks that are ever more spatialized, connecting more people and more places. Increasingly, eating and food represent an important expression of our identity, both as individuals and in reference to broader groupings.

EATING IN, EATING OUT: IDENTITY AND DIFFERENCE

French gastronome Brillat Savarin's oft-quoted 1825 aphorism 'Tell me what you eat and I will tell you who you are' (1825/1970: 13) reveals an interlocking relationship linking food, identity and difference. Food and eating constitute who we are. But who we are is not only marked by a system of differences including **gender**, age, class and **ethnicity** – **modern** and **postmodern** food habits also increasingly reflect how changing practices of **consumption** constitute changing identities and new ways of negotiating difference.

Consider gender difference as an example. The question of eating and food is a complex one that includes not just the actual practices of eating and food, but also the preparation of meals (and clearing up afterwards). Feminist theories have exposed the gendered nature of work where the provisioning of food remains largely the remit of women in a domestic replication of the **gendered division of labour** (Counihan 1999). Women are responsible for feeding the family in a manner that is budget-conscious and healthy; women also cook to suit the preferences of the family (often husbands, sons and male partners). The response 'It's a pleasure to cook for him' encapsulates this myth. Men who cook tend to do so less frequently and are more likely to prepare snacks rather than meals, or to cook meals considered particularly appropriate for men: for example, barbecues. As mothers, women are expected to practise 'maternal altruism' towards their children and male partners, and deny themselves food when there is not enough to go round. Gender is also tied to eating disorders and dieting: women are more likely than men to be on weight-reducing diets, and are more likely to develop eating disorders such a anorexia nervosa and bulimia nervosa (Orbach 1986; Bordo 1998). These practices show how gender difference expresses power ambivalently. On one hand, women's bodies and shapes and sizes are **overdetermined** by cultural forces (women are powerless, in this sense); on the other hand, women have the power to control their bodies, not only through control over appetite, but also of social relations, particularly those of the family. Through cooking and the selling of home-cooked food (e.g. cake stalls, bake-offs, country fares, etc.), women have also creatively developed alternative economies of sociality and income.

Changing food practices also reflect changes in our identities as a result of how, when, where and with whom we eat. The transformation of the meal brought about by the great increase in eating ready-prepared food inside and outside the home has shifted from Douglas's structure of the meal as a powerful metaphor for the family to one that is symptomatic of changing lifestyles, work patterns and leisure. When one eats without meals, or eats when and what one wants, eating can be an expression of freedom, choice, individuality or modern alienation. In a study of eating patterns among Canadian teenagers, Gwen Chapman and Heather Maclean (1993) divide food into two categories – junk food and good food – and discover that teenagers and children still consume junk food despite being aware that sweets, for example, are not good for them. Good food is associated with the family and domesticity; junk food represents freedom from parental control and fun with friends, and is treated as a means of resistance against adult norms and values.

The convenience of take-away fast foods and lifestyle dining in restaurants has transformed the practice of eating out in recent years. In the West, eating out has its origins in the Middle Ages in inns that accommodated travellers. In the eighteenth century, coffee houses served as meeting places for the bourgeoisie. Later, the emergence of restaurants as places that served meals for pleasure added to the democratization of luxury. An activity that was once considered a luxury for the elite has come within reach of almost the whole population. This practice has been applauded for its promotion of social participation. The café, for example, has been considered a site for democratic participation, a place where people can discuss political issues and express an opinion about them.

Joanne Finkelstein (1989) considers the restaurant as a metaphor for a democratic public space and points to the negative aspects of dining out. She sees the restaurant experience as limiting and controlling of diners' sociality. Diners are manipulated by the distraction of décor, service and atmosphere; they are not encouraged to interact with others. They become conventional, lazy and lose the ability to be self-critical. Although the restaurant is a site for maintaining social harmony and mutual tolerance among a wide variety of customers, according to Finkelstein it is a myth to consider it as a public space. It is a hierarchical space with clear demarcations abutting private reservations and drinks-only sections. People seldom talk to each other across tables. Eating in this manner is an ambivalent practice, a private act conducted in the presence of strangers. One's behaviour is controlled by the gaze and power of others.

In a study documenting the rate of satisfaction with eating in restaurants in Britain, sociologists Lydia Martens and Alan Warde (1999) report that most people generally agree that eating out is a pleasurable experience, supporting a 1997 British National Food Survey showing 28.3 per cent of expenditure was on food and drinks away from home. They argue that Finkelstein wrongly constructs the consumer as victim of false consciousness. Warde and Martens' 1998 study also diagrams the popularity of eating out in pizza houses, fast-food and burger restaurants, as well as Indian, Chinese and Italian meals. The **globalization** of food and the increase in the varieties of fast-food eating have clearly contributed to changing tastes and identities.

Take-away fast foods such as fish and chips in Britain were first associated with the working class. The availability of convenience food at unsocial hours, and canteens suited the shift pattern of industrial workers' lives. Restaurants serving European cuisine gradually became important sites of eating out in the first part of the twentieth century. Then the arrival of South and East Asian immigrants in the 1960s introduced culinary diversity to restaurants and 'ethnic foods' emerged as a new source of take-away fast-food eating. Food ecologists Peter Atkins and Ian Bowler (2001) argue that since the 1980s, the trend in developed and developing countries toward highly standardized American franchised burgers, chicken and pizza has dominated the global fast-food eating culture (p. 286).

The development of fast-food eating highlights the consumption of **ethnicity**. The corporate globalization of food has seen 'ethnic foods' such as fried chicken, hot dogs and hamburgers become standard fare in contemporary eating (Gabbacia 1998). 'Ethnic foods' lose their ethnic identities when they are assimilated into mainstream cultures. Here, the notion of ethnicity, as a synonym for descent or heritage, is shifted to another notion of ethnicity, as a practice of everyday life. The consumption of 'ethnic foods' has also produced what Anne Goldman (1992) criticizes as *culinary imperialism* among Western consumers in search of exotic foods in order to enhance their taste and class. According to Goldman, eating ethnicity in this way, without any real understanding of the origins of these foods or the cultural contexts in which they are consumed, colonizes and appropriates the dominated other. Here, eating ethnicity can be considered a strategy of **orientalism**, a process of exoticization practised by dominant groups to further subjugate the 'other'.

In her study of Anglo-Indian curry culture Uma Narayan (1997) argues for a different perspective: thinking about 'ethnic foods' from the point of view of diasporic immigrants. She shows the colonial invention of curry powder by the British and its orientalized incorporation into British everyday life by comparing Indian food in Britain to the authenticity of India's regionally based cuisines. She suggests that diasporic immigrants turn the metaphor of 'eating the other' around through serving the British fabrication of 'Indian' food in their 'ethnic' restaurants. Her study credits **agency** and self-sufficiency to diasporic immigrants, highlighting how the civilizing strategy of the British can be resisted through the self-orientalizing tactic of eating ethnicity. Self-orientalism has become an empowering process that is increasingly re-appropriated by minority groups for transforming themselves from a previously subjugated status into self-fashioning subjects.

Contemporary eating practices express identity and reflect the tension between sameness and difference. The consumption of food reveals anxieties about the desire for the familiar and the fear of the unknown. These practices challenge the so-called omnivore's paradox where, on the one hand, there is a suspicion about food that may not fit in the traditional food networks; on the other hand, there is also a curiosity about novelties from new places to the extent that multicultural fusion foods are being created through the mixing of different cuisines. Whether it is culinary conservatism or 'tastebud tourism', if we are what we eat, then contemporary shifts in eating practices must signal a shift in the way we express and experience our identities.

CONTEMPORARY MULTICULTURAL AND GLOBAL PRACTICES OF EATING

The migration of people and the globalization of food cultures have contributed to multicultural eating practices and evolving identities. Viewing multiculturalism as food is often criticized as the most banal and unproductive way of negotiating cultural difference in various national contexts (Gunew 1994). Multiculturalism recognizes the diversity of ethnicities and different practices of everyday life. For migrant communities, the celebration of food practices enables them to undo the cultural effects of assimilation. Eating practices mark the boundaries of cultures as familiar foods bind taste and engender group loyalty. Comfort food, for example, is usually associated with the security, love and nostalgia of childhood homes, and migrant women (as food preparers and as bearers of culture) help to maintain culture and act as a buffer against the alienation of a new place. As migration continues to produce new communities of consumption that generate niche markets for small businesses to serve the needs of distinctive tastes, the introduction of new culinary diversity also succeeds in reaching out to other consumers. Migrant foods are becoming increasingly popular in their cross-over appeal. Through mass production, they are slowly hybridizing food cultures and transforming national identities.

The consumption of multicultural food remains an important expression of national identity in Singapore. The Singapore Tourism Board advertisement (Figure 10.1) shows an official endorsement of the relationships between food, multiculturalism and national identity. The text 'more than just nourish the body' reveals food to be serving more than its straightforwardly biological need. The **connotation** of 'food' to 'table', supported by the image of outdoor dining, demonstrates how food functions as a cultural platform for people of different racial backgrounds to come together. As 'cuisine' denotes the particularity of style and the manner of preparation, the anchorage of food to 'national cuisine' further illustrates the cultural function of food as a metaphor for national identity. Style expresses the **politics** of national identity through the multiracial **ideology** of the country and an orientalized **cosmopolitanism** that self-exoticizes the practice of eating 'with our fingers'.

As an endorsement from the Tourism Board, the advertisement produces national identity for use both domestically and abroad. Within Singapore, a collective identity based on the multiculturalism of food coheres the disparate races. Outside of Singapore, such an identity helps to promote the place as a desirable tourist destination. Both uses are supported in the slogan 'Singapore New Asia: So easy to enjoy'. The

Why must a day **only** have **three meals?**

Does there always have to be only one national cuisine?

Can food do more than just nourish the body?

Can people of different races share the same table?

Who said we can't eat with our fingers?

Are we really asking too much?

Singapore

So easy to enjoy

Figure 10.1: Dining out in Singapore. Advertisement from Singapore Tourism Board. Courtesy Singapore Tourism Board.

pleasure of multicultural eating functions here as a strategy of national pride and economic wealth creation.

As a strategy of national pride, the practice of multicultural eating reflects Singapore's popular image as a multiracial country consisting of a variety of different ethnic groups (namely Chinese, Malay, Indian and Eurasian) living together in harmony and peace. Similar to eating ethnicity, multicultural eating expresses the desire to experience other cultures and signifies identities that are in affiliation with others. Just as food retailers and producers market with both innovative and traditional strategies, food consumers convey their consumption choices through the desire for both the novel and the familiar. Multicultural eating can suggest a curiosity for the unfamiliar or a desire to engage in the complexities of cultural interaction and co-existence. In the advertisement, the dining crowd details a somewhat monocultural group of food consumers: young, modern, urban, apparently middle class and predominantly Chinese. This monocultural image shows that what makes Singapore multiracial is not so much the recognition of its many races as the desire for multicultural food. It reveals Singapore's racial ideology by exposing Chinese hegemonic dominance. For the predominantly Chinese crowd, just like the tourists, eating with the fingers functions as a form of tastebud tourism, reflecting a desire to experience the 'authenticity' of Malay and Indian cultures, and highlighting the fetishization of such a practice. The nationalization and indigenization of multicultural eating also resonates with the metaphor of the melting pot where ingredients lose their distinctive tastes through a process of hybrid amalgamation. Multicultural eating as national cuisine is a practice of fusion that incorporates the specificities of all ethnic cuisines into a homogenizing mix where racial and economic difference are replaced by cosmopolitanism as a state strategy for generating economic wealth.

As a strategy of economic wealth creation, tastebud tourism uses multicultural eating to express literal and gastronomic travel. It engages the impersonal rules of commercial exchange to help ease the fears of cultural difference. Encouraged to enjoy the pleasure of multicultural eating, food-consuming tourists can cross cultural boundaries with minimal obligation; they do not need to know a culture in order to enjoy eating it. Cultural anxieties are allayed in the advertisement through the promotion of cosmopolitanism. Against the backdrop of towering skyscrapers, outdoor eating in Singapore combines the comfort of capitalist modernity, the exoticism of eating differently and the culinary cool of European alfresco dining. Eating in this way reflects both sameness and difference. For the Australian tourists the advertisement was marketed to, the orientalized practice of eating with the fingers is negotiated through the familiarity with alfresco dining. For the urban Singapore crowd, the self-orientalizing practice of eating with the fingers is made newly traditional through the riverside's heritage renewal development, which saw the once-dilapidated warehouses in this area transformed into world-class restaurants, cafés and pubs. Multicultural eating evinces the multi-directional flows of transnational *foodways* (networks and practices created by the globalization of food cultures) and their cross-cultural effects (Howes 1996). It shows the political processes of how ethnic and exotic foods have been naturalized, indigenized and mobilized across time and contexts. In this instance, multicultural eating conveys an atmosphere of worldliness through the privileges of mobility and class, constituting the tourist and the local food consumer as cosmopolitan subjects in an increasingly globalized world of universal sameness. Such a practice is 'easy to enjoy' because cultural difference is elided through the **discourse** of worldliness that cosmopolitanism provides (Cheah and Robbins 1998). Through the globalization of food, tastebud tourism shows that *it is how more than what we eat that constitutes who we are.*

The globalization of food has resulted in changing eating habits that are becoming increasingly homogenized because of the standardization of food industries and the growth of food corporations. As food becomes more and more mass produced for mass-market consumption, advertising that once sought to encourage *sameness* in taste is now encouraging consumer *diversity* through new niche marketing that produces difference and choice. From Pepsi generation to the local adaptation of global food products, food and eating practices are used by both producers and consumers to develop an identity that marks them as different; as particular types of subject.

An example that uses the McDonald's franchise to illustrate the debate surrounding global homogeneity and local adaptation is *Autumn Moon*, a Hong Kong film about the friendship between a jaded Japanese tourist, Tokio, and a local adolescent schoolgirl, Pui Wah (Clara Law, 1992). During their second meeting, Tokio, on a tourist mission in search of Chinese food, urges Pui Wah to take him to her favourite restaurant that serves 'traditional' food not catalogued in where-to-eat travel guidebooks. She obliges and takes him to McDonald's where she feasts on French fries and hamburgers whilst he looks on and laments the loss of 'tradition'. For the well-travelled Tokio who has visited similar outlets in Toronto, Singapore, Taipei and London, McDonald's is the same all over the world. For the young Pui Wah who has experienced the emigration of her friends and family, and is herself in the process of relocating to Canada, this particular McDonald's is different. She remembers it as the venue for her childhood birthday celebrations and a sanctuary where she and her friends have sought refuge from sadness and sorrow.

This scene's eating practices show a **geography** of food networks intersecting the global and the local. For Tokio, although McDonald's hamburgers are global food commodities and they are universally similar, eating with Pui Wah becomes locally meaningful as it demythologizes his search for the imaginary authenticity of Chinese culture. Global eating in this manner produces eating as practices of incorporation and indigenization. As a strategy of culinary imperialism, global eating dominates and incorporates the specificities of local Cantonese cuisine. Tokio's tastebud tourism also demonstrates how eating ethnicity helps to negotiate the otherness of a different culture that cannot be overcome by language. Both practices of incorporation, the sameness of global eating and the difference of ethnic eating transform the self by incorporating fragments of the other. They constitute Tokio's identity as a cosmopolitan Japanese food **subject**, as one who is similar to the local hybridized Hong Kong subjects, but also slightly different. As a practice of indigenization, Pui Wah's creative transformation of a global product to a local taste challenges the authenticity of Chinese cuisine as the authoritative signifier for Chinese culture. Her localization further domesticates memories of friendship, family bonding and belonging, transforming the adolescent schoolgirl by consolidating her hybrid identity as a diasporic and transnational Hong Kong-Chinese subject. Eating in this film reveals McDonald's as a global and local site of intersection, highlighting the globalization of food as a complex process that converges cultures and changes identities.

Global, cosmopolitan and multicultural eating show how transnational food networks connect people and places. Central here are the values of power as cultural or culinary imperialism and resistance as heterogeneous localization. As eating practices become more complex in the contemporary marketplace where multi-directional foodways abut conflicting ethics, bodies and lifestyles, the cross-cultural effects of eating remain an important and necessary engagement for the politics of consumption and cultural identity.

Summary

In this chapter we have argued that:

- eating is a practice of consumption that produces new meanings;
- eating is a practice that is both mundane and specific;
- although food is a sign that communicates meaning about the world, its universal function is only meaningful when it is mobilized in particular social contexts;
- eating joins and separates the world – it is an ambivalent practice entwined in a system of representation about regimes of power, norms and regulations, and the politics of difference; as a practice of transformation, eating can also be resistant and tactical;
- eating constitutes the identity of the food consumer as a self-fashioning subject who exercises both will and intent;
- meanings about the self and others are constructed in relation in to how we eat;
- as foodways continue to connect more people and places, and global vectors accelerate to complicate contemporary eating practices, an analysis of eating helps to focus on the myriad ways in which our tastes can lead us from our guts to the backbones of who we are.

EXERCISES

1. Using a food example such as chocolate, discuss the general and specific contexts of eating. How are power and resistance mobilized? List three strategies and tactics. (The practice of teenagers eating 'junk' food despite parental disapproval, for example, would be a form of resistance.)

2. Consider the effects of cross-cultural eating by comparing the menus from a trendy café and an 'ethnic' restaurant. Critically examine the term 'fusion food' using concepts such as cultural hybridity, multiculturalism and the politics of ethnicity.

3. The globalization of food cultures has produced patterns of consumption that are universal and adaptive. Using the example of a food outlet in your local neighbourhood, critically discuss the impact of global eating. Key concepts that are useful include cultural homogeneity, cultural heterogeneity, localization and indigenization.

REFERENCES

ATKINS, P. and BOWLER, I. 2001: *Food in Society: Economy, Culture, Geography*. London: Arnold.

BAKHTIN, M. 1984: *Rabelais and His World*. Bloomington, Indiana: Indiana University Press.

BARTHES, R. 1961/1997: Towards a psychosociology of contemporary food consumption. In Counihan, C. and van Esterik, P. (eds), *Food and Culture: A Reader*. London: Routledge, 20–7.

BORDO, S. 1998: Hunger as ideology. In Scapp, R. and Seitz, B. (eds), *Eating Culture*. New York: University of New York Press, 11–35.

BOURDIEU, P. 1984: *Distinction: A Social Critique of the Judgement of Taste*. Cambridge, MA: Harvard University Press.

BRILLAT-SAVARIN, J.A. 1825/1970: *The Physiology of Taste*. Drayton, A. (trans.), Harmondsworth: Penguin.

CHAPMAN, G. and MACLEAN, H. 1993: 'Junk food' and 'healthy food': meanings of food in adolescent women's culture. *Journal of Nutrition Education* 23(3), 108–13.

CHEAH, P. and ROBBINS, B. (eds) 1998: *Cosmopolitics: Thinking and Feeling Beyond the Nation*. Minneapolis: University of Minnesota Press.

COUNIHAN, C. 1999: *The Anthropology of Food and Body: Gender, Meaning, and Power*. New York: Routledge.

DE CERTEAU, M. 1984: *The Practice of Everyday Life*. Randall, S. (trans.), Berkeley: University of California Press.

DE CERTEAU, M., GIARD, L. and MAYOL, P. 1998: *The Practice of Everyday Life, Volume 2: Living and Cooking*. Randall, S. (trans.), Minneapolis: University of Minnesota Press.

DOUGLAS, M. 1975/1997: Deciphering a meal. In Counihan, C. and van Esterik, P. (eds), *Food and Culture: A Reader*. London: Routledge, 36–54.

FINKELSTEIN, J. 1989: *Dining Out: A Sociology of Modern Manners*. Cambridge: Polity.

GABACCIA, D. 1998: *We are What we Eat: Ethnic Food and the Making of Americans*. Cambridge, MA: Harvard University Press.

GOLDMAN, A. 1992: 'I yam what I yam': cooking, culture and colonialism. In Smith, S. and Watson, J. (eds), *De/Colonizing the Subject: The Politics of Gender in Women's Autobiography*. Minneapolis: University of Minnesota Press, 169–95.

GOODY, J. 1982: *Cooking, Cuisine, and Class: A Study in Comparative Sociology*. New York: Cambridge University Press.

GUNEW, S. 1994: *Framing Marginality*. Melbourne: Melbourne University Press.

HOWES, D. 1996: *Cross-Cultural Consumption: Global Markets, Local Realities*. New York: Routledge.

LEVI-STRAUSS, C. 1970: *The Raw and the Cooked*. New York: Harper Torchbooks.

MARTENS, L. and WARDE, A. 1999: Power and resistance around the dinner table. In Hearn, J. and Roseneil, S. (eds), *Consuming Cultures: Power and Resistance.* Basingstoke: Macmillan, 91–108.

MINTZ, S. 1989: *Sweetness and Power: The Place of Sugar in Modern History.* New York: Penguin.

NARAYAN, U. 1997: Eating cultures: incorporation, identity and Indian food. In *Dislocating Cultures: Identities, Traditions, and Third World Feminism.* New York: Routledge, 161–88.

ORBACH, S. 1986: *Hunger Strike: The Anorextic's Struggle as a Metaphor for Our Age.* London: Faber.

PROBYN, E. 2000: *Carnal Appetites: Food, Sex, Identities.* New York: Routledge.

WARDE, A. and MARTENS, L. 1998: Eating out and the commercialization of mental life. *British Food Journal* 100, 147–53.

FURTHER READING

ALBALA, K. 2002: *Eating Right in the Renaissance.* Berkeley: University of California Press.

APPADURAI, A. 1981: Gastro-politics in Hindu South Asia. *American Ethnologist* 8, 495–511.

BENTLEY, A. 1998: *Eating for Victory: Food Rationing and the Politics of Domesticity.* Urbana: University of Illinois Press.

CAMPBELL, J.R. and REW, A. (eds) 1999: *Identity and Affect: Experiences of Identity in a Globalizing World.* London: Pluto Press.

CAPLAN, P. (ed.) 1997: *Food, Health, and Identity.* London: Routledge.

CHUA, B.H. (ed.) 2000: *Consumption in Asia: Lifestyles and Identities.* New York: Routledge.

GLICKMAN, L.B. (ed.) 1999: *Consumer Society in American History: A Reader.* Ithaca, NY: Cornell University Press.

HESSE-BIBER, S.J. 1996: *Am I Thin Enough Yet?: The Cult of Thinness and the Commercialization of Identity.* New York: Oxford University Press.

HEYWOOD, L. 1996: *Dedication To Hunger: The Anorexic Aesthetic in Modern Culture.* Berkeley: University of California.

MENNELL, S. 1996: *All Manners of Food: Eating and Taste in England and France from the Middle Ages to the Present.* Urbana: University of Illinois Press.

WARDE, A. 1997: *Consumption, Food, and Taste: Culinary Antinomies and Commodity Culture.* London: Sage Publications.

WITT, D. 1999: *Black Hunger: Food and the Politics of US Identity.* New York: Oxford University Press.

Chapter Eleven

EVERYDAY TECHNOLOGY ☐

Brett Farmer

Film discussed in this chapter:
- *The Electric House* (Edward F. Cline and Buster Keaton, 1922).

INTRODUCTION: THE ELECTRIC HOUSE IS BORN

In 1922 the legendary silent film comedian, Buster Keaton, produced what many regard as one of his greatest shorts, *The Electric House* (Cline and Keaton, First National Pictures Inc.,1922). In the film Keaton plays a character who, mistaken for an electrical engineer, is contracted to modernize a middle-**class** family's home with the latest in electrical **technology**. With only a beginner's manual as a guide, Keaton wires up the house with all manner of fanciful mechanical gadgetry including an in-built escalator, a fully automated kitchen and a mobile bathtub. Inevitably, the machinery goes awry and the stage is set for a riotous display of Keaton's signature physical comedy: the escalator speeds up and torpedoes people out the window, the dishwasher starts hurling plates, and the bathtub chases the family around the house.

One of the reasons Buster Keaton is still widely remembered and celebrated, other than his enormous talents as a screen comic, is that his films serve as a rich and insightful barometer of the early twentieth-century *Zeitgeist*. Living through what was arguably the most transformative period of Western history, Keaton used his comic cinema to represent and explore the massive upheavals of **modernity** and the concomitant 'shock of the new'. The physical pratfalls, accidents and collapsing structures that characterize Keatonesque humour constitute what Tom Gunning (1995) describes as a metaphoric staging of 'the plight of modern man', trying to absorb and find a place in the brave new world of 'fast-moving traffic and demonic machinery' (p. 14). *The Electric House* furnishes a clear example of this sort of social allegory. Its manic visions of mechanized domesticity run amok give clear voice to the competing desires and anxieties circulating throughout the modern era around the technologization that was rewriting the scripts of social life in general and domestic life in particular.

In the first few decades of the twentieth century, home life in Euro-American societies was radically transformed by a series of technological innovations. Electricity, telephony, radio and other such 'miracles of the modern age' were rapidly incorporated

173

into the spaces of domesticity. In the process, they fundamentally changed those spaces, and the meanings and **practices** they supported. Where in 1900, for example, the average home would have been lucky to have, at most, gas lighting, by 1930 it was a veritable beehive of technological industry: fully illuminated by electricity, abuzz with mechanical appliances, plugged into national and even international networks of communication, and made readily mobile by new means of private automotive transport. Not surprisingly, these changes were met with considerable ambivalence. There was widespread excitement at their novelty and the possibilities they provided, but the technological transformations of modernity also evoked considerable consternation, with many commentators worrying about their effects on traditional domestic organization and family cohesion. In 1926 the Catholic Church, for example, held public forums across the United States to debate whether 'modern inventions help or mar character and health', warning parishioners that new technologies like the automobile and the telephone had the potential 'to break up home life' and counselling them that 'unless they individually master these things, the things will weaken them' (cited in Fischer 1992: 1). Such responses may strike the contemporary reader as quaintly amusing, but in fact they are not all that dissimilar to the sort of moral concerns regularly raised today about the social impact of more recent technologies, especially those that are domestically oriented. To wit, one need only consider the furore that has met the advent of home computing and the Internet, which is regularly ascribed all manner of deleterious potential, from an erosion of personal privacy to infantile sexual exploitation.

The persistence and intensity of these anxious responses is clear evidence of the significance that technology has come to assume in modern social life. While a constitutive engagement with technology has arguably been a vital part of all human societies since *homo sapiens* first tamed fire and started to fashion implements for hunting, *contemporary* **culture** *is characterized by an unprecedented level of technological use and integration.* Today we have at our disposal a vast range of different technologies with which we engage in ways both big and small. Writing these words, for example, I sit in a house that is positively immersed in technology. I type on a computer using word-processing software. The computer is net-connected via cable modem and every so often a window pops up on my screen and a robotic voice tells me of an in-coming e-mail, usually a bothersome piece of advertising spam mail, but sometimes a communication from a friend on the other side of the country or even the world. Occasionally, I receive interruptions of a different kind when the telephone rings. If I get tired or bored with my work, I might take a break and surf the net or maybe insert a DVD and watch a movie. Elsewhere in the house, my partner is doing the cleaning – vacuuming the floor, putting the breakfast dishes into the dishwasher and the dirty laundry in the washing machine – all the while listening to music on his personal Discman. Through my open window, I can hear a variety of neighbourhood sounds: the children next door playing Nintendo, the woman on the corner mowing her lawn, the faint strains of someone's radio, and the occasional rumble of a car motoring up the street or an aeroplane flying overhead. These are the sorts of mundane activities of everyday life that are intimately familiar to most of us – and each one depends centrally on technology. Technologies are such an integral part of our everyday experiences and are so resolutely stitched into contemporary cultural life that many of our most basic **ideological** beliefs about who we are and how we relate to the world and each other are constitutively framed by technologies. Put simply, *contemporary culture is a* **technoculture**, *a culture saturated by and fundamentally invested in technologies* (Penley and Ross 1991; Green 2001).

In this chapter, we address some of the technocultural dynamics of contemporary life, paying particular attention to how technology informs everyday **practices** and **identities**. While it would be impossible to offer a comprehensive analysis of the full range of contemporary technologies and their varied uses, this chapter seeks to furnish a critical context within which to think about and understand the technocultures of everyday life. We start with a consideration of how best to theorize the relationship between technology and **culture**.

THEORIZING TECHNOLOGY

We've all heard the story of Archimedes' bathtub and how, when hopping into it one day, he caused the bath water to overflow and thus realized his classic theory of hydrostatic balance: immersed in fluid, a mass will always displace its equal measure. Often dubbed the Eureka principle – because, as legend relates, Archimedes was so enthused by his discovery that he ran naked into the streets shouting 'Eureka! I've found it!' – it is a story that crystallizes the dominant Western way of thinking about discoveries and inventions. We commonly mythologize inventions as the result of epiphanic moments of intellectual breakthrough and personal innovation, particularly in the case of technologies. Whether it is Thomas Edison and the electric light bulb, the Wright brothers and aviation, Marconi and radio, or the Lumière brothers and motion pictures, we have developed a collective archive of folkloric narratives for conceiving and representing new technologies as products of individual inspiration that burst suddenly onto the social scene and change the course of history.

This way of thinking about technology is often called **technological determinism**: the belief that technology is an independent force with its own logic and progress. In this schema, technological change is understood as a given, an autonomous series of unfolding innovations that intervene on society from outside and produce substantive, and often unpredicted, effects. It is a reading that suggests we as social subjects can do little in the face of the inexorable march of technological progress except try to harness its energies for our collective and individual benefit, while seeking to minimize its damaging impact. At its most extreme, technological determinism holds technology to be the primary – if not sole – engine of social change and progress. Thus, for example, it is not uncommon in this tradition to represent the course of human history in terms

175

of technological catalysts. Think of the way that prehistory is regularly divided into Stone and Iron Ages or, closer to home, modern history is read in terms of a series of technologically driven 'revolutions' and epochs: the Industrial Age, Electrical Age, Atomic Age and, most currently, the Information or Digital Age. In all these examples, the guiding assumption is that technology exists in a sphere of its own and that it directly determines the shape of society in a systematic, unilateral fashion.

Recently, this popular mode of theorizing the relationship between technology and culture has been challenged and revised. As many critics point out, the problem with technological determinism is that it abstracts technology from its social and historical contexts. *Technologies do not exist in some sort of idealist vacuum from which they spring fully formed onto an unsuspecting public, but are themselves the fully constituted effects of social trends and conditions.* Economics, governmental policy, religious and moral **discourses**, military imperatives, educational practices, marketing **strategies**, and so forth, play a vital role in determining how technologies are developed, circulated and used. In other words, *technology is just as centrally determined by society as society is by technology.*

Donald Mackenzie and Judy Wajcman (1999) refer to this revisionist approach as the *social shaping of technology.* As they point out, social dynamics are absolutely crucial to the inception and incorporation of technology, and we should thus consider technology 'like our economy and political system, an aspect of how we live socially' (p. 2). Any technology, they suggest, will always consist of a three-layered complex – the physical artifact, human activity and human knowledge – with each layer shaping the other in mutual complementarity. Thus, a given technology will always exist in relation to both its contexts of use and the surrounding knowledges that frame its **production** and **consumption**. From such a perspective, technology becomes an irremediably social phenomenon, bound into the network of ideologies, economics and **power** relations that govern human society and its productions.

TECHNOLOGY AS CULTURAL PRACTICE

The argument for the social shaping of technology has been very influential in **cultural studies**, where it has been taken up and elaborated in relation to a wide range of technologies and associated cultural forms. In an early contribution, Raymond Williams (1974) develops a detailed reading of television as a technology shaped to its core by cultural dynamics. In explicit opposition to technological determinist accounts, Williams argues that the development and use of a technology like television is not 'a matter of some autonomous process directed by remote engineers' but 'a matter of social and cultural definition' (p. 134). The 'invention' of television, he points out, was a complicated process involving competing industrial, political, military and commercial imperatives. Together these social forces dictated the shape that television assumed as a cultural form, determining among other things its cast as a domestic-based rather than public medium, and its development as a unidirectional broadcast system rather than one of multidirectional communication. In addition, Williams argues that any account of television as a cultural technology must also take on board the myriad ways in which it is incorporated and used in material contexts: in other words, the way television is *pract_ised* in everyday life. The consumption of technology, he suggests, is not some discrete action that occurs after the fact, but an integral part of the very process of technological constitution. By using technology, we actively play a role in how it is fashioned and experienced as a cultural form, locating it within and relating it to the manifold artifacts and rituals of everyday life. These uses are undoubtedly cued to a greater or lesser extent by the ideological discourses and institutional imperatives that frame a given technology, but they can equally produce variable and 'unforeseen effects, among them the desire to use the technology for oneself' (p. 133). In this way, Williams advances a compelling argument for television as a **cultural practice**, something that is articulated across and actively incorporated into the lived networks of culture.

This emphasis on cultural practice has been central to how cultural studies conceives and theorizes technological forms. For cultural studies, technology is not something that simply engages scientists or industrial designers, nor is it merely an element of hardware, a piece of machinery or electronic circuitry. *Instead, it is an integral part of how we live as a society and it functions as a vital site of cultural production and negotiation wherein meanings and identities are constructed, exchanged, struggled over and reformed.* Summarizing the core assumption behind this work, Hugh Mackay (1997) writes that 'technology is cultural – not simply in that it exists in a cultural context, that technological artifacts are surrounded by culture, but is cultural through and through, in its design, its meaning, its use and thus its very form' (p. 268).

One of the more sustained attempts to think through and provide an analytic framework for this type of reading of technology as cultural practice is offered by Paul du Gay *et al.* (1997) in the collaboratively authored book, *Doing Cultural Studies: The Story of the Sony Walkman*. Using the Walkman as an extended case study, the book maps the multiple registers through which a technology circulates and is produced as a cultural practice. As the authors state, a technology like the Walkman 'is not only a part of our culture' but 'has a distinct culture of its own' (p. 10). Through its imaging in various cultural discourses, its connection with distinct social activities, and its association with certain kinds of people and places, the Walkman has developed as more than just a technological device. *It is a dynamic convergence of social meanings and values, a symbolic artifact that is produced by, and simultaneously reproduces, the distinctive culture of late modern, **consumer** society and its ways of life.* When we use a Walkman, we engage in a complex practice of cultural articulation, relaying and negotiating pre-existing meanings and identities encoded into the object and its constitutive discourses, while also potentially forging new meanings and identities through our variable uses and acts of consumption.

In order to tease out and read the full range of elements operative in the **construction** of a symbolic technology like the Walkman, du Gay *et al.* propose a heuristic model of analysis that they term the *circuit of culture*. It is a model that consists of five levels or processes through which a technology – or any cultural form, for that matter – is constructed and circulated as a cultural practice. The five levels in the circuit are:

- **production** – the physical manufacture of an object and all that it entails (science and technological knowledge, economics, industry), and also how these processes are organized culturally (scientific and corporate philosophies, working patterns, market research);
- **regulation** – how an artifact and/or its uses are regulated by social institutions and agencies (governments, legal bodies, consumer advocacies, religious groups);
- **representation** – the ways an artifact is imaged and defined through representation (advertising, press and media reports, **popular culture**);
- **consumption** – the actual and varied uses of an object in material contexts, how it is deployed, its rituals of use;
- **identity** – how an object impacts on and/or is mobilized for the articulation of **subjectivity** or social selfhood.

The benefit of this model lies in its comprehensiveness and flexibility. It encourages recognition of the full range of registers active in the cultural articulation of a given technology, while also focusing attention on the moments of interaction between registers. Because it is a circuit, all of these processes interrelate and none of them takes precedence over another. An analysis of a given technology could conceivably start with any one of these five processes, as long as account is taken of the entire nexus, and it is observed that each process relies upon the others for meaning to emerge. Furthermore, the multiform dimensions of the model allow for a reading of technology as a continuous process of renewable social action and struggle. Positioned within the endless circuit of culture, technology is not a static or isolable object, but a dynamic cultural practice of everyday life with varied functions and effects.

Using the circuit of culture as a guiding frame, we want to illustrate some of the theoretical points we have been covering with a brief case study of the telephone. Like television and the Walkman, the telephone is a central and popular technology within contemporary culture, and thus it serves as an ideal focus for the sort of culturalist analysis of technology argued for here.

CALLING HOME: THE TELEPHONE AS CULTURAL TECHNOLOGY

Of all contemporary technologies, arguably none is more ubiquitous or fully integrated into the texture of everyday life than the telephone. In **postindustrialized** countries, the telephone has an almost universal market penetration, with over 90 per cent of households in possession of at least one telephone connection (Smith 1990). The telephone is the dominant medium for interpersonal communication, and most of us use it on a daily basis for a host of routine activities, from simple conversation to business and shopping. The familiar everydayness of the telephone imbues it with a strong degree of mundanity, making it what Paul Wisener (1984) calls an 'anonymous object [...] so imbedded in daily routine as to have become undifferentiated from the rest of our immediate landscape' (p. 23). There is a certain sense of natural inevitability about the telephone and, even if intellectually we may know otherwise, we can't help but think of it as an intrinsic part of life that is simply 'meant to be'. Like any cultural technology, however, the telephone is in fact the constructed effect of interacting social and historical discourses, and the site of competing cultural projects.

The **production** of the telephone as a cultural technology has been a long and complicated process. Indeed, to the extent that the global expansion of telephony is an ongoing project and modern telecommunications are constantly being revised through the incorporation of new technologies, it could be argued that we are still negotiating the cultural production of the telephone. Born of nineteenth-century cultures of technological modernity and urban expansion, the telephone developed through a combination of technical, industrial and social transformations. Advances in electronics, telegraphy, wiring and acoustics enabled the development of the telephone as a technical possibility, but the actual form it assumed was the result of entirely cultural imperatives. In fact, the telephone we know today was not always the anticipated end-result of early cultures of telephony (Marvin 1988; Martin 1991). Following the first successful trials of electronic voice transmission in the 1870s, there were various 'visions' as to how this technology could be used. The primary telephonic function of interpersonal conversation that is so familiar to us today was simply one of several possibilities. Another major future envisioned for telephony was as a broadcast medium, and throughout the late nineteenth century the telephone was widely used to transmit various acoustic performances such as concerts, sermons, political speeches and sporting events (Marvin 1998: 209–16). That the broadcast potentials of telephony were not further realized, and were largely dropped in preference of the telephone's eventual cast as a carrier of point-to-point communication among individuals is due to several intervening factors. In part, the reason was industrial and economic: the large corporations driving telephony were able to realize greater profits from a network of individual subscribers. In part, the reason was political: Michele Martin (1991), for example, details how in Canada, agencies serving **hegemonic** interests conspired to ensure that telephony developed as a commercialized system of communication controlled by private monopoly. But in equal part, the reason was a result of persistent **ideological** currents.

In his study of television discussed earlier, Raymond Williams (1974) argues that the development of modern communication media has been profoundly shaped by a prevailing socio-historical dynamic that he dubs *mobile privatization*. Since the late nineteenth and early twentieth century, industrialized cultures have been prone to two seemingly antithetical but deeply interrelated trends. On the one hand, the new urban and suburban cultures of modernity have served to fracture traditional structures of

179

community and collective identity, fostering a new ideological economy centred on the private individual. On the other hand, expanded systems of automated transport and mass communications have afforded these privatized subjects an unprecedented degree of both physical and symbolic mobility. Williams contends that this hybrid regime of mobile privatization is a foundational logic of modern cultures, driving and shaping many of our most characteristic cultural forms, from popular entertainments such as television and radio, to autoculture and our collective love of the car. Though Williams does not explicitly address telephony in his argument, it is reasonable to surmise that the emerging culture of mobile privatization played a decisive role in the development of the telephone as a private communicative technology. Indeed, it is instructive that much of the regulation of telephony in the early period was explicitly geared towards increasing its individuated, private dynamics. Substantial social and political pressures were brought to bear on telephone companies to ensure maximum privacy for individual subscribers, and a battery of 'secrecy devices' was implemented across the early twentieth century. Most of these devices failed miserably – in fact, it wasn't until the phasing out of communal telephone wires, or 'party lines', and the gradual implementation of individual lines in the 1930s that real privacy was achieved – but, as Martin (1991) opines, 'the large number of attempts to increase telephonic privacy demonstrates the importance of the issue for users of the time' (p. 21).

If the social function of the telephone changed and narrowed over time to emerge finally as a means of private communication for an individuated user, how that user has been conceived and defined has been equally prone to revision. The history of telephonic representation reveals that for much of its early existence, the telephone was almost entirely conceived and promoted as an instrument of commerce and 'a means of circulation of capital' (Martin 1991: 9). Its primary business was business, and it was all but inconceivable that it could ever be used as a means of everyday social conversation. Even with the expansion of telephone networks into residential areas and the accelerating introduction of home telephone sets, the telephone was still viewed as a commercial tool to be used only for 'serious' business such as domestic management or civic communication. It was well into the 1920s, notes Hugh Mackay (1997), 'before the telephone began to be promoted as suitable for sociability, as opposed to practical, economic matters' (p. 273).

Not surprisingly, this early cultural representation of telephony obtained profoundly **gendered** dimensions. The telephone was originally seen as the primary preserve of men (Figure 11.1). Women either had little access to telephones or were actively discouraged from using them. The major exception was of course the telephone operator, who was almost always female, but whose sole role was to mediate the important business communication of men. The early social coding of the telephone as a masculine artifact seems particularly striking to the contemporary observer because today the telephone is, if anything, more commonly associated with women than men. Contemporary popular **mythology** routinely represents women as the primary subjects

Figure 11.1: The telephone as a serious tool of masculine industry.

of telephony and, while in real terms both sexes make regular use of the telephone, there is empirical evidence to suggest that, in Anglo-American cultures at least, women on average make many more and substantially longer telephone calls than men (Dordick and La Rose 1992; Haddon 1997). The radical turnaround of the gendered economies of telephony not only provides further evidence of the contingent and mutable cultural definitions of technology, but furnishes a concrete example of the impact of **consumption** on those definitions.

As the telephone expanded its reach from the public realm of business into the private realm of domesticity, it also entered new contexts of meaning and use. Dominant discourses and social representations continued to construct the telephone as a masculine tool of industry but once in the home, women – in their historical capacity as primary agents of the domestic sphere – started to use this new means of communication in variable ways. In particular, women were quick to use the telephone for what Martin (1991) terms 'delinquent activities': familial conversation, neighbourly chats, and other forms of 'social visiting' (p. 169). Male commentators initially remonstrated that women's conversation was a misuse, if not abuse, of telephony – as Marvin (1988) points out, the received wisdom of the time was that 'women's use of men's technology would come to no good end' (p. 23). Despite this, however, the telephone industry itself was eventually influenced by women's widespread mobilization of telephonic technology for sociability and, recognizing the potential it offered for commercial expansion, incorporated social use of the telephone into its own representations. From the 1920s onward, telephone advertising started to promote sociability as a possible function of telephony and by mid-century, sociability, not business, was arguably the dominant register of telephone culture. Thus, while it is almost inconceivable for us to think that the telephone could have developed otherwise, its role today as a 'natural' medium of interpersonal socialization is in no small measure a result of women's **resistant** (mis)use of the technology in its early period of social diffusion. As Martin asserts, 'Women ... were largely responsible for the development of a culture of the telephone, as they instigated its use for purposes of sociability' (p. 171) (Figure 11.2).

While relations between women and telephony intensified across the twentieth century, it should be noted that there is considerable debate about how to read and evaluate these relations. Some critics argue that the telephone has been an emancipatory tool for women and this is one of the reasons it has developed as a vital focus for women's cultural practices (Moyal 1992; Frissen 1995). In an era when women were largely confined to the home, the telephone provided a welcome means of bridging women's

Figure 11.2: The telephone as a tool of feminine sociability.

Figure 11.3: The telephone as a means of keeping women 'happy in the home'.

social isolation and fostering communicative bonds with others. It has also been suggested that the telephone served to increase women's access to (semi-)public communication, and thus their sense of social assertiveness and independence. Male commentators of the early twentieth century, for example, often complained that 'the telephone permitted girls to be bolder in their approach' and to 'acquire a sudden and surprising self-assurance and aptitude' (cited in Martin 1991: 164–5). These arguments cut both ways, however. To the extent that the telephone offered housebound women opportunities for outside contact, it equally furnished a potential pacifier to those women and a continued legitimation of feminine subordination and domestic containment. Indeed, advertising campaigns across the mid-century often actively sold the telephone as a way of keeping women 'happy in the home' (Figure 11.3).

While debates over the political status of women's relations to telephony are fraught and possibly irresolvable, they certainly highlight the potential significance of the telephone – or any cultural technology for that matter – to the articulation of social **identity**. Elsewhere in this book, we have discussed how the use of commodities has become an increasingly central focus of identity projects in late modernity. The notion of **lifestyle** as a pursuit of self through cultural consumption is a characteristic feature of contemporary society, and technologies such as the telephone often assume a key role in this process. As a domestic technology, the telephone has been instrumental for women in constructing and negotiating feminine identities, particularly as these have been realized historically in the everyday spaces of the home. Gender is not, of course, the only site of identity construction in which the telephone features: it is also mobilized in identities based upon, among other categories, class, nationality, religion, and generation or age. The identity category of the teenager, for example, has a long history of association with the telephone. The image of the self-indulgent teen tying up the family phone as s/he chats with friends for hours on end has been a stock feature of popular representation since the 1950s and, while teen uses of the telephone are invariably cast as a source of amusement, we shouldn't overlook their social significance and value. Like women, teenagers inhabit subordinate positions in cultural economies of power and more often than not they are constrained – in discursive if not necessarily physical terms – by a primary location in the domestic sphere. Given this, the telephone arguably operates as a tool for teenagers with which to renegotiate their position in social hierarchies and achieve some measure of self-empowered identity. The virtual mobility of telephonic communication – which, as suggested earlier, is a defining feature of so many contemporary technologies – provides teenagers with a degree of social mobility that may not otherwise be available to them in everyday life.

The use of telephony for the production and negotiation of teen identities has assumed new and quite striking forms with the recent advent of cellular phones and pagers. In a way that again nicely mirrors the earlier feminine **appropriation** of telephonic technology, cell phones and pagers were originally designed and marketed for business and commercial ends, but in recent years they have been taken up and popularized by young people as key fashion accessories and (sub)cultural artifacts. To the vocal chagrin of parents and educators, young people routinely use these telephonic technologies to forge social relations with peers, evade authority and discipline, and generally foster a distinctive sense of teen identity. A recent report on teenage cell phone use in, of all places, the *British Medical Journal*, suggests that the appeal of the technology for young people lies in its potential for 'individuality, sociability, rebellion, peer group binding, and adult aspiration' (Charlton and Bates 2000: 1155). Predictably, the communications industry has been quick to note and cash in on this trend. Contemporary advertising campaigns for cellular phones are routinely pitched to a young demographic and will often espouse an explicit rhetoric of teen identity production (Figure 11.4).

The speed with which the telecommunications industry has **incorporated** teen cultures of telephony into its mainstream marketing operations should serve as a sobering check against any over-romanticized celebration of these cultures as purely oppositional. As discussed on several occasions in this book, late capitalist culture is nothing if not enormously adept at re-deploying potential points of resistance as so much grist to the consumerist mill. The voracious opportunism of corporate culture does not, however, diminish the fact that everyday technologies such as the telephone can be and are used to produce and negotiate a variety of different social identities and meanings. Throughout its history, the telephone has been the site of a continuous struggle between competing discourses, projects and interests. Articulated across the mobile

Figure 11.4: The telephone as a tool for teen identity production.

circuits of culture, its meanings have never been singular, its functions never static. It may be co-opted and routinized to the point of mundanity but, like so many of the other technologies that saturate and define the spaces of the contemporary social landscape, the telephone functions as a rich resource for diverse practices within the cultures of everyday life.

Summary

In this chapter, we have argued that:

- we live in a technoculture – a culture whose practices, values and identities are centrally invested in technologies and their use;
- technology does not exist in an independent sphere but is fully constituted by sociocultural forces;
- an integral part of technology is its circulation and consumption within everyday contexts;
- people use technologies in varied ways and this informs both how technologies develop and the cultural significances they assume;
- technologies can become sites of social struggle and resistance as different social groups deploy them for competing social uses and/or identity projects.

EXERCISES

1. Write down all the different technologies you would use on a regular basis and then rank them in order of their personal importance to you. What criteria did you use to make your rankings? Why are some technologies more important to you than others? What do your answers reveal about the relationship between technology and everyday life?

2. It is often claimed that the practices and uses of technology in contemporary culture are profoundly gendered, with many technologies coded as explicitly masculine or feminine. Do you think this is true? Why? Discuss in relation to your own everyday knowledges and experiences of technology.

3. We have argued among other things that teenagers have appropriated telephonic technology for their own identity projects. Do you think that telephones and/or associated technologies such as pagers, SMS, et cetera are a vital part of contemporary youth cultures? Can you think of other technologies that are used by young people or other social groups to define a distinctive sense of social identity?

4. Select a technology from everyday life and, using the model outlined in this chapter, map its constitution across the five registers of the *circuit of culture*. You may have to do a little background research, but think about how each register contributes centrally to the construction of the technology as a significant cultural form.

REFERENCES

CHARLTON, A. and BATES, C. 2000: Decline in teenage smoking with rise in mobile phone ownership: a hypothesis. *British Medical Journal* 321(7269), 1155.

DORDICK, H. and LA ROSE, R. 1992: *The Telephone in Daily Life: A Study of Personal Telephone Use*. Philadelphia, PA: Temple University Press.

DU GAY, P. *et al.* (eds) 1997: *Doing Cultural Studies: The Story of the Sony Walkman*. London: Sage.

FISCHER, C.S. 1992: *America Calling: A Social History of the Telephone to 1940*. Berkeley: University of California Press.

FRISSEN, V. 1995: Gender is calling: some reflections of past, present, and future uses of the telephone. In Grint, K. and Gill, R. (eds), *The Gender–Technology Relation: Contemporary Theory and Research*. London: Taylor & Francis.

GREEN, L. 2001: *Technoculture: From Alphabet to Cybersex*. Crows Nest: Allen & Unwin.

GUNNING, T. 1995: Buster Keaton or the work of comedy in the age of mechanical reproduction. *Cineaste* 21(3), 14–16.

HADDON, L. 1997: *Empirical Research on the Domestic Phone: A Literature Review*. Brighton: University of Sussex Press.

MACKAY, H. (ed.) 1997: *Consumption and Everyday Life*. London: Sage.

MACKENZIE, D. and WAJCMAN, J. (eds) 1999: *The Social Shaping of Technology: How the Refrigerator Got its Hum*, 2nd edn, first published 1985. Milton Keynes: Open University Press.

MARTIN, M. 1991: *Hello Central?: Gender, Technology and Culture in the Formation of Telephone Systems*. Montreal: McGill-Queen's University Press.

MARVIN, C. 1988: *When Old Technologies Were New: Thinking about Electric Communication in the late Nineteenth Century*. New York: Oxford University Press.

MOYAL, A. 1992: The gendered use of the telephone: an Australian case study. *Media, Culture and Society* 14, 51–72.

PENLEY, C. and ROSS, A. (eds) 1991: *Technoculture*. Minneapolis: University of Minnesota Press.

SMITH, T.W. 1990: Phone home: an analysis of household telephone ownership. *International Journal of Public Opinion Research* 2(4), 369–90.

THOMS, D., HOLDEN, L. and CLAYDON, T. (eds) 1998: *The Motor Car and Popular Culture in the 20th Century*. Aldershot: Ashgate.

WILLIAMS, R. 1974: *Television: Technology and Cultural Form*. London: Fontana.

WISENER, P. 1984: Put me on to Edenville: one hundred and six years of the telephone. *Mind and Nature* 3(1), 23–31.

FURTHER READING

GREEN, L. and GUINNERY, R. (eds) 1994: *Framing Technology: Society, Choice and Change*. St Leonards: Allen & Unwin.

HUTCHBY, I. and MORAN-ELLUS, J. 2001: *Children, Technology and Culture: The Impacts of Technology in Children's Everyday Lives*. London and New York: Routledge.

NELSON, A., TU, T.L.N. and HINES, A.H. (eds) 2001: *Technicolor: Race, Technology and Everyday Life*. New York: New York University Press.

ROBINS, K. 1999: *Times of the Technoculture: From the Information Society to the Virtual Life*. London and New York: Routledge.

SLEVIN, J. 2000: *The Internet and Society*. Malden, MA: Blackwell.

TERRY, J. and CALVERT, M. (eds) 1997: *Processed Lives: Gender and Technology in Everyday Life*. London and New York: Routledge.

WINSTON, B. 1998: *Media Technology and Society, a History: From the Telegraph to the Internet*. London and New York: Routledge.

Chapter Twelve

GETTING AROUND

Audrey Yue

Film discussed in this chapter:
- *Beijing Bicycle* (Wang Xiaoshuai, 2000).

INTRODUCTION

This chapter examines the everyday **practices** of transport and travel. It provides a detailed discussion of the materiality of some of the forms these practices take today, by means of theoretical frameworks introduced elsewhere in this book. We will argue that the rise of mass transportation in **modernity** and **postmodernity** has led to the emergence of novel forms of **culture** that are centrally structured by mobility and travel, rather than by fixity in place. This discussion also draws on some of the ideas introduced in the previous chapters on the accelerated information flows enabled by new media and communication **technologies**.

TRAVEL, DISPLACEMENT AND MOBILITY

From walking, cycling and commuting on public transportation to driving, touring and virtual teleporting, the rise of mass transportation, the popularity of global tourism and the novel interconnections enabled by new communication technologies have decisively reconfigured the ways in which we can get around today in everyday life. This chapter suggests that getting around is a series of practices structured by displacement and mobility. As a material practice, getting around signifies the geographical movement from here to there, and vice-versa. Whether it is the everyday routine of bus commuting, the once-a-year holiday ritual of overseas travel or the trauma of long-term migration, geographical travel, as mundane and specific, can be both **hegemonic** and **resistant**. It functions as hegemonic, for example, in a tourist journey where empowered travellers visit underdeveloped Third World countries in search of exoticism and leisure, or disempowered immigrants are seduced by a falsely **utopian** image of the metropolitan centres of the West. As Chapter 10's section on 'tastebud tourism' suggests, this practice, more often than not, perpetuates the centre–periphery dichotomy and reproduces unequal **power** relations. Travel can be considered resistant, though, when it involves a two-way exchange between the **strategies** of power and the **tactics** of **resistance**. Fare evasion, for example, reveals public transportation culture as a site of negotiation between commuters' tactics and the strategies of the providers of public services. As a tactic of evasion, fare evasion undermines the ticketing strategies of purchase and **surveillance**. As a practice of protest against the privatization of government services and the increased costs of consuming 'public' resources, fare evasion highlights the under-resourced and over-utilized state of current economically rationalized, privatized, 'public' transportation in many contemporary societies. It also calls into question the transformation of the travelling **subject**, from the citizen (with access to public services provided by the state) to the user-pays **consumer**. Clearly, as mundane and specific practices of getting around, travel is a critical everyday practice that can question hegemonic power relations and reveal tactics of resistance.

Travel can also be thought of as an epistemological and metaphoric practice that highlights the ways in which knowledge-claims about the world and ourselves are only ever contingent, partial and ambiguous (Kaplan 1996). Many current cultural technologies and practices draw in some way upon the idea of, and desire for, travel. Fashion, food, music, tourism, global commodities, television and new media function *metaphorically* as sites of 'virtual travel', in that they facilitate symbolic interaction with other cultures and other people. 'Critical travel' – thinking in a sensitive and politically engaged way about such everyday interactions – challenges the presumptively fixed relations between subjects and objects, the East and the West, and the empowered and disempowered, because such relations are in fact constantly contested and negotiated. Whether it is via virtual travel in watching television, consuming fashion or multicultural eating, or geographical travel by means of the automobile or the aeroplane, the everyday cultures that are produced (we might call them 'travelling cultures') merge cosmopolitan experience with local specificity in a way that complicates commonly held notions of **cultural imperialism** and global homogenization (Clifford 1997).

Getting around is an everyday practice that can produce travelling cultures through travel-as-displacement and mobility rather than always or only reinforcing existing power relations through one-way interaction. Displacement describes the movement from one place to another. As many theorists of **postcolonial** culture and migration have argued, such a movement spurs the displaced subject to consider questions about **identity** and difference because traversing the geo-cultural space between 'here' and 'there' is a process that questions the self ('I') and other ('not-I') (Kaplan 1996; Robertson *et al.* 1994; Hall 1987). Thus, travel-as-displacement is a process that allows subjects to constitute **identities**.

CAR CULTURES

Car culture is a good example of how travelling cultures produce new identities. The automobile has been described as the machine that changed the world (Womack *et al.* 1990). Ford's mass assembly line that made the Model T revolutionized and modernized work, leisure and recreation (Cross and Szostak 1995: 257). The automobile and the individualized mobility it provides have transformed social subjects and their experiences of space and time. Offering an alternative to older forms of leisure activity such as walking to the neighbourhood pub, the automobile perpetuates the **myth** of freedom and facilitates a desire to live away from urban centres. As we saw in Chapter 5, it has enabled the sprawling growth of suburbs (and new ideals of home), as well as the emergence of new forms of leisure such as drive-in cinemas, roadside museums, theme parks, auto-touring and auto-camping country holidays, and shopping malls (Jennings 1990; Thoms *et al.* 1998). The automobile also led to a decline in public transportation and the decentralization of workplaces right across the industrialized societies of the West. No longer constrained by the timetables of the railways and public transportation, the mass consumer is produced by the automobile as a subject that is highly individualized and privatized.

The image of the car and the distinctions it assumes has produced different car cultures that signify highly differentiated identities. A pickup truck used for daily work has a different status than the luxury status of the weekend car. Barthes suggests that 'an object becomes a symbol when it acquires through convention and uses a meaning that enables it to stand for something else' (Barthes 1977: 24). Illustrating this, automotive manufacturer Holden Ltd has conducted a study of national car industries which shows that consumers purchase cars in order to attain the identities represented by some aspects of the car's national culture: 'Thus Audi and BMW represent German quality engineering and efficiency. ... The Citroën DS 19 represents French élan and style; Volvo and Saab, Swedish safety and welfarism' (Thoms *et al.* 1998: 38).

The meanings that cars symbolize and the identities they produce may change through time and in different contexts, and the myths and **ideologies** that cars signify have also been appropriated to signify resistance to normative strategies. The formation of a 'rice boy' **subculture** in the Asian diasporas in the West is an example of how appropriation has become a tactical force for new identity formations. A rice boy is an Asian identified by his car (or rice rocket) and what he does to it. The rice boy usually drives a Japanese car, but unlike a normal performance enthusiast, he is more concerned with the image of speed than he is about performance, carrying out extensive aesthetic modifications to his car – these flashy modifications are the primary visual signifier of the 'rice rocket' (Hong 1998). The rise of the rice boy is connected to the rise of the New Rich in Asia, where sustained economic growth in the last two decades has translated into a rapid expansion of consumerism as part of everyday life. Chua writes that the body has emerged as the site for consumerism with 'adornment as its primary modality' (2000: 14). In the case of rice boy culture, the image of speed becomes a form of new Asian **cultural capital** that expresses a resistance to the body politic of (emasculated) Asian **masculinity** in the West. Here, the desire for Occidental muscularity is displaced by the hybrid display of materialism. Western **consumption** practices (purchase of cars) is mixed with an 'Eastern' practice (adornment of cars). Globally familiar branding is replaced by a regionally specific form of customizing, and modern, urban street savvy is subverted by the amateur car enthusiast (Figures 12.1–12.3).

Figure 12.1

Figure 12.2

Figure 12.3

Figures 12.1–12.3: A rice boy Toyota Celica. Note the rear spoiler, the custom paintwork, decals, wheel trim, petrol tank cover and steering wheel, and a Chinese woven ornament hanging from the rear-view mirror beside the earphones. Photographs by Audrey Yue.

CAR CULTURES AND IDENTITY: DECALS AND BUMPER STICKERS

Fran Martin

A few hours spent cycling around the northern Melbourne suburb where I live turned up a wealth of examples of decorated cars representing various aspects of their owners' identities: from **ethnicity**, national affiliation (Figures 12.4 and 12.5) and religious beliefs (Figures 12.6 and 12.7) to hobbies including musical theatre, drag racing and shopping (Figures 12.8 and 12.10), and some widely disparate opinions regarding pets (Figures 12.11 and 12.13).

Figure 12.4

Figure 12.5

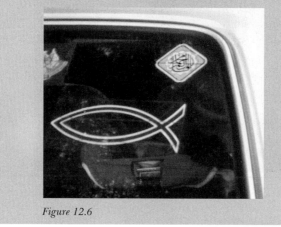

Figure 12.6

Figure 12.7

Figure 12.8

Figure 12.9

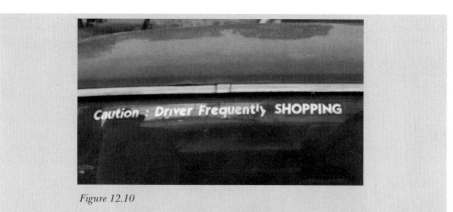

Figure 12.10

Figure 12.11

Figure 12.12

Figure 12.13

Some cars expressed their drivers' **gendered** identities (Figure 12.14); others made statements about environmental politics (Figure 12.15); others offered potted versions of their drivers' widely variant beliefs and philosophies of life (Figures 12.16–12.20).

Figure 12.14

Figure 12.15

Figure 12.16   *Figure 12.17*

Figure 12.18

Figure 12.19

Figure 12.20

Some cars, too, expressed composite or hybrid forms of identification. The truck in Figure 12.21, for example, declares a preference for the rock music played on Melbourne radio station FOX FM, with the FOX stickers, as well as an ethnic affiliation, with the hand-painted decals in Arabic. And the station wagon in Figure 12.22 declares its owner's personal identification along three axes: sexual orientation (the rainbow sticker of lesbian and gay pride); environmental politics (the anti-uranium mining sticker); and favourite football team (Essendon).

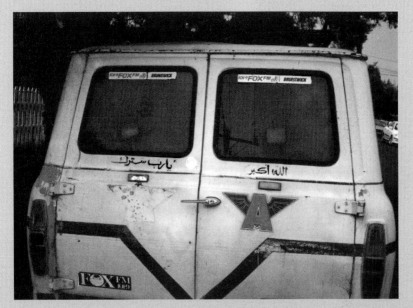

Figure 12.21

Figure 12.22

Figure 12.23, meanwhile, seems to express an interesting tension or contradiction. On the one hand, the peeling sticker with the Australian flag, nationalistically quoting the Australian national anthem, declares the car's driver to be 'young and free' (in the photo the words are partly obscured by the peeling sticker). On the other hand, the sticker beneath, calling the van 'Mums taxi' [*sic*], invokes a gendered identity that is possibly less 'young', and certainly less 'free', as 'Mum' declares herself constrained to serve as a personal taxi service for her children.

Figure 12.23

Figures 12.4–12.23: Photographs by Fran Martin.

Taken as a group, these examples illustrate the function of vehicle decoration in helping drivers express and negotiate complex forms of public identity. They suggest that vehicle decoration not only expresses existing identities, but also allows individuals to re-construct and 're-mix' their identities via their cars, and even to express some of the structuring contradictions inherent in (post)modern subjecthood, such as the contradictions between freedom and constraint; or between individual identity and group affiliation.

This study only looks at bumper stickers and decals, but one could extend it to consider other aspects of vehicle customization, like dashboard and mirror ornaments; personalized number plates; customized wheels and other accessories – even the kinds of music sometimes audible from cars when they are being driven. Take a walk around your own neighbourhood and see what other examples you can come up with!

Not only do car cultures signify different identities that are highly individualized as the foregoing photo essay shows, the automobile also shores up a culture of the individual in another way: by producing a culture in which isolated individuals increasingly spend time alone in the car. Morse extends the idea of travel-as-displacement to point out how such a culture helps to produce 'mobile identities'. She uses the practice of driving on the freeway to show how displacement from context produces dislocation (Morse 1990: 199) The freeway is a **nonspace**, a site in between the city and the suburb. Like the experience of walking in the mall discussed in Chapter 8, driving on the freeway is a practice characterized by distraction, because it allows one to tune out and momentarily escape. Such a practice is experienced contradictorily as both motion and stasis, exterior and interior, private and public. Contained in the intensely interior, private space of the car, yet surrounded by the rapidly changing landscapes of the road, the driver is dislocated and transformed into a privatized mobile subject:

> In nonspace, the body in motion is no longer a kinesthetic key to reality, for at the wheel of the automobile ... engaged in small motor movements which have become highly skilled and automatic, it explores space as an inert mass, technically or electronically empowered with virtual or actual speed. Indeed what we experience is not an erasure, circumvention, or fragmentation of the body but its investment with a second and more powerful skin within which a core remains secure, intact, and at rest in a vortex of speed. (Morse 1998: 204)

Mobility highlights four frames of reference that relate to the practices of getting around. It points to:

- *displacement* from one location to another, as examined in the concept of travel;
- *freedom* of movement, exemplified in the social mobility afforded by the automobile;
- the *ephemerality* of transient cultures enabled by new media technologies, and
- *labour* and the occupational flexibility brought about by global **capitalism**.

In recent years, new media technologies and the effects of global capitalism have transformed the means by which we get around. New media technologies produce 'mobile cultures' characterized by inter-connectivity. In their recent edited collection on the consumption of new media technologies by emergent gay and lesbian communities in Asia, Berry, Martin and Yue show how the tactical uses of mobile and Internet technologies such as chat rooms, bulletin boards, beepers and cell phones have connected isolated, individual queer subjects and enabled the expression of new and collective sexual identities (2003). While they point to how queer cultures are emerging in Asia despite the widespread illegality of homosexuality, the case studies collected in their volume on Internet censorship and regulation also warn that such tactical mobility and connectivity have resulted in increased strategies of surveillance.

TELEMATICS

The paradox of mobility as both freedom and containment, and the increased surveillance it produces for the highly privatized and mobile subject is also evident in communication and information technologies. One such area that relates to everyday life practices of getting around is telematics. Telematics involves the use of interactive multimedia touch screens and/or Internet or Ethernet technologies to distribute and provide information between providers and customers/citizens (Nijkamp *et al*. 1996) One popular use of telematics is in the public service provision sector, where information kiosks are located at shopping malls, petrol stations and convenience stores in order to facilitate citizens' access to public, voluntary and private information. Another use is in transportation telematics where interactive information is exchanged to enhance public transportation and car driving behaviour via collective road-based information signs such as Variable Message Signs (VMS) or individual in-vehicle terminals. Telematics is promoted as an information and network tool that facilitates mobility because information is easily packaged, distributed and retrieved, and is also extremely accessible from remote regions.

Morse notes that such technology represents a means for social cohesion and control because it 'can dispense with the need for any "central" or panoptic position of surveillance, visible display of force, or school of discipline, because [it is] fully congruent with the values of **individualism** and hedonistic pleasure, as well as desires for social recognition and dreams of community' (1990: 208–9). Because telematics narrates official information, its form functions as a hegemonic strategy for producing only desirable subjects – citizens who pay taxes, consumers who are prompt in their bill payments, customers who can afford to access information or users with the correct identity profile. The use of automatic tracking and tracing technologies, bar codes, magnetic striped cards and smart cards to facilitate identification processes attests to the technology's strategic monitoring of individual subjects. In transportation, telematics is also a strategy for influencing travel practices. Route changes and detours are prescribed from above, rather than tactical. Some trips may be cancelled or rescheduled if there is traffic congestion or if a road is closed. Parking choices and the mode of transportation may also be altered depending on the information accessed. Where providers see strategic potential, some of the practices may also be appropriated to suit the user. For example, a decision not to drive, and to use public transportation instead may prove to be a resistant response to road congestion and environmental pollution. Standing at the bus stop waiting for the bus to turn up instead of following the bus timetable and setting out for a particular bus may be more desirable for the infrequent commuter who practises public commuting as a form of sociability.

Notwithstanding the tactical uses of telematics, the system also functions as a hegemonic strategy for control implemented through the ideologies of information access and 'consumer choice'. Central to this is the changing role of the citizen as an informed, user-pays consumer of services. Wessels examines this in her study of the community use of public information kiosks in Newham in London's East End. She argues that although the implementation of the kiosks promotes a form of citizenship based on consumerism, its users are unable to exercise consumer choice because they are disadvantaged by 'lack of awareness, low expectations and social and cultural deprivation as well as language difficulties' (2000: 441) Wessels' study questions the ideology of the citizen-as-consumer and problematizes the rhetoric of choice and participatory democracy in our late modern capitalist culture. More significantly, it highlights the role that information plays in contemporary everyday life and the ways in which the travel metaphor has produced a new type of subject who is not only a highly individualized, private, informed and mobile consumer, but is also characterized by a new kind of occupational flexibility brought about by the increasing decentralization of work.

Flexibility and mobility have been the central paradigms of capitalism and modernity. Marx states that the fragmentation of modern life resided in the principle of 'value in motion', where capital is constantly in circulation in search of new profits (cited in Harvey 1990: 109). Harvey extends this to suggest that since the early 1970s, the flexible subject has come to represent the practice of capital accumulation˙ (1990). Harvey, like Morse, also points to the paradox of flexibility and notes that although flexibility often connotes decentralization in the international workplace – because occupational flexibility is opposed to governmental regulation and market segmentation – flexibility is in fact used as a strategy for maintaining centralized control through decentralization. Flexi-time, a practice where workers are able to negotiate their conditions of employment, for example, functions more as a disciplining and de-skilling strategy than one of worker empowerment. For example, this strategy ensures that workers self-conform to efficient practices of time management when working from home. People who work from home or are part of a flexible labour force may also miss out on training opportunities that are otherwise available to people who work on-site.

That information is the new form of capital in our postmodern, global everyday life is evident in how the practices of getting around have been transformed through the deployment of new technologies and the adaptation of traditional modes of transportation. Contemporary practices of getting around have produced a highly flexible and mobile subject, one who is bombarded by images from billboards and graffiti while walking on the street, trades in e-data, commutes on a bus to work for the knowledge economy, and perhaps even holidays at national forests with coordinates provided by park rangers and four-wheel drive magazines. What follows in the next section is an analysis of the bicycle as a case study to extend these ideas; in particular, we argue that bicycle cultures expose the strategies of informational and global capitalism as well as the tactics of local and transnational resistance.

BICYCLE POLITICS: FLEXIBILITY, SUSTAINABILITY AND CRITICAL MASS

This section applies concepts such as displacement, mobility and flexibility, discussed in the first section, to a case study on the bicycle. It uses the material culture of the bicycle, its cultural history and the Chinese film *Beijing Bicycle* (Wang Xiaoshuai, 2000), to show how the bicycle, as an object of everyday life, functions as a site for contesting different local, national and transnational travel ideologies.

The bicycle produces many meanings and assumes many different kinds of status. Tricycles or one's first BMX bike evoke memories of childhood and adolescence. A mountain bike used on the weekend connotes off-road cycling as a leisure pursuit. The bicycle is a work necessity in many professions, including postal delivery services and police patrols. In addition, cycling is an eco-friendly alternative practice of getting around. Anti-car protesters have also organized Critical Mass rides in city centres to demonstrate and raise public awareness about automobile dependency, environmental pollution and street safety.

Although driving is now the desired mainstream practice of getting around, in the nineteenth century the bicycle was instrumental in providing personal freedom and speed to those who did not desire the public transportation offered by horse-drawn coaches and trains (Rosen 2002: 26). Women in particular gained greater mobility

Figure 12.24: Women riding bicycles on Revere Beach driveway in the 1890s, Revere MA, USA. Courtesy Frances Loeb Library, Graduate School of Design, Harvard University.

through their newly acquired freedom (Figure 12.24). The bicycle not only redefined female beauty and but also transformed women's social and political roles. Debates over women cycling ranged from debates over women in public spaces and what women should wear when cycling. Predominantly male objections to women cycling were soon replaced by debates on what women should wear (McGurn 1987: 101). Women's fashion began to change with the invention of the bloomer and the knickerbocker, and the adoption of what was called 'Rational Dress' (shorter skirts and looser waists) (Dodge 1996: 122–3). Cycling liberated isolated women from their domesticity and provided an acceptable public culture for women to participate in. Suffragettes used the bicycle as an important symbol of women's empowerment.

Cycling was originally a leisure pursuit among the bourgeois elite in France and Britain. In their colonies, cycling in the parks was promoted as a recreational amusement for bored expatriate housewives. As the mass **production** of bicycles in the 1890s made the bicycle accessible to the working **class**, cycling soon became a popular practice of getting around. With the cost of the bicycle approximately equal to the cost of a suit, the demand for the bicycle changed consumption patterns and everyday life. Smith reports that in America, 'it was the first big-scale assault of American technology on institutionalized religion' (1972: 72). Instead of going to the church on Sunday, people would go out riding their bicycles, and as a further consequence, barbers, tailors, cigar-makers, booksellers, piano manufacturers and saloon keepers reported a decline in trade (1972: 72). Embraced by the working class as a sign of social mobility, the bicycle was crucial to lessening the appearance of class differences.

Although bicycle technology has changed comparatively little through the years, the technology of the bicycle has also been significant in contemporary culture. The technique for the mass production of bicycles was a blueprint for the automobile industry to build cars, which were to become a key aspect of national industries and cultures as well as an intrinsic aspect of everyday life, as discussed above (Dodge 1996: 6). Despite the modern car replacing the bicycle as the preferred mode of transportation, the bicycle has regained its popularity in the last two decades in the West and in some parts of Asia as a result of the movement towards sustainable technology. Protest movements and new road management policies have used the bicycle as a tool for raising awareness about environmental conservation and traffic congestion. In Britain, a 1996 Department of Environment planning policy promoted the bicycle as a new mode of sustainable transportation (Rosen 2002: 161). By identifying the car as the major cause of pollution and the bicycle as a form of sustainable mobility, this strategy highlights two competing ideologies: car economy versus sustainable economy. The rise of the latter ideology has resulted in the introduction of cycling lanes on some roads, bicycle parking at train and bus stations, and car-free zones in new road programmes in many Western countries. National, state and local governments have also supported and funded cycling campaigns in order to encourage the everyday utilitarian use of the bicycle.

Public debates are also raised through unofficial tactics such as Critical Mass bike rides. Since the first Critical Mass ride in 1992 in San Francisco, regular monthly mass rides have been organized throughout the Western world. These bicycle rides take place en masse around congested city streets to protest against car pollution and demonstrate the advantages of cycling over driving. One related tactical deployment is by a transnational activist group, Reclaim The Streets (RTS). This group organizes illegal street parties as direct action tactics to demonstrate against the negative impact of the automobile on street life. These global street parties have appropriated highways, train stations, parks and major arterial roads in cities including London, San Francisco, Berlin, Birmingham, Bogotá, Vancouver and Sydney. Eclectic devices such as mixing decks, walkmans and mini-discs are used to create a carnival-like atmosphere where activists, music and street performers disrupt traffic order, pedestrian rules and road regulations, and subvert the street's strategic use to expose the **politics** of its space.

The technology of the bicycle has also generated a strategy of transnational flexibility through the global consumption of the mountain bike: 'the globally flexible bicycle has [...] emerged since the 1980s, centred on several interlocking features: new production methods and new ways of organizing the industry [...] new products; new ways in which consumers perceive and use bicycles' (Rosen 2002: 122). *Flexible production* practices are evident through the mountain bike's American, British, Taiwanese or French design, with some of its parts manufactured in Japan or generically mass supplied by Taiwan, while assembly happens in China or India. *Flexible consumption* is evident through self-specification where consumers can choose from catalogues a range of tubings, forks, brakes, frames and transmissions. Self-specification creates distinctions and different types of subjects including tourers, trekkers, weekenders, BMXers and utilitarians. Mountain bikes can be seen as both modern and postmodern sites of contradiction. While postmodern subjects are produced through their pastiche of self-customization and transnational production, the ideology of mountain bikes as hi-tech, weekend, country bikes also demonstrates the contradictions of modernity, evoking at once technology and nature; work and leisure; the **postindustrial** city and the non-industrial rural ideal.

These contradictions are evident in *Beijing Bicycle*, a film about the lives of two 17 year olds – Gui, a bicycle messenger, and Jian, a high schooler – in 1990s Beijing. It uses the mountain bike as a site for challenging the politics of an urban space created by capitalism, post-socialism, modernity and **globalization**. Gui is a village boy who comes to Beijing to find employment. He lands himself a job as a delivery boy and must earn the ownership of his bike through the deliveries he makes. A day before he finishes paying off the bike, it is stolen. Jian is an urban dweller who needs a bike to impress his friends and his girlfriend. His father promises to buy one but never does. He steals his father's money, buys a bike at the flea market and gains social acceptance amongst his peers. When Gui discovers that Jian now has his bike, he is desperate to have it back. Jian is even more desperate to keep it. In their desperation, both set out to negotiate their respective ownership and use of the bike.

The mountain bike stages urban/rural, class and generational divides against the backdrop of a rapidly transforming modern cityscape. These divides signify displacement and produce a politics of mobility. The juxtaposition of Gui and Jian exposes the distinctions between the city and the village. Gui is in awe when he finds himself delivering messages to hotels, high-rise apartments and saunas. He is often contemplatively silent, not because he is afraid of the city, but because he is cautious about what the city may mean. He possesses an ethics that still has faith in the rewards of hard work and truth. Jian is at home in the video arcades. His rage against his father shows a rebellion against his parents' class and tradition, and he steals and lies to attain a **commodity** that will provide him with personal freedom. Both protagonists are displaced, Gui from the country, and Jian from his father and the values he represents. Both boys desire mobility, one upward social mobility to enable him to fit in with the **lifestyles** of his middle-class friends, the other geographic mobility enabling him to succeed – and possibly attain upward class mobility – in the city. The politics of this mobility is evident in the film's use of space. Beijing is presented as a contrast of old and new. Tall skyscrapers, new hotels, half-built apartments and crane-supported construction sites sit alongside ancient alleys, laneways, and dwellings with clay rooftops and courtyards. In such a space, old men sunbathe, drink tea and practise daily t'ai chi; city dwellers drive fast cars, dress in designer clothes and have frequent saunas; and country folk work hard or pretend that they are who they are not. Mobility and displacement express the rapid transformation of a city that is caught between tradition and modernity.

As a signifier of high technology and mobility, the mountain bike produces distinctions that negotiate the transition between the old and the new. Gui's bicycle is not just new and fast in and of itself, it also signifies newness and speed because Gui uses it to courier information to businesses in a city eager to integrate in the global economy. Gui's bicycle not only symbolizes global flexibility in its mode of production, it also represents a wider strategy of capital accumulation through the value of information that is being couriered. As media theorist Paul Virilio expounds, information is speed and speed is capital (1995). For Jian, the same bike has become a commodity and is valued for the glamour that it signifies. His friends and their bicycle culture epitomize such a distinction: they sport trendy coloured hair, wear racing sunglasses and BMX gloves and dress in the latest hip-hop fashion, all global signifiers of capitalist modernity. In a country where the bicycle is almost a national icon and car ownership is rapidly on the rise, the mountain bike functions as a site of transition between those who have and those who have not. Gui even rejects his friend's old boneshaker and opts to run, instead of having to pedal without the aid of Shimano gears. Although the mountain bike acquires a new form of cultural capital in its aspirational functionality (for Gui) and pleasurable distraction (for Jian), overall it represents the dislocation felt by the city's inhabitants as old communal values are replaced by new desires brought about by the fragmentation of modernization and globalization, and speaks to their yearning for belonging in a rapidly changing place.

Summary

In this chapter, we have argued that:

- getting around is an everyday practice involving displacement and mobility;

- travel, mobility and displacement are experienced at the level of both the local and the transnational;

- the material cultures of transportation and travel have been configured and reconfigured by modernity and postmodernity;

- travelling cultures can be both hegemonic and resistant; both strategic and tactical;

- new communication technologies have changed traditional modes of transportation, travelling and connecting;

- getting around is a practice that forms and consolidates individual subjects' personal identities.

EXERCISES

1. List and discuss three tactics and three strategies in relation to: walking in the mall, driving to the movies and riding a bicycle.

2. Critically evaluate how the camper-van or an auto-touring holiday helps travellers negotiate identity through mobility.

3. Discuss how the tools of the World Wide Web (e.g. e-mails, chat rooms, bulletin boards, messenger services, etc.) have enabled new practices of 'getting around', or becoming mobile, within contemporary cultures. List three such practices.

REFERENCES

BARTHES, R. 1977: *Image-Music-Text*. London: Fontana.

BERRY, C., MARTIN, F. and YUE, A. (eds) 2003: *Mobile Cultures: New Media in Queer Asia*. Durham, NC: Duke University Press.

CHUA, B.-H. (ed.) 2000: *Consumption in Asia: Lifestyles and Identities*. New York: Routledge.

CLIFFORD, J. 1997: *Routes: Travel and Translation in the Late Twentieth Century*. Cambridge, MA: Harvard University Press.

CROSS, G. and SZOSTAK, R. 1995: *Technology and American History: A History*. New Jersey: Prentice-Hall.

DODGE, P. 1996: *The Bicycle*. Paris: Flammarion.

HALL, S. 1987: Minimal selves. In Appignasesi, L. (ed.), *Identity/The Real Me*. London: ICA Documents, 134–8.

HARVEY, D. 1990: *The Condition of Postmodernity: An Enquiry into the Origins of Cultural Change*. Cambridge, MA: Blackwell.

HONG, B.M. 1998: Bryan's Rice Boy Page, 17 September 2000, <http://www.riceboypage.com>. Accessed 27 September 2000.

JENNINGS, J. (ed.) 1990: *Roadside America: The Automobile in Design and Culture*. Iowa: Iowa State University Press.

KAPLAN, C. 1996: *Questions of Travel: Postmodern Discourses of Displacement*. Durham, NC: Duke University Press.

McGURN, J. 1987: *On Your Bicycle: An Illustrated History of Cycling*. London: John Murray.

MORSE, M. 1990: An ontology of everyday distraction: the freeway, the mall and television. In Mellencamp, P. (ed.), *Logics of Television: Essays in Cultural Criticism*. Bloomington: Indiana University Press, 193–221.

NIJKAMP, P., PEPPING, G. and DANNISTER, D. 1996: *Telematics and Transport Behaviour*. New York: Springer.

Reclaim The Streets Website, 1 December 2002, <http://www.reclaimthestreets.net/>. Accessed 29 January 2003.

ROBERTSON, G., MASH, M., TICKNER, L., BIRD, J., CURTIS B. and PUTNAM, T. (eds) 1994: *Travellers' Tales: Narratives of Home and Displacement*. London: Routledge.

ROSEN, P. 2002: *Framing Production: Technology, Culture, and Change in the British Bicycle Industry*. Cambridge, MA: MIT Press.

SMITH, R.A. 1972: *A Social History of the Bicycle*. New York: American Heritage Press.

THOMS, D., HOLDEN, L. and CLAYDON, T. (eds) 1998: *The Motor Car and Popular Culture in the 20th Century*. Aldershot: Ashgate.

VIRILIO, P. 1995: *The Art of the Motor*. Minneapolis: University of Minnesota Press.

WESSELS, B. 2000: Telematics in the East End of London. *New Media and Society* 2(4), 427–44.

WOMACK, J.P., JONES, D. and ROOS, D. 1990: *The Machine that Changed the World*. Maxwell Macmillan International, Oxford.

FURTHER READING

BEST, S. 1999: Driving like a boy: sexual difference, embodiment and space. In Barcan, R. and Buchanan, I. (eds), *Imagining Australian Space: Cultural Studies and Spatial Inquiry*. Nedlands, WA: University of Western Australia Press.

COWAN, R. S. 1997: *A Social History of American Technology*. Oxford: Oxford University Press.

HALL, S. 1996: Cultural identity and diaspora. In Rutherford, J. (ed.), *Identity: Community, Culture, Difference*. London: Lawrence & Wishart, 222–37.

JORDAN, T. 1999: *Cyberpower: The Culture and Politics of Cyberspace and the Internet.* London: Routledge.

KAUR, R. and HUTNYK, J. (eds) 1999: *Travel Worlds: Journeys in Contemporary Cultural Politics.* London: Zed Books.

LAVIE, S. and SWEDENBURG, S. (eds) 1996: *Displacement, Diaspora, and Geographies of Identity.* Durham, NC: Duke University Press.

MARLING, K.A. 1994: *As Seen on TV: The Visual Culture of Everyday Life in the 1950s.* Cambridge, MA: Harvard University Press.

MILLER, D. (ed.) 2001: *Car Cultures.* Oxford: Berg.

MORSE, M. 1998: *Virtualities: Television, Media Art, and Cyberculture.* Bloomington: Indiana University Press.

PINCHES, M. (ed.) 1999: *Culture and Privilege in Capitalist Asia.* London: Routledge.

ROJEK, C. and URRY, J. 1997: *Touring Cultures: Transformations of Travel and Theory.* London: Routledge.

ROSZAK, T. 1994: *The Cult of Information.* Berkeley: University of California Press.

GLOSSARY

Fran Martin, with contributors

advanced capitalism: see **capitalism**

aesthetics: the consideration and judgement of the properties of an object that are perceived by the senses (sight, hearing, etc.), according to a particular regime of **cultural value**.

agency: the role of someone or something whose actions have a real effect on a situation or course of events.

alienated labour: Karl Marx proposed that in a capitalist society, the worker's labour-power is no longer her or his own – since it is no longer used directly for his or her own personal benefit – but instead it is sold to the **capitalist** employer, who then effectively owns this labour-power and uses it for her or his own profit, rather than that of the worker. Alienated labour is labour that, as a result of this process, is used for the profit of the capitalist and has ceased to be under the control of the worker.

appropriation: the act of taking up an object or practice and using it in ways different from or contrary to those in which it was originally used.

bricolage: the **resistant appropriation** and reconfiguration of mainstream forms and objects in ways that disrupt **hegemonic** systems of social order.

capitalism: the economic system that is now globally dominant, in which the surplus value created by the labour of workers is taken as profit by capitalist classes that control the means of **production**. Capitalism progresses in stages. **Industrial capitalism** refers to the mode of economic organization first enabled by the Industrial Revolution, and which became dominant with the spread of the industrial mode of production through the nineteenth century. **Advanced capitalism** is the kind of economic system found in advanced economies post-Second World War. Characteristic of **postindustrial societies**, it is organized less centrally around secondary industries (the transformation of primary resources into commodities through manufacturing) and more around the forms of secondary production found in the service industries (such as advertising, leisure, education and media).

class: the division of individuals into groups based on their position within the **capitalist** economic system and the social and cultural systems that attend it. A central class distinction is that between the working class and the bourgeoisie. Class divisions are expressed through distinct cultural practices as well as through individuals' relationship to the means of **production**.

commodification: the process by which everything in a **capitalist** society tends to assume the form of the **commodity**.

commodity: in a **Marxist** analysis, a product circulating within a capitalist society whose **exchange value** dominates its **use value**. The commodity's value comes from its equation with the abstract form of money, rather than from how directly useful it is to its owner.

commodity culture: the form that **culture** takes in **modernity**, which intensifies in **postmodernity**, when the **commodity** form dominates social life.

commodity fetishism: originally a **Marxist** concept, commodity fetishism refers to the process whereby any sign of the labour that goes into producing a **commodity** is effectively erased by the commodity form, and the commodity then seems, as if by magic, to appear in culture devoid of any social history. The concept of commodity fetishism also refers to the relationship between the commodity and the **consumer**, whereby the commodity is invested with the quasi-magical ability to satisfy the consumer's desires. These desires have been created not 'naturally', but through the workings of **commodity culture** and, by definition, such desires can in fact never be finally satisfied.

connotation: the 'second layer' of associative meaning attached to a given sign, beyond the surface meaning of **denotation**. For example, a photograph of a steamed dumpling in an advertisement denotes merely 'steamed dumpling', but may be designed to connote 'deliciousness', 'nutrition', or 'family togetherness'.

construct (n.): designates the 'reality-effect' produced by a given cluster of cultural beliefs, which is in fact thoroughly **ideological**. For example, we might refer to the **discourse** of **racism** as producing **race** as a cultural construct. Construct can also be used as a transitive verb (to construct) designating the process of creating a construct.

construction: the action of given cultural beliefs in producing the **ideological** 'reality-effect' known as a **construct**.

consumer: a **subject** in a **capitalist** society that is defined by its practices of **consumption**. Arguably all subjects within contemporary capitalist societies are defined by their positioning as consumers or potential consumers, although historically in the West, consumption has been culturally coded as an activity particularly associated with women and **femininity**.

consumption: the moment at which the economic activity of exchanging goods for money and the cultural practices of the **consumer** coincide.

cosmopolitanism: an interest in other cultures and a sense of worldliness as a result of the ability to travel. Cosmopolitanism depends on a mobility enabled by social, economic and cultural privilege. The term is flexible, and implies at once a sense of global citizenship (non-affiliation to a nation state) and intercultural experience (both appropriation and exchange).

cultural capital: a term popularized by Pierre Bourdieu. It refers to acquired knowledge that enables an individual to interpret particular cultural codes (like the codes of classical ballet or of rave culture). Cultural capital is comparable to economic capital in that it is unevenly distributed across **classes**.

cultural imaginary: the ensemble of images and fantasies, thoughts and expectations, feelings and values that we mentally attach to the idea of something. For example, we might speak of the cultural imaginary of the city as an urban imaginary; the cultural imaginary of the suburb as a suburban imaginary, and so on. Our urban imaginaries might include ideas about density, excitement, modernity and alienation; suburban imaginaries frequently draw on notions of expansive space, family life, peacefulness and banality. See also **imaginary**.

cultural imperialism: describes the dominance of one culture over another – most frequently, the dominance of Euro-American cultures over non-Western ones – and the consequent loss of local cultures. See also **globalization** and **glocalization**.

cultural studies: a discipline that emerged initially in Britain in the 1960s, whose object of study was forms of social and cultural organization and expression in contemporary, Western, industrialized societies. Since the 1960s the discipline has spread to the USA, Australia, New Zealand, East Asia and elsewhere, and over the past decade it has begun also to address everyday cultures outside the West.

cultural value: refers not to any inherent value, but instead to the value ascribed to particular cultural forms by a given, historically and socially embedded regime of cultural valuation. For example, forms of **high culture** are routinely accorded a greater cultural value than examples of **low culture**.

culture: in cultural studies, refers to 'a whole way of life' – the whole complex network of values, beliefs and practices that characterize a given society. In this sense 'culture' does not refer only to specific artistic forms, such as those designated by 'high culture'.

denotation: the 'first layer' of meaning attached to a given sign. For example, the typographic letters 'T-R-E-E' denote a large, trunked plant with multiple leaves. See also **connotation**.

disciplinary power: according to Michel Foucault, a form of **power** that emerged in the seventeenth and eighteenth centuries along with the rise of **modern capitalism**. Disciplinary power relies on individual self-**surveillance** rather than brute force exercised by power's representatives; cf. **sovereign power**.

discourse: a term drawn from the work of Michel Foucault to designate a cluster of statements, beliefs and practices that cohere to produce a particular object of knowledge at a particular moment in history. For example, one might say that an anatomy textbook, a television commercial that declares sore throats to be the result of bacterial infection, and 'common-sense' beliefs that children should be vaccinated against childhood diseases all contribute to a medical discourse, which **constructs** human bodies in particular ways and arose in the West as the result of **modern** developments in scientific thought. Equally, one might speak of a religious discourse, an educational discourse, a discourse on **gender**, a discourse on **race**, and so on.

dystopia: the inverse of **utopia**: an imagined hellish or intolerable place.

essentialism: an **idealist** way of thinking that assumes the existence of an inherently 'natural' and proper state of being for particular people or things, imagined as an irreducible, interior 'essence'. For example, an essentialist view of **gender** might hold that women are 'naturally' less aggressive and more nurturing than men, because their inherent, feminine essence makes them so. Essentialist views of cultural phenomena like gender are frequently challenged by more **materialist** views.

ethnicity: a cultural identity based on an individual's own identification with a particular, geo-culturally derived set of practices and/or beliefs. For example, we can speak of 'Native American ethnicity', 'Japanese ethnicity', etc. Distinguished from **race**, which is based on more scientistic, determinist ideas about bodies, rather than culture.

Eurocentrism: A way of thinking that privileges Western cultures over non-Western ones. Eurocentric thought takes 'Western-ness' as the norm against which all other cultures should be measured, and effectively **constructs** Western culture as the most important and meaningful culture in the world, compared to which all other cultures are peripheral and relatively insignificant.

exchange-value: the value of a thing measured by how much money it can be exchanged for rather than by what useful purposes it can serve. See also **use-value**.

femininities: those forms of **gendered** identification and **practice** available primarily to **subjects** who identify as women or girls within a given cultural context. Femininities might be understood as a range of 'ways of being culturally female'.

feminism: a critical movement whose central object of analysis is **gender**. Feminist cultural studies considers women's role as active producers of **culture**, and draws attention to the power relations that produce gendered categories within culture as a whole.

flâneur: the concept of the *flâneur* was popularized by the writings of Walter Benjamin on Charles Baudelaire's poems about nineteenth-century Paris. The *flâneur* was a poet of **modern**, urban life who was most at home wandering amid the crowds of the metropolis, observing and interpreting the city's commercial and human **spectacle**. Later writers continue to draw upon the *flâneur* as a narrative device for theorizing the experience of inhabiting **postmodern** cities and spaces.

gender: refers to attributes that are culturally ascribed to women and men. Gender denotes the cultural system that produces some subjects as feminine and some as masculine. Distinguished from **sex**, which is sometimes used to refer to biological attributes understood to differentiate male bodies from female ones. Gender is the central object of analysis of **feminism**.

gender performativity: an idea taken from the work of Judith Butler. Gender performativity refers to the way in which the cultural **construct** of **gender** is produced not by **identity** or what one essentially is, but instead by acts, or what one does. This is a radically anti-**essentialist** view of gender.

gendered division of labour: the tendency for the paid workforce to be divided along the lines of gender, with some jobs tending to be done by, and considered appropriate for, men (e.g. construction work, corporate management) while other kinds of work tend to be done by, and are considered appropriate for, women (e.g. primary teaching, sewing). The persistence of the gendered division of labour contributes to the discrepancy between men's and women's pay, since the types of work considered more appropriate for men are, overall, better paid than those considered more appropriate for women.

geography: the geography of a given place refers to the relationships among all of the sites located within that place (for example, we might consider the geography of a shopping mall; or the geography of a domestic home). Cultural geography is a critical approach that analyses the power relationship between people, place and resources.

globalization: the increased interconnection of the world as a result of the mobility of people, capital, things, media and markets since the mid-twentieth century. Spatial expansion is accompanied by a shrinking sense of time as people in different parts of the world become increasingly connected to each other. One view of globalization concerns the effects of unequal development where traffic flows uni-directionally from one culture to another. Another view suggests that globalization is a chaotic and irregular flow creating disjunctive new worlds formed by finance, media, technology, people and ideology. See also **cultural imperialism** and **glocalization**.

glocalization: describes the resistant process where local cultures creatively appropriate and transform global forms to suit their own needs. Glocalization enables **tactics** of indigenization and localization, and produces difference. See also **globalization** and **cultural imperialism**.

habitus: defined by Pierre Bourdieu as the set dispositions, based on the power relations that structure a class-based society, which are internalized at the level of the body in the processes of early acculturation. These predispose individuals to act in certain ways – for example, showing particular formations of personal **taste** – without being fully conscious of what structures their decisions.

hegemony: defined by Antonio Gramsci as a 'moving equilibrium' that binds a society together without the use of physical force. It works by generating the consent of subordinate **classes** to the ideas, values and beliefs – the **ideologies** – of dominant classes. The result is that the social distribution of **power** appears legitimate and 'natural'. Hegemony is never completely stable: it must constantly be won, reproduced and sustained.

high culture: a term originally used in the nineteenth century to draw a class-based distinction between elite and '**low**' cultural forms. High culture also defines itself in aesthetic terms as being 'serious' or 'true' culture as opposed to 'inauthentic' **mass culture**.

idealism: a way of thinking that takes the abstract qualities of mind or spirit as primary over the concrete forms of matter and history. Idealism is the opposite of **materialism**.

identity: within cultural studies, identity is not usually treated in an **essentialist** way, which would assume that we all have a 'true self' waiting to find expression. Instead, identity is understood in a **materialist** way that sees identities as produced out of **subjects**' interactions with different options for personal identification that are available to them in a particular cultural context. See also **subjectivity**.

ideology: a concept from the work of Louis Althusser. Ideology is the system of beliefs and assumptions, the entire system of common-sense knowledges through which we all make sense of our 'selves' and our place within culture. Ideology always seems 'natural', but is in fact fully **political** and saturated by relations of **power**. Althusser explains that subjects are brought into social life in ideology through the mechanism of **interpellation**.

imaginary (n.): a set of ideas, beliefs, images and assumptions that creates a mental 'picture' of a particular place. For example, we might speak of the urban imaginaries of particular cities: our imaginary of the city of Paris, for example, might be dominated by ideas about 'art' and 'romance', and images of cobbled streets and the Eiffel Tower; whereas our imaginary of Shanghai might be dominated by ideas about Chinese colonial and postcolonial **modernity** and images of street markets juxtaposed with towering skyscrapers. See also **cultural imaginary**.

incorporation: the mechanisms by which **hegemonic** culture is able to contain and thereby neutralize various forms of **resistance**.

individualism: a way of thinking based on the assumption that individuals are free agents of their own will, and that each individual has a unique character. In individualist thought, it is the free choices made by individuals that ultimately decide their destiny.

industrial capitalism: see **capitalism**

interpellation: a term coined by Louis Althusser to designate the mechanism by which **ideology** 'calls on' individuals and constitutes them as **subjects** of and to itself. Althusser uses the metaphoric example of a policeman calling out in the street 'Hey, you there!' When an individual recognizes that this call is directed at her or him, s/he turns around in answer, and has then been successfully interpellated by the policeman's call. Similarly, when we recognize that the call of ideology is meant for us (it is always meant for us), we are interpellated by ideology.

lifestyle: a fundamentally **modern** concept that assumes that people's everyday lives in advanced **capitalist** cultures are vehicles for the expression of personal style achieved primarily through **consumption**.

low culture: culture judged, according to a particular, class-based system of **cultural value**, to be the inverse of **high culture**; cultural forms excluded from the definition of 'serious culture', often including popular rather than elite forms; '**mass culture**'; or '**commodity culture**'.

Marxism: a theory of economy and culture first developed by Karl Marx and Frederick Engels. Marxism assumes that economic formations play a crucial role in society, and advances a theory of how **capitalism** works.

masculinities: those forms of **gendered** identification and **practice** available primarily to **subjects** who identify as men or boys within a given cultural context. Masculinities might be understood as a range of 'ways of being culturally male'.

mass culture: a term often used disparagingly, as by critics associated with the Frankfurt School (Adorne, Horkheimer), to designate **culture** in the age of mass media and communication. In this theory, the 'mass' of media **consumers** is imagined as passive, undifferentiated and inert.

materialism: a way of thinking that attends to the concrete forms of matter and history, and assumes that these have a more determining influence over events than abstract qualities like mind, spirit or essence. Materialism is the opposite of **idealism**. Materialism sees material conditions (such as **power** relations and historical positioning) as determining, rejecting explanations that appeal to transcendent causes. Cf. **essentialism**.

modern: an object or practice that is characteristic of the historical period known as **modernity**.

modernity: the historical period in the West between approximately the eighteenth century and the present, commencing after the Enlightenment in eighteenth-century Europe. Modernity is also defined by the passage of the Industrial Revolution at that century's end, and sees the rise to dominance of industrial **capitalism** in Europe and the peak years of European colonial expansion in the rest of the world. The **ideology** of modernity emphasizes the progress of science, the rationality of thought, a new type of social subject, and a belief in the new as inherently better than the old. Many argue that the subjective experience of modernity is characterized by uncertainty and ambiguity driven by flux, change and the ephemerality of culture. Some now argue that non-Western 'alternative modernities' should also be considered.

myth: a term from the work of Roland Barthes, which refers to the multiple sites of **ideological** effect in everyday life. Barthes argues that the forms and practices of

215

everyday life in contemporary, industrialized societies function similarly to the myths of pre-modern cultures by representing and communicating our collective social beliefs. Importantly, myth is not opposed to 'reality'; rather, myth creates our very sense of what counts as 'real'.

nonspace: An in-between space on the border between public and private, interior and exterior, artificial and natural, individual and communal. Paradigmatically **postmodern** spaces like freeways and shopping malls are often defined as nonspaces: spaces that problematize previously assumed categorizations of social space.

orientalism: defined by Edward Said as a **discourse** that originated in the West, which constructs 'the orient' (primarily the Middle East in Said's account, but the term is now also often used to include East Asia) according to the values and desires projected onto it by Western interests. For Said, orientalism has historically been and remains a very powerful discourse because its effect is not just to describe 'the East' but, effectively, to **construct** it as an object of Western knowledge, and as the inferior and subject of the West.

overdetermination: This term has been used, differently, in psychoanalytic theory, where Freud used it in relation to dream interpretation, and in Marxist theory, where Louis Althusser, among others, used it to analyse the complex relations among ideology, state institutions and lived culture. For our purposes, overdetermination refers to the complex webs of influence and counter-influence at work within culture, such that processes within culture are not the result of pure chance or a free play of possibilities, but result instead from the determining impact of over-arching structures, such as ideology and existing configurations of power. Hence, we might speak, for example, of the overdetermination of **taste** by **cultural capital**.

patriarchy: refers to a particular organization of gendered **power** in which men are accorded social and material dominance over women. Patriarchy is a primary target of **feminist** critique.

performativity: see **gender performativity**

phallocentrism: a way of thinking that privileges men or **masculinity** over women or **femininity**. Phallocentric thought assumes that **hegemonic** masculinity is the norm against which all other forms of gender expression should be measured, and effectively positions 'man' and masculine **power** as the taken-for-granted centre of social life and philosophical inquiry. Phallocentrism is a key target of **feminist** critique.

politics: In cultural studies, this term is used not in the narrow sense that designates the machinations of organized political parties, but instead in the broad sense that refers to the ways in which culture is saturated by multiple forms of **power**.

popular culture: popular culture is often defined as the everyday culture 'of the people', in opposition to **high culture**, **mass culture** or **hegemonic** culture. Cultural studies has been instrumental in opening up the space for popular culture to be studied as 'seriously' as high culture traditionally has been.

positivism: a way of thinking that assumes the existence and accessibility to human understanding of absolute truths that exist independent of human action.

postcoloniality: the general state of the world and of particular nations following the impact of imperialisms and colonialisms. Some understand the 'post' in 'postcolonial' to mean 'after the end of'; others take it to mean 'under the continuing influence of'. Generally, postcoloniality is understood to refer to the European colonialisms that flourished between the mid-eighteenth and the mid-twentieth centuries. However, some are now keen also to include in the definition the effects of other imperial and colonial powers such as Japan.

postindustrial society: refers to societies in advanced **capitalism**, in which the industrial stage has been eclipsed by a 'postindustrial' stage in which economic activity is concentrated in the service, media, leisure, education and other tertiary industries rather than in the secondary industry of manufacturing.

postmodernity: the historical period in industrialized societies since the conclusion of the Second World War in the mid-twentieth century. Postmodernity is characterized by the rise of the mass market and increased automation, travel, and mass communication and media. Some view postmodernity as a passage beyond **modernity**; others consider it an intensification of modern forms of social and economic organization.

power: following the theory of Michel Foucault, power is understood not as merely repressive, but importantly also as productive, since it is inevitably attended by resistances. Power is understood not as a monolithic force that controls **subjects** 'from above', but rather as produced and negotiated in the micro-level interactions of the everyday. Power is expressed in everyday life through the effects and contestations of such formations as **patriarchy**, **sexism** and **racism** – among many others.

practice: an activity performed by a social **subject** within a particular cultural and historical context. Practices are shaped by the values and beliefs of the particular cultures in which they occur and which they help to define.

production: a term that originates in **Marxist** accounts of economy and society, in which the control of the means of production by a certain **class** equates to the control of capital itself. Production refers not only to the manufacture of **commodities**, but also to the linked creation of intellectual and cultural items. The moment of production and the moment of **consumption** are each crucial to analysing a product's passage through **culture**.

race: an idea invented by European scientists across the eighteenth and nineteenth centuries to classify all the people of the world into supposedly biologically differentiated groups based on people's outward physical appearance. The idea of race has historically been aligned with **racism**, but it has also been **appropriated** as **resistance** by subordinated groups, including African-Americans and others. See also **ethnicity**.

racism: social and material prejudice against a particular people based on assumptions about that people's **race**, when it is considered different from one's own.

rationalism: a way of thinking that places ultimate faith in the capacity of human reason to account for phenomena by discovering the absolute truths that underlie events.

relativism: a way of thinking that assumes there is no absolute truth, but instead that particular 'truths' apply to particular situations. In relativist thought, 'truth' is determined contingently, by the specificity of a given historical or cultural context, and does not apply universally.

resistance: refers to the many ways, both conscious and sometimes partly unconscious, in which people assert their **agency** to symbolically contest oppressive forms of **power** in everyday life.

semiotics: the study of signs, developed most significantly by Swiss cultural linguist Ferdinand de Saussure. The sign is composed of the signifier – the sign's physical form, for example, the letters that spell the word 'shop' – and the signified – the mental association called up by the signifier: the idea that comes to mind when we read the word 'shop'. The identification of **denoted** and **connoted** elements in a sign's meaning is a method taken from semiotic analysis.

sex: see **gender**

sexism: social and material prejudice against particular people based on assumptions about that person's **gender**. In **patriarchal** societies, sexism has usually taken the form of prejudice against women and the privileging of men.

shopper: The shopper is a distinctively **modern** and **postmodern identity** that has come into being with the rise of **commodity culture** in the West since the late eighteenth century. The shopper is the concrete individual defined by the activity of **shopping**. Shoppers have skills and knowledge that enable them to read, negotiate and select from the cultural meanings of the goods consumed. The shopper can be understood as **gendered feminine**. Historically, the majority of the labour of purchasing goods has been done by women, which produces the association between the idea of shopping and the category 'women' that we're familiar with today. As a subject of consumption, the shopper is an agent who is actively engaged in producing an identity by acquiring commodities that mark his/her difference and distinction.

simulation: a term taken from the work of Jean Baudrillard. Baudrillard argues that with the hyper-development of the media, advertising and entertainment industries in **postmodernity**, everyday life experience is structured more by our interaction with representations of events and things than with actual events and things themselves. Thus, simulated events and things come to usurp the place of the 'real'. 'Simulation' refers to this paradigmatically postmodern phenomenon of mediatized representation effectively becoming our experiential reality, so that to speak of unmediated 'reality' no longer makes sense. See also **spectacle**.

sovereign power: according to Michel Foucault, a pre-modern form of **power** by which authority was centralized in an agency such as the crown or the state, and was physically enforced on the people by deputized representatives. Cf. **disciplinary power**.

spectacle: following the analysis made by Guy Debord in his *The Society of the Spectacle*, this refers to the ideological role of electronic media in the domination of the 'real' by representations. Debord draws on Marx's theory of the commodity form to describe the electronic media's representation of the world to us as a flattened-out series of images: a spectacle. 'Spectacle' can also refer more broadly to any social power relationship between people that is mediated by images or an exchange of looks and gazes.

strategies: an idea taken from the work of Michel de Certeau. For de Certeau, everyday life is the terrain on which the powerful seek to maintain their dominance and the powerless seek to contest it. A 'strategy' is a method deployed by the powerful, who enjoy the security of a fixed place from which to launch their bids to maintain power. Cf. **tactics**.

subcultures: cultures that exist within mainstream cultures, made up of individuals who share common interests, values, styles and knowledges, and pursue common practices. Subcultures are often taken to refer to postwar youth cultures in the West – for example, mods, punks, skinheads or goths – but might equally refer to any other micro-community bound by shared knowledges and practices.

subject: the subject is distinguished from the 'self' or individual of humanist discourse because the subject is viewed not as existing independently of broad social structures, but rather as being the effect of such structures. For Louis Althusser, for example, the subject is produced by **ideology** and does not exist prior to its call (or **interpellation**).

subjectivity: the interiorized experience of being a **subject** in culture; the experiential 'life-world' inhabited by individuals in a given cultural and historical context.

surplus value: in **Marxist** theory, surplus value refers to the extra value created in products, in addition to the value of the raw materials from which they are made, by the labour-power of the worker. This surplus value is the object of a struggle between the worker and the **capitalist**, as the latter tries to extract it from the worker as cheaply as possible. Surplus value is what enables the capitalist to realize a profit, by paying the worker less than the amount for which the capitalist can effectively sell her or his **alienated labour**.

surveillance: a mechanism by which **subjects** are disciplined by being made to feel that they are constantly under observation by the representatives of **hegemonic power**. Michel Foucault proposes that surveillance is the key strategy of **modern, disciplinary power**, and that it is exercised indirectly, by causing subjects to internalize the gaze of power and effectively police themselves through self-surveillance. See also **sovereign power**.

tactics: an idea taken from the work of Michel de Certeau. For de Certeau, everyday life is the site of countless tactics of **resistance** to the **strategies** of broader **power** structures. A 'tactic' is a method deployed by the socially powerless, who unlike the powerful lack the security of a fixed place from which to launch their bids for power.

taste: for Pierre Bourdieu, taste defines not the idiosyncratic aesthetic judgement of a unique individual, but rather is the result of knowledges that are determined by a subject's **class** positioning. Taste thus functions as a means by which social distinctions are sustained and reproduced.

technoculture: a culture, like those that most of us inhabit today, that is saturated by, fundamentally invested in, and in important ways defined by, contemporary **technologies**.

technological determinism: a way of thinking which assumes that **technology** is a force that exists independently of cultural context, possessing its own internal logic and inevitable teleology.

technology: any human-made tool or implement produced to enable people to achieve or expedite a particular task. As the term is used in this book, it refers primarily to those mechanical, electronic and digital technologies invented since the late nineteenth century and popularized for domestic usage.

universalism: a way of thinking which assumes that particular truths hold for any historical and/or cultural situation. Universalism assumes that all phenomena can be explained by recourse to generally applicable principles.

use-value: the value of a thing measured by how directly useful it is to its owner, as happens in non- or pre-capitalist societies. See also **exchange-value**.

utopia: etymologically meaning 'no place', this term designates an imagined paradise or ideal place that by definition cannot exist in reality. Cf. **dystopia**.

INDEX